How New Languages Emerge

New languages are constantly emerging, as existing languages diverge into different forms. To explain this fascinating process, we need to understand how languages change and how they emerge in children. In this pioneering study, David Lightfoot explains how languages come into being. He explores how new systems arise, how they are acquired by children, and how adults and children play different, complementary roles in language change.

Lightfoot distinguishes between "external language" (language as it exists in the world) and "internal language" (language as represented in an individual's brain). By examining the interplay between the two, he shows how children are "cue-based" learners, who scan their external linguistic environment for specified structures, making sense of the world outside in order to build their internal language. The internal properties of human brains provide the means to interpret speech.

Engaging and original, this book offers a pathbreaking new account of language acquisition, variation, and change.

DAVID LIGHTFOOT is Professor of Linguistics at Georgetown University and Assistant Director of the National Science Foundation, heading the Directorate of Social, Behavioral and Economic Sciences. He has published ten books, including *The Development of Language* (1999), and *The Language Organ* (with S. R. Anderson, 2002, also published by Cambridge University Press).

D0898313

How New Languages Emerge

David Lightfoot

CAMBRIDGE UNIVERSITY PRESS

CAMBRIDGE UNIVERSITY PRESS
Cambridge, New York, Melbourne, Madrid, Cape Town, Singapore, São Paulo

Cambridge University Press
The Edinburgh Building, Cambridge CB2 2RU, UK

Published in the United States of America by Cambridge University Press, New York

www.cambridge.org
Information on this title: www.cambridge.org/9780521676298

First published 2006

Printed in the United Kingdom at the University Press, Cambridge

A catalogue record for this book is available from the British Library

Library of Congress Cataloguing in Publication data
Lightfoot, David, 1945–
How new languages emerge / David Lightfoot.
    p.   cm.
Includes bibliographical references and index.
ISBN 0-521-85913-1 (hardback) – ISBN 0-521-67629-0 (pbk)
1. Linguistic change.   2. Language acquisition.   3. Language and languages –
Variation.   I. Title.
P142.L543   2006
417'.7 – dc22   2005015819

ISBN-13 978-0-521-85913-4 hardback
ISBN-10 0-521-85913-1 hardback
ISBN-13 978-0-521-67629-8 paperback
ISBN-10 0-521-67629-0 paperback

Contents

Preface

Newspapers tell us that languages are dying out at an alarming rate but they do not tell us that new languages are always emerging. To explain the emergence of new languages with new structures, one needs to understand how languages change and how they emerge in children, like new plants growing and spreading. In fact, we need some new understanding, because the most usual models of change and of the acquisition of language by children make it hard to think of how new languages can emerge; we need new models.

This book aims to investigate not new meanings or new pronunciations but how new systems might arise and be acquired by children, who are the vehicles for structural shifts, I argue. Languages undergo big changes from time to time and adults and children play different, complementary roles.

Linguists have always been interested in language change. Linguistics first became an independent discipline in the nineteenth century and at that time it was concerned exclusively with the history of languages, trying to understand how languages became the way they are. The nineteenth century can be seen as the century of history. Linguists wanted to know how languages changed, biologists wanted to know how species changed, and political thinkers wanted to know how societies and political systems changed; they read each other and gave similar kinds of answers.

That nineteenth-century work has profoundly influenced linguists of subsequent eras as the field has expanded to encompass many branches: phonetics, language acquisition, syntax, discourse analysis, sociolinguistics, semantics, neurolinguistics, and much more. However, the early, influential work on language change had little understanding of how languages emerged in children, and very little interest in the topic. As a result, it never achieved the levels of explanation that it sought, ambitiously. I shall argue that a significant part of change needs to be understood through the mechanisms of children's language acquisition.

In the second half of the twentieth century, language came to be studied alongside other aspects of human mental life and some linguists saw themselves as cognitive scientists. This brought remarkable developments in syntactic theory and in our understanding of how children acquire language, involving quite new concepts. Language came to be seen as emerging in children rather as a plant develops, unfolding according to an inner program. This book will examine those concepts and show how some of them help us to understand better how new languages emerge.

The book addresses people who have thought a little about language but who do not necessarily work on syntactic theory, who have no concern whether syntax is minimalist or cognitive or unificationalist or systemic, but who might be interested in the implications of that work for understanding how new systems can develop. I aim to describe the key concepts of the new work, particularly the distinction between internal and external languages, in a way that avoids unnecessary technicality and enables us to see how new languages emerge. I want to be comprehensible for colleagues, both faculty and graduate students, in areas like anthropology, sociology, psychology, and neuroscience, colleagues who view language with the special lenses of those disciplines. Such readers may not be interested in the nineteenth-century antecedents of the new work and may skip chapters 2 and 8.

Within linguistics, syntacticians need to understand work in discourse analysis and the USE of grammars, if they are to achieve their goals. To explain language change, one needs to understand grammatical theory, language acquisition, discourse analysis, and social variation in grammars. The book will draw on all of these different areas, making connections through language change, and, in some cases, I shall be introducing practitioners to each other.

I address old themes of language change but from a new angle, asking how new systems emerge, where there are different syntactic structures. That question is most often asked within an independent branch of linguistics dealing with creoles, sometimes called "creolistics," but I aim for a broader understanding of new languages that integrates the study of language change, acquisition, and creoles and shows how new languages of many sorts emerge naturally. This yields a new, broad-based kind of historical linguistics, embracing internal and external languages, language change, acquisition, use, grammatical theory, and creoles.

I believe that linguists have developed a more sophisticated analysis of history and change than evolutionary and developmental biologists and political historians, and I hope to demonstrate that. I shall draw on earlier work, particularly my *Development of Language*, but here I will undertake a more comprehensive treatment of change than in my earlier work, which focused on change in internal languages. In this book I shall explore the interaction between change in external and internal languages, showing how they feed each other, thereby addressing critics of the earlier work.

I am indebted to people at many different levels. We stand on other people's shoulders and readers will see whose. I build on and reconstrue the work of many people, and sometimes my thinking has been clarified and sharpened by rejecting certain work. Historical linguists as a group have always had a great interest in explanations, perhaps greater than other linguists, and have been willing to think broadly in order to find them; I like to think that I am following in that tradition. Noam Chomsky's work has been a major influence on almost everything I have written and here I make crucial use of his distinction between internal and external languages. I have also benefited a great deal from the work of the Diachronic Generative Syntax (DIGS) community and the discussion at those lively and productive biennial meetings.

One is also influenced by one's immediate environment. For many years I was at the University of Maryland in a highly focused department that I helped to set up. However, a few years ago I moved to Georgetown University as Dean of the Graduate School, working with colleagues from a more diffuse department and, indeed, with colleagues from the full range of graduate programs. This drew me into a different kind of discourse that has helped to shape this book.

More immediately, thanks to the generosity of Curt Rice and Jürgen Meisel, I digested the book into a series of lectures at the University of Tromsø and for the multilingualism research group at the University of Hamburg. The Hamburg group has a broad vision of linguistics, studying acquisition and change in the context of grammatical theory, discourse analysis, multilingualism, and translation. It is just such a broad range of people that this book addresses and the book emerges from the notion that in order to understand how languages change and how new languages may emerge, one needs to understand many different branches of the field.

As with almost everything else I have written over the last thirty years, Norbert Hornstein has read the whole manuscript wisely and forced me to think through various points from different angles. Over the same period, Noam Chomsky has read most of my book manuscripts, usually being the first to reply and with the richest commentary. I thank these two old friends now for reading a draft of this book, offering helpful advice, and raising important questions.

I thank Christina Villafana and Kay McKechnie, CUP's copy editor, for their fast, graceful efficiency in the preparation of references and the final shape of the book.

New languages emerge through an interplay of internal and external language. This needs to be understood through a non-standard approach to language change, where there are no principles of history. That approach, in turn, requires a non-standard, cue-based analysis of language acquisition by children. We need models that differ from those generally used by linguists, including by modern generativists.

Now to the rich substance of the matter.

1 Internal languages and the outside world

1.1 Languages and the language capacity

Languages come and languages go. We deplore it when they go, because the disappearance of a language is a loss for the richness of human experience. These days, linguists are devoting much energy to documenting expiring languages. That documentation itself may increase the use of the language, which may increase its chance of surviving in some form. For example, simply finding a written version of a language facilitates its use for new purposes and new uses lead the language to be spoken more widely. Adapting computer software to accommodate the language may bring further advantages. Ultimately, however, people cease to speak a language because they come to identify with a different group, perhaps encouraged by factors of economic interest, perhaps influenced by governmental policy favoring one language above others in schools and official discourse.

Nettle & Romaine (2000: ix) note that "the greatest linguistic diversity is found in some of the ecosystems richest in biodiversity inhabited by indigenous peoples, who represent around 4% of the world's population, but speak at least 60% of its 6,000 or more languages." Expiring languages tend to be spoken by small, underprivileged groups that lack resources. The disappearance of languages is a complicated matter that began to generate widespread concern in the 1990s, when funds were invested in investigating the death of languages and efforts were made to document endangered languages. Now the National Science Foundation and the National Endowment for the Humanities have begun to fund work jointly on endangered languages.

The *Ethnologue*, a website maintained by SIL International, reports that there were 6,912 languages spoken in the year 2005 – 239 in Europe, 2,092 in Africa. One can argue about how the languages were counted. English is listed as a single language, although it embraces varieties that are mutually incomprehensible, but the very similar Norwegian and Swedish are listed as distinct languages (Grimes & Grimes 2000). Conventionally, we often speak of Chinese and Arabic as single languages, although they include mutually incomprehensible varieties – "Chinese" seems to encompass eight very different languages.

Whatever the best number is for the world's languages, it will be smaller in a short time. A total of 497 languages are listed as "nearly extinct," which means that "only a few elderly speakers are still living." Some linguists, the *Ethnologue* reports, believe that over half of the world's languages will not be passed on to the next generation.

Meanwhile new languages are emerging and we often deplore that, too, on the grounds that new forms represent a kind of decay and degenerate speech that violates norms that we have been taught in school. Nonetheless, Latin became Portuguese, Spanish, French, Italian, Romanian, and other languages, Dutch became Afrikaans in nineteenth-century South Africa, and early English developed into distinct forms of West Saxon and Mercian, into London, Scots, and Lancashire English, and later into Texan, Australian, Delhi, Jamaican, and many other forms. Within the last generation, we have even been privileged to witness the sudden emergence *ex nihilo* of some new signed languages in Nicaragua and Israel, as we shall discuss in chapter 7.

The emergence of new languages is harder to track than the loss of languages. It is sometimes an identifiable event when the last native speaker of a language dies, e.g. Dolly Pentreath in 1777, allegedly the last speaker of Cornish, but there was no comparable discrete event when, say, Portuguese became a new language as opposed to just the form of Latin spoken around the River Tagus. We now think of Australian and Jamaican as particular forms of English, and they may one day become as distinct as Portuguese, Spanish, and Italian, distinct languages with their own names, perhaps Strine and Jamenglish. If so, there will be no identifiable day or even year in which this happens, no matter how alert the recording linguists.

We may wonder what might have happened if the Romans had lost the Second Punic War in 202 BCE and Hannibal's descendants had brought to western Europe forms of Phoenician, which would have become as different from each other as modern French, Italian, and Sardinian. However, we could not provide a precise date for the emergence of a Semitic language spoken along the River Seine, any more than we can provide a date for the emergence of Latin-based French.

Languages diversify, and not just languages that spread over large areas through conquest and other forms of social domination. The phenomenon, like language death, connects to the way that people identify themselves with groups, adopting modes of speech that characterize the group. People, teenagers from every generation, speak differently as they feel themselves to belong to a distinct group, just as they may dress differently or wear their hair differently. The tendency for languages to diversify reflects the fact that linguistic change is a constant of human experience.

Like it or not, human languages are in constant flux. They flow around something that does not change, the human capacity for language, a biological property. That capacity is common to the species, is not found outside our species, and has not changed, as far as we know, over the period in which recorded human languages have been coming and going and changing in subtle and in bigger, more dramatic ways. That invariant capacity is one of the constants of human nature and helps us understand how brains deal with the shimmering world outside and impose an internal order, and how that interaction with the world outside yields the diversity of human languages.

Indeed, from certain points of view, there is only one human language. If one asks how many human hearts there are, a reasonable answer is one. The human heart has distinctive properties and is uniform across the species. There are differences, but not of a kind to suggest that there are different types of heart, each genetically determined in the way that, say, eyes may differ in color. At the genetic level, there is one heart, and that is the crucial level for answering such a question. Similarly, if one asks how many languages there are, seen from a biological point of view and given the current state of biology, a plausible answer is ONE, the human language, Human. This is not a new idea: Wilhelm von Humboldt held that "the form of all languages must be fundamentally identical" (1836/1971: 193) and they differ as human physiognomies differ: "the individuality is undeniably there, yet similarities are evident" (1836/1971: 29).

When human beings examine the communication systems of other species, herring gulls, honeybees, or dolphins, we establish the distinctive properties, showing how honeybees differ from herring gulls, and the differences are radical. Species differ in big ways that are genetically determined. Honeybees communicate the direction and distance to nectar sources through their "dance language," by wiggling their rear ends at different rates (von Frisch 1967), herring gulls communicate fear and warning by various body movements and calls (Tinbergen 1957), geese mimic social behaviors through imprinting (Lorenz 1961), and, more controversially, dolphins communicate instructions for finding food through high-pitched tones (Lilly 1975) (von Frisch, Lorenz, and Tinbergen shared the 1973 Nobel Prize in Physiology or Medicine).[1] Only after establishing the major species properties are we able to detect differences within the species and rarely do we make much progress in that regard, although different "dialects" of honeybee communication and of passerine birdsongs have been identified.

If colleagues from the Department of Biology, following their usual methods, were to examine the communication systems of life forms on this planet, putting humans alongside honeybees and dolphins, in the way that, say, Niko Tinbergen investigated herring gulls, they would find a number of properties shared by the

---

[1] The dance of the honeybees appears to be unique in having at least some apparent similarity to human language: infinite range and the ability to communicate information about things not in the sensory field.

human species and by no other species, the human language organ (Anderson & Lightfoot 2002). These properties constitute the biggest discovery of modern linguistics. For example, the human language system is not stimulus-bound (not limited to elements within the sensory field), but it is finite and ranges over infinity, it is compositional, algebraic, and involves distinctive computational operations, as we shall see in a few pages. The properties are general – everybody has them – and they facilitate the emergence of the system in young children. The way the system emerges in children also has distinctive properties. For example, the capacity of a mature individual goes far beyond his/her initial experience, unlike birds, for instance, who usually sing pretty much exactly what their models sing (Anderson & Lightfoot 2002: ch. 9; Marler 1999). These are big, distinguishing properties that are biologically based and define the species and its language, Human; Human is very different from any other communication system in the natural world.

Whatever the biological perspective, people do speak differently in Tokyo and Toronto, in the Bronx and in Brooklyn. London is said to have over 300 languages spoken by its citizens, and people's speech is as distinctive as their thumbprint – it often takes only a second or two to know who is on the other end of the telephone line. Why does human speech vary so much and change so readily, if the capacity for language is uniform and static? I shall argue that postulating an invariant CAPACITY for language enables us to understand how we communicate in the context of such rich diversity, where not even sisters speak identically and speech patterns differ in a lottery of linguistic influences. We can understand central aspects of language change and variation, and understand them better than in the past. In particular, we can understand how new systems and new languages emerge.

The POSSIBILITY of variation is biologically based but the actual variation is not. For example, we know that there are distinct systems represented in the language most commonly used in Hamburg and in the most common language of Chicago: verb phrases (VP) are basically object–verb in Hamburg (*Ich glaube, dass Gerda* $_{VP}$*[Tee trinkt]* 'I think that Gerda drinks tea') and verb–object in Chicago (*I think that Gerda* $_{VP}$*[drinks tea]*); finite verbs raise to a high structural position in Hamburg (occurring to the left of the subject of the sentence) but not in Chicago (*In Hamburg* **trinkt Gerda** *Tee* 'In Hamburg Gerda drinks tea,' lit. in Hamburg drinks Gerda tea), and people speak differently. This kind of variation represents something interesting: the language capacity is a biological system that is open, consistent with a range of phenotypical shapes. This is not unique in the biological world – there are plants that grow differently above or below water and immune systems develop differently depending on what people are exposed to (Jerne 1985) – but it is unusual.

One could think of this variation in the way that we think about differences between species. The biology of life is similar in all species, from yeasts to humans. Small differences in factors like the timing of cell mechanisms can produce large differences in the resulting organism, the difference, say, between a shark and a butterfly. Similarly the languages of the world are cast from the same mold, their essential properties being determined by fixed, universal principles. The differences are not due to biological properties but to environmental factors: if children hear different things, they may grow a different mature system. Linguists want to know how differences in experience entail different mature systems.

Observed variations between languages are secondary to the general, universal properties, and they are not biologically based: anybody can become an object–verb speaker and there is nothing biological about it. Such differences amount to little compared to the distinctive properties that hold for all forms of Human, compositionality, structure dependence, and all the particular computational possibilities (see the next section). That is what distinguishes us from other species and constitutes Human, not the Hamburg–Chicago variation. What distinguishes us from other species must be represented in the human genome; what distinguishes a German speaker from an English speaker is not represented in the genetic material but is represented somehow in brain physiology, although not in ways that are detectable by the present techniques of biologists and neuroscientists. We have no significant knowledge yet of the biochemistry of acquired physiological properties. In fact, fundamental matters are quite open: neuroscientists have traditionally focused on neurons but brain cells of a different type, the glia, are now attracting more scrutiny and outnumber neurons nine-to-one. Glia "listen in" on nerve signals and communicate chemically with other glia. Until we know more, a biologist or neuroscientist using currently available techniques will not detect the differences between German and English speakers and will conclude that there is just one human language, Human, which has the rich kinds of properties we have discussed.

At this stage of the development of biochemistry and imaging techniques, biologists cannot determine physiological properties of the Hamburg–Chicago phenotypical variation. However, they are used to teasing out information that must be provided genetically and we are now beginning to learn about genes like FOXP2, which seem to be implicated in the human language capacity. This work is in its infancy but it has begun. Investigators have found families with mutant forms of the FOXP2 gene and mutant forms of language (Gopnik & Crago 1991). We should not expect a simple solution under which there is a small number of genes specifically controlling language organs. We know that the FOXP2 gene, for example, occurs in other species in somewhat different forms and controls aspects of respiratory and immune systems. Work on smell by Richard Axel and Linda Buck, honored in the 2004 Nobel Prize in Physiology or Medicine, showed a family of one thousand genes controlling a mammalian olfactory system that can recognize 10,000 different smells, and it is possible that many genes play a role in controlling the operation of language organs.

We may identify more genes involved in the operation of language organs and that is in prospect, as we learn more about the functioning of genes quite generally. We can also imagine a day when we can examine a brain and deduce something about acquired characteristics, perhaps that it is the brain of a Japanese-speaking, cello-playing mother of two children, but that day seems to be much further off.

In the first few years of life, children grow systems that characterize their particular, individual linguistic range; adapting traditional terminology for new, biological purposes, we call these systems GRAMMARS. Despite all the personal diversity, we know that individuals each have a system and that certain properties in a person's speech entail other properties, systematically. A person's system, his/her grammar, grows in the first few years of life and varies at the edges depending on a number of factors.

We observe that from time to time children acquire systems that are significantly different from pre-existing systems – they speak differently from their parents, sometimes very differently, and they have new languages. New "Englishes" have emerged in postcolonial settings around the globe. Crystal (2004) argues that English has recently recovered from a few centuries of pedantry and snobbery on the part of elite groups who sought to impose their own norms on others, and literature in non-standard Englishes is flourishing again. Schneider (2003) claims that, for all the dissimilarities, a uniform developmental process has been at work, shaped by consistent sociolinguistic and language-contact conditions.

Sometimes there are big changes, which take place quickly in ways that we shall examine carefully. Those big changes will be the focus of this book and we shall need to understand what the systems are, how children acquire their linguistic properties, and how languages change. We can understand certain kinds of change by understanding how acquisition happens, and, vice versa, we can learn much about acquisition by understanding how structural shifts take place.

Understanding how new grammars emerge involves understanding many aspects of language; a modern historical linguist needs to be a generalist and to understand many different subfields – grammatical theory, variation, acquisition, the use of grammars and discourse analysis, parsing and speech comprehension, textual analysis, and the external history of languages. We shall consider diachronic changes in general, changes through time, but particularly syntactic changes in the history of English, treating them in terms of how children acquire their linguistic range.

I shall ask for a three-way distinction between the language capacity, internal languages, and external language. That distinction, incorporating what we now call I-language and E-language (Chomsky 1986), has been revitalized in modern generative work but its origins go back a long way. For example, Humboldt wrote that language "is not a mere external vehicle, designed to sustain social intercourse, but an indispensable factor for the development of human intellectual powers . . . While languages are . . . creations of nations, they still remain personal and independent creations of individuals" (1836/1971: 5, 22). E-language is to the nation as I-languages are to the citizens that constitute it.

Internal languages are systems that emerge in children according to the dictates of the language capacity and to the demands of the external language to which they are exposed. Internal languages or grammars (I use the terms interchangeably) are properties of individual brains, while external language is a group phenomenon, the cumulative effects of a range of internal languages and their use. Individuals typically acquire some particular form of English, an I-language and not the external language of English as a whole.

1.2   Internal languages

A core notion is that of a grammar, sometimes called an I-language, "I" for internal and individual. This is what I mean by an "internal language" and a grammar, in this view, is a mental system that characterizes a person's linguistic range and is represented somehow in the individual's brain. This is a person's language organ, the system. For example, English speakers – and "English" is a rough-and-ready notion that cannot be defined in any precise way, an external language – have grammars that characterize the fact that the first *is* may be reduced to *'s* in a sentence like *Kim is taller than Jim is*, but not the second *is*; they would say *Kim's taller than Jim is* but not **Kim's taller than Jim's* (the * indicates a logically possible sentence that does not in fact occur). They might say *Jim said he was happy* with *he* referring either to Jim or to some other male, but *Jim likes him* could only be used to refer to two separate people. The plural of *cat* is pronounced with a VOICELESS hissing sound, the plural of *dog* is pronounced with a VOICED buzzing *z* sound, and the plural of *church* involves an extra syllable – if a new word is introduced, say *flinge*, we know automatically what its plural sounds like, like the plural of *binge*. All of this is systematic, characterized by a person's internal language system, his/her grammar.

Linguists know many things about people's grammars; in fact, our knowledge has exploded over the last fifty years. Since grammars are represented in people's brains, they must be FINITE even though they range over an infinitude of data. That is, there is an infinite number of sentences within an individual's range. Give me what you think is your longest sentence and I will show you a longer one by putting *He said that* . . . in front of it; so your *The woman in Berlin's hat was brown* is lengthened to *He said that the woman in Berlin's hat was brown.* And then *She thought that he said that the woman in Berlin's hat was brown.* And so on. If we had the patience and the longevity, we could string relative clauses along indefinitely: *This is the cow that kicked the dog that chased the cat that killed the rat that caught the mouse that nibbled the cheese that lay in the house that Jack built.* All of this means that grammars have RECURSIVE devices that permit expressions to be indefinitely long, and therefore indefinitely numerous. Finite grammars, therefore, generate indefinite numbers of structures and involve computational operations to do so. That's part of the system.

Grammars are also ALGEBRAIC and generalizations are stated not in terms of particular words but in terms of category variables like verb, noun, preposition, etc. The VERB category ranges over *die, like, speak, realize*, and the PREPOSITION category ranges over *over, up, through*, etc.

Also, grammars consist of different kinds of devices and are therefore MODULAR. Some device derives *cats*, with a voiceless *s*, from *cat+plural*, as opposed to *dogs*, with a voiced *z*, from *dog+plural*, and as opposed to *churches*, with an extra syllable, from *church+plural*. A different device relates a structure corresponding to *What do you like?* to *You like what*, with *what* in the position in which it is understood, namely as the direct object (or COMPLEMENT) of the verb *like*. That device "displaces" any phrase containing a wh- word and creates a structure in which the displaced wh- phrase (in square brackets) is followed by an auxiliary verb (italicized) (1). Again, this is systematic.

(1)   a. [What] *do* you like?
       b. [What books] *will* she buy?
       c. [What books about linguistics written in English] *have* you read?
       d. [Which books about linguistics that the guy we met in Chicago told us about] *could* they publish?

So grammars are generally supposed to be finite and ranging over an infinitude of data, algebraic, and modular (consisting of different types of mechanisms), and to involve computational operations of a special kind. These are some very basic, general properties of people's grammars, all grammars, and I shall discuss more as we go along. For the moment, we just need to grasp that people's language capacity is systematic.

A fundamental property of people's grammars is that they develop in the first few years of life and, again, our knowledge of how they develop has exploded over the last few generations: we have learned a great deal about what young children say and what they do not say, using new experimental techniques. Also in this domain, there is a great deal of systematicity, much of it newly discovered and different from what we find in other species. A person's grammar emerges on exposure to particular experiences in conformity with genetic prescriptions. An English speaker's system arose because, as a child, he/she was exposed to certain kinds of experiences. Children raised in Hamburg are exposed to different experiences and develop different systems. One empirical matter is to determine which experiences trigger which aspects of people's grammars, not a trivial matter.

Linguists refer to what children hear, to the crucial experiences, as the primary linguistic data (PLD). Somehow grammars are acquired on exposure only to PRIMARY linguistic data but characterize secondary data in addition to the primary data. For example, children might hear expressions like *Kim is tall* or *Kim's tall* and thereby learn that *is* may be reduced to *'s*. So primary data might trigger an operation mapping *is* to the reduced *'s*. However, the grammar must also characterize the secondary fact, already noted, that the second *is* does not reduce in *Kim is taller than Jim is*. That is a secondary fact, because the non-occurrence of **Kim's taller than Jim's* is not something that children hear. You cannot hear something that doesn't occur.

This is crucial and constitutes part of the POVERTY-OF-STIMULUS problem, which will turn out to be important for our general story. Somehow the stimulus that children have is rich enough for them to learn that *is* may be reduced, but not rich enough to determine that it not be reduced in the longer sentence. The fact that the second *is* cannot be reduced cannot be learned directly from experience.

Children converge on a system, subconsciously, of course, in which certain instances of *is* are never reduced, even though their experience doesn't demonstrate this. These poverty-of-stimulus problems are widespread. In fact, there are very few, if any, generalizations that work straightforwardly; all but the most superficial break down and reveal poverty-of-stimulus problems, like the reduction of *is* to *'s*. The problems are solved by postulating information that is available to children independently of experience, represented in some fashion in the genetic material, directly or indirectly. This is a central part of our reasoning and we shall illustrate the logic in chapter 3.

The reason why poverty-of-stimulus problems are pervasive is that there are genetic factors involved, and those genetic factors solve the problems. Careful examination of the poverty-of-stimulus problems reveals the genetic factors that must be involved, just as Gregor Mendel postulated genetic factors to solve the poverty-of-stimulus problems of his pea-plants.

In this view, children are internally endowed with certain information, what linguists call Universal Grammar (UG), and, when exposed to primary linguistic data, they develop a grammar, a mature linguistic capacity, a person's internal language or I-language (2a). The essential properties of the eventual system are prescribed internally and are present from birth, in much the way that Goethe (1790) saw the eventual properties of plants as contained in their earliest form in a kind of E N T E L E C H Y , where the *telos* 'end' or potential is already contained in the seed.[2]

To summarize, grammars are systems: formal characterizations of an individual's linguistic capacity, conforming to principles of a universal initial state, UG, built from its elements, and developing as a person is exposed to his/her childhood linguistic experience. A grammar, in this terminology, is a mental organ, a person's language organ, and is physically represented in the brain, "secreted" by the brain in Darwin's word. The grammar characterizes not only the primary but also the secondary data. One can think of the Primary Linguistic Data (PLD) as the triggering experience that makes the linguistic genotype (UG) develop into a linguistic phenotype, a person's mature grammar (2).

(2)   a. Primary Linguistic Data (UG → grammar)
         b. Triggering experience (genotype → phenotype)

Grammars emerge through an interplay of genetic and environmental factors, nature and nurture. A task for linguists is to distinguish the genetic from the environmental factors, teasing apart the common properties of the species from the information derived from accidental experience, the source of the diversity.

Two analogies with chemistry are appropriate here. As noted, these grammars characterize a person's linguistic capacity and are represented in the brain. Damage to different parts of the brain may affect a person's language capacity differently. Grammars or I-languages consist of structures and computational operations, of a kind that we shall see, and not of neurons, synapses, and the stuff of neuroscientists, but nonetheless they are represented in that kind of matter. The claim here is that there are significant generalizations statable in these linguistic terms and that internal languages constitute a productive level of abstraction in the same way that chemical elements make up a level of analysis at which productive generalizations can be stated. The elements of chemistry can also be reduced to some degree to other levels of abstraction, to quanta and the elements of physics. However, they don't need to be so reduced. In fact, there are few instances of such reductions in science and for the most part scientists work at different levels of abstraction, each justified by the kinds of generalizations that it permits. Chemists and physicists work at different levels, each able to state interesting generalizations.[3] Likewise biologists, physiologists, and medical doctors.

---

[2] For Goethe, plant growth consisted of repeated replication of the same structure, the stem and the leaf. These ideas, embodying repeated mathematical forms, were taken up by D'Arcy Thompson (1917) and Alan Turing (1952), and are discussed accessibly in Stewart (1998).

[3] A historian of chemistry points out that its triumphs were "built on no reductionist foundation but rather achieved in isolation from the newly emerging science of physics" (Thackray 1970). In fact, Chomsky (2002: 69) points out that chemistry was eventually U N I F I E D with physics but not reduced to it; "physics had to undergo fundamental changes in order to be unified with basic chemistry," while chemistry remained virtually unchanged.

So with internal languages. We are interested in understanding the relation between different levels of abstraction, in understanding the findings of colleagues working on the neurological bases of the language capacity and how they may relate to generalizations stated in terms of grammatical categories and computations, but this does not entail that all work should be conducted at one or the other level. Scientists are opportunistic and work where they can discover interesting generalizations and explanations. Linguists' ideas of I-language constitute one level where interesting generalizations can be stated.

This is to adopt what physicist Steven Weinberg (1977), following Husserl, has called the "Galilean style," whereby "physicists give a higher degree of reality to [their abstract mathematical models of the universe] than they accord the ordinary world of sensation," dedicated to finding understanding and not to covering data and phenomena. Scientists of this type see beyond the thing at hand to the mysterious relation it might have to other things at hand, mediated through the mathematical models. They observe and leap to new models as poets leap to new metaphors. We know very little about the relevant genes and next to nothing about how the brain secretes the language organ, but our models of I-language have been productive and permitted considerable understanding, as we shall see in chapters 3–7. We pursue our understanding where we can, opportunistically, hoping for an eventual convergence between cognitive psychology and neurobiology, but aware that convergence often brings surprises and emerges from changes and developments in one or another level of analysis.

Second, the chemists' periodic table defines the chemical elements of the natural world and grammatical theory has been described intriguingly in similar terms, defining the structural elements from which natural languages are composed (Baker 2001). Particular I-languages are made from elements provided by the language capacity, Universal Grammar, and triggered by the external language to which children are exposed. In a sense, UG constitutes the periodic table, the elements from which particular grammars are made up.

So a child grows a certain grammar if he/she hears certain things. The only way that a different grammar develops is if somebody hears different things. There is no one-to-one relation here. Grammars are abstract and formal and children may develop the same grammatical structures, despite a variety of initial experiences. No two children have exactly the same experiences, but two sisters, despite variation in experiences, may perhaps acquire the same system, so variation in experience does not necessarily entail different mature systems and the relationship between PLD and grammars is many-to-one. Consequently, if a new grammar emerges in a population, it can only be because the PLD, the expressions that people hear, have shifted in a SIGNIFICANT way.

We should allow for the possibility that the PLD that trigger a grammatical property may not have any obvious connection with that property. Niko Tinbergen (1957: ch. 22) once surprised the world of ethologists by showing that young herring gulls' behavior of pecking at their mothers' mouths was triggered not by the fact that the mother gull might be carrying food but by a red spot. Mothers typically have a red spot under their beak and Tinbergen devised an ingenious series of experiments showing that this was the crucial triggering property. So the chicks would respond to a disembodied red spot and not to a bird carrying food but lacking the strategic red spot. Similarly, grammars may have certain mechanisms and devices because of properties in the primary data that are not obviously related to those mechanisms; I shall discuss such examples in chapter 5.

People have their own internal system, a grammar, which develops in them in the first few years of life as a result of an interaction between genetic factors common to the species and environmental variation in primary linguistic data. Such a grammar represents the person's linguistic range, the kind of things that the person might say and how he/she may say them. If they hear different things, children may converge on a different system, a new grammar, perhaps the first instance of a particular, new I-language. We want to find out what triggers which aspect of a person's I-language, therefore how new I-languages might emerge.

1.3   External language

Internal languages exist in people's brains, and external, E-language is part of the outside world.

External language is amorphous and not a system. It is language out there in the world and it includes the kinds of things that a child might hear. This is a function of the various grammars in the child's environment and of people's USE of those grammars and does not reflect any single system. No two children hear exactly the same things and no two people speak exactly the same way.

External language is affected by the fact that some people might use "topicalization" constructions more frequently, expressions like *War, I hate and it always has unexpected consequences.* Anybody might use such expressions because their structures are generated by the grammars of most English speakers, and therefore fall within their linguistic range, but some individuals might use them more frequently than others, affecting the ambient E-language.

Similarly, for a brief period a few years ago some people were using constructions like *War is fun, not* self-consciously as a means of emphasizing negation; these unusual negations were popularized by *Wayne's World*, a weekly skit in the television program *Saturday Night Live*. These expressions were a feature of some television-watchers' E-language but were not systematic and not a function of their internal systems, their grammars. They were not systematic, because they were "frozen" and did not interact with other grammatical operations. For example, people did not say *Is war fun, not?* by analogy to *Isn't war fun?*, nor *She said that war was fun, not*, to mean that she said that war wasn't fun (negating the embedded clause).

E-language, then, is fluid, in constant flux. It incorporates the kinds of things that groups of people say. "English," "German," etc. are E-language, group notions, but they are not systematic, nor can they be: "English" incorporates the things that somebody from New York might say but not people from Cornwall, and it also includes the things that Cornishmen say that a New Yorker wouldn't understand. The group notion goes beyond any individual's capacity and no individual knows all of English, partly because some data are contradictory, different in different individuals.

1.4   Change

We have distinguished between individual I-languages and group E-language, but they interact. Changes in E-language cause changes in I-languages and changes in I-languages cause changes in E-language (chapter 5). Put differently, if people hear different things, they may attain a new grammar; if they attain a new grammar, they will say different things.

Language change as a whole is a group phenomenon. External languages like English and German, whatever they may be precisely, reflect the output of grammars, the varying use of those grammars in discourse, and social variation in the set of grammars that are relevant for any particular language. Language change can sometimes be tracked geographically, as one sees some new variant attested in different places at different times. And change at the level of languages often seems to take place gradually, spreading through the population from place to place and from group to group. People's speech, external language, is intrinsically amorphous, ever moving, and E-language is inherently fluid, unstable, always changing. As a result, no two people have the same initial experiences.

One aspect of global language change is that individual grammars may change over time: people developed certain grammars in London in the thirteenth century and different ones in the fifteenth century. The only way a different internal grammar may grow in a different child is when that child is exposed to significantly different primary data, to different external language. In that case, the linguist wants to find how grammars changed and how the relevant childhood experience might have changed just prior to the change in grammars, in such a way that the new grammar was the only possible outcome.

In this perspective, the study of grammar change is fused with work on variation and the growth of grammars in children. We explain the emergence of the new grammar and the explanation illuminates the nature of the child's triggering experience and the way in which children acquire their linguistic capacities;

the study of grammar change has implications for grammatical variation and for theories of language acquisition.

Grammars differ sharply: a person either has an internal grammar with a certain property, or not (although he/she may have more than one system, multiple grammars, each of them discrete; we will discuss coexisting systems in chapter 6). While the primary linguistic data (PLD), the kinds of things that people hear, vary indefinitely, grammars do not; there is a finite number of grammatical structures, resulting from different settings of a finite number of option-points. If we treat the parameters of variation in terms of CUES, as we shall argue (chapter 4), there is a finite number of cues, elements of structure, for which a child scans his/her linguistic environment. A child scans the PLD and seeks the cues prescribed by UG and the innate (pre-experience) system grows to a mature grammar (2). In that case, grammars may differ by one or more cues. If grammars and the cues that make them up are finite and abstract, then they change only occasionally and sometimes with dramatic consequences for a wide range of constructions and expressions; grammar change, therefore, tends to be "bumpy," manifested by clusters of phenomena changing at the same time, as we shall see.

Grammatical change is also contingent, dependent on the details of the use of language (for example, changing morphology, changing distribution of words and construction types), language contact, perhaps even social attitudes and second language acquisition. Grammar change is linked to changes in people's speech, external language; we can only know about it by studying what people say, usually through written texts, and it must be studied in conjunction with other kinds of change. Nonetheless, grammar change constitutes a distinct type of change, a reaction to external language, to contingent factors of language use, and the new grammars emerge subject to the usual principles of UG. The study of the contingent events is complementary to the search for the general organizing principles of UG, but there is a different focus. To focus on grammar change, on I-language, is to attend to one aspect of language change, an important part and one that illuminates the variation and acquisition of grammars by children, but one that is dependent on other kinds of language change.

In chapters 5–7, I make a clear distinction between I-language changes and E-language changes. From our perspective, E-language changes are changes in the trigger experience, the input available to a child during language acquisition, paving the way for a possible I-language change, that is, formal change in grammars that takes place with a new generation acquiring the language.

An approach to language that incorporates I-language and postulates universal principles of grammar formation common to the species entails approaching changes very differently from more traditional approaches, which focus pretty much exclusively on what we are calling E-language. We shall want to know about the nature of I-languages, how they are acquired on the basis of exposure to E-language, and how E-language might change in critical ways such that it triggers new grammars.

Linguists describe grammars before and after a change. Different I-languages are analyzed and compared, as in synchronic comparative syntax. What makes historical syntax a particularly interesting form of comparative syntax is that sometimes, when we are lucky enough to have appropriate records, we can identify points of change along with prior changes in the external language, what children might reasonably be thought to have heard, such that we can link the E-language change to the I-language change (chapter 5).

Grammars grow in children in the first few years of life and reach their adult form by puberty (chapters 4 and 8). Consequently, grammar change most usually does not occur through a child or an adult changing his/her grammar; the changes in grammars take place from one generation to another. However, E-language is always in flux and may change in some particular context in a critical way that has the effect of triggering a new I-language. If there were no change in E-language, there could be no new I-language.

Children acquire I-language systems that go far beyond the external language that they experience and that happens on an everyday basis in every child. Sometimes it happens more dramatically, when children are exposed to modestly different E-language experiences which, although only modestly different, trigger a new grammar; in that event, the new generation speaks differently from their parents. And sometimes it happens much more dramatically, when children acquire systems that generate data spectacularly different from what they experienced. This is when new productive systems emerge out of fragmentary experiences and the first stages of a "creole" language appear. We have gained new insight into this process in recent years through the study of new signed languages emerging under conditions similar to those of new creoles (chapter 7). In each of these cases, we have new languages.

All of this will entail a rethinking of language change as an interaction of changes between E-language and changes in I-languages. And that will provide a new historical linguistics with a firmer naturalistic base, deeply connected to other aspects of language study. The goals are not modest.

1.5   Plans

In the next chapter I shall identify the traditional work of historical linguists, one of the two bodies of work that we are rethinking, showing that it focuses on E-language and gets into conceptual tangles because of its exclusive focus on languages as external objects, entities out there, more or less independent of people.

In chapter 3 I develop our notion of grammars, examining the properties of I-languages and how they instantiate UG. I examine some poverty-of-stimulus problems, showing how they can be solved by identifying relevant properties of UG and learnable grammatical properties. I will write a little about the history of some of these ideas, about how ideas about the human language faculty have changed over time and why.

Chapter 4 focuses on the growth of grammars in children, and the second body of work that we are rethinking, again considering how researchers' ideas about acquisition have changed and why. Here we will develop the non-standard notion of cues, showing how it differs from other approaches to the acquisition and growth of grammars. We shall translate the analyses of chapter 3 into claims about cues, showing how children can acquire the analyses under natural conditions.

Chapter 5 treats the cuing of new grammars, examining the emergence of new I-languages and how they were triggered by changing E-language properties. We shall examine a sequence of changes involving the syntax of verbs in the history of English and consider the syntactic effects of changes in morphology.

In chapter 6 I link a change in discourse function, the shape of names, to a structural change involving "split genitive" constructions in Middle English. Then we will study the change from object–verb order to verb–object order. A number of European languages have undergone such a change and I will focus on the change in English and Icelandic, showing that while the structural change was the same, it took place at different times in the two languages but in each case triggered by changes in the use of structures.

Chapter 7 focuses on how new grammars may emerge quite suddenly, erupting like volcanoes. I shall consider new work dealing with creoles, new languages emerging from bilingual settings in which simple pidgins constitute part of children's linguistic experience, and discuss work on new signed languages.

And then in the last chapter I consider how this approach to acquisition and change influences the way we might think about traditional issues of historical linguists: the role of adults vs. children, the gradualness of change, notions of directionality, how one might be able to reconstruct properties of prehistoric languages, how changes spread through populations, and more.

2   Traditional language change

2.1   Introduction

I should elaborate on the skepticism about languages like English and Dutch, which are undefinable and at best rough and ready notions. In general, an individual either has some grammatical property or not. Ella Fitzgerald pointed out that some say *tomeyto* and some say *tomahto*, and the word is different for different people. Some people might say something like *Who did Kim say that visited Baghdad?* and others might not. There are problems of observation: sometimes a person might agree that some sentence type is part of their competence, while at other times denying it, and we are not good observers of our own speech. Nonetheless, in principle, we will either observe somebody with a certain property or not, with some gray areas. But that is demonstrably not so of an external language like English.

A person brought up in Tennessee might say *Kim might could sing that song* but a person brought up in Polperro, Cornwall, would not speak that way (with what linguists call a "double modal"). Our Cornishman might ask if she is happy by saying *Bin her happy?*, but not our Tennesseean. You might agree that our Tennesseean and our Cornishman are both speakers of English and indeed they might communicate with a significant degree of success, but what does this discrepancy mean for "English"? Are *Kim might could sing that song* and *Bin her happy?* sentences of English, or not? Well, yes in the first case for somebody living in Memphis and not for our Cornishman, and vice versa for the second case. And what about *Who did Kim say that visited Baghdad?*? Children acquire some form of English, not English as a whole.

The very notion of a language like English is an idealization, a useful idealization for certain purposes, and we will use it in this book in a pretheoretical way. For example, it is intended to provide a rough approximation of who understands who. Two speakers of "English," whether they are from Cornwall or Tennessee, will understand each other to a degree, whereas neither understands a speaker of Dutch. The approximation is very rough and our Cornishman may, in fact, understand a particular sentence of Dutch (maybe *Maria drinkt whisky*) more readily than some sentence uttered by a woman in Memphis, and there are notorious problems in characterizing the boundaries of languages. Is a speaker of some form of Jamaican really a speaker of English, when much of what he says is not understood by our Cornishman? Does it make sense to call two people speakers of Chinese when one comes from the hills of Taiwan and understands little of the banker from Shanghai? And is it right to say that a teacher from Oslo is a speaker of Norwegian and that a teacher from Stockholm is a speaker of a different language, when they understand each other to a large degree? Resorting to dialects does not help us define a language, and many of the same problems of definition arise as much for dialects as for languages. And similarly for stages of a language: I shall refer, as is customary, to Old English, Middle English, and Early Modern English, but these are approximate categories for classifying texts and there is no clear cut-off.

Sometimes it is convenient to use problematic idealizations. Everybody knows that the earth rotates but it is convenient to think in terms of the sun rising and setting. A closer analogy to language is the notion of race. At least 150 years of determined efforts to find a biological explanation of race have failed. Scientists studied skull sizes, facial features, bone shapes, compiling vast tomes of data that have added up only to the unhelpful notion that black people look black and white people look white. Human beings turn out to be genetically more homogeneous, more like each other than unlike; the traits that seem to make us most unlike (skin color, eye shape, hair texture) are, in biological terms, both very new and extremely superficial. There is more difference within racial categories than across those categories (Lewontin 1972) and, now that human genomes have been decoded, it turns out that a fully specified genome gives us no way of knowing whether the person is black or white: looking at the genetic code, we can tell who is male and who is female but we cannot determine who is Chinese, Hispanic, African-American, or Caucasian (Venter 2002). Racial divisions are social constructs, essentially biological fictions, but nonetheless used for social purposes. So with languages, as people usually talk about them.

In fact, this book concerns the interplay of external and internal languages, both idealizations: the idealization involved in speaking of external languages like "English" and the idealization in speaking of internal languages represented in the brains of individuals. In a sense these are competing idealizations and I argue that one can achieve better understandings of how languages change and how new languages emerge, if one takes a biological perspective and incorporates I-language in one's toolbox, a system that grows in an individual's brain when exposed to specific triggering conditions. However, the fact of the matter is that almost all work on language change so far has focused exclusively on external languages like English and this has proven problematic. In this chapter, I shall examine how this is the case and where the difficulties have lain, and then I will proceed in the next chapter to examine ideas about internal, individual languages.

Linguistics emerged as a distinct discipline in the nineteenth century and the discipline was concerned exclusively with language change. Linguists thought of texts as the essential reality and took languages to be entities "out there," existing in their own right, waiting to be acquired by groups of speakers. For them, languages were external objects and changed in systematic ways according to "laws" and general notions of directionality. Languages were related to each other to different degrees, modeled in tree diagrams (*Stammbäume*), and they changed at certain rates that could be discovered. Linguists of the time focused on the products of human behavior rather than on the internal processes that underlie the behavior. By the end of the nineteenth century, the data of linguistics consisted of an enormous inventory of sound changes but there were no general principles: the changes occurred for no good reason and tended in no particular direction. The historical approach had not brought a scientific analysis of language, of the kind that had been hoped for, and there was no predictability to the changes. The historicist paradigm – the notion that there are principles of history to be discovered – was largely abandoned in the 1920s and linguists moved to other concerns, focusing less exclusively on language change. That is often the way it is with the demise of research paradigms: they are just abandoned after a period of diminishing returns (Kuhn 1962). However, the core notions of our nineteenth-century predecessors have been resilient, even though research paradigms have changed, and they were taken up again by linguists in the last decades of the twentieth century, in ways that are worth examining, as we shall see later.

2.2   The nineteenth century[1]

The study of language goes back to classical Greece and India, and there has been much productive work. Pāṇini's grammar, the *Aṣṭādhyāyī*, formulated more than 2,500 years ago, contains some 4,000 sutras, formal rules for the word forms of Sanskrit that occur in the written texts, and remains "one of the greatest monuments of human intelligence" (Bloomfield 1933: 11). The study of language was often closely linked with the study of mind, taking language to be a "mirror of the mind" and assuming that the study of language would give special insight into human thought. This was a conspicuous line of thought for several seventeenth-century philosophers.

Not much of the early work on language dealt with change and historical relationships, but some did. An unknown Icelandic scholar of the twelfth century, canonized now as the "First Grammarian," postulated a historical relationship between Icelandic and English. He was interested primarily in spelling reform; his *Treatise* was published only in 1818 and even then remained

---

[1] This chapter draws heavily on chapter 2 of Lightfoot (1999).

largely unknown outside of Scandinavia. Dante in his *De vulgari eloquentia* divided the Romance languages and dialects into three groups: each language was descended historically from one of three vernaculars, which in turn were descended from Latin. Other writers had alternative models of the historical relationships among languages, often deriving modern languages from a favored religious language, usually Hebrew, Latin, or Sanskrit.

Then came Sir William Jones. He was a British judge serving with the East India Company, and he worked in Calcutta. In an after-dinner speech in 1786 he suggested that Greek, Latin, and Sanskrit were similar in ways that indicated that they descended historically from some common source, which may no longer exist. The key idea was that the origin of particular languages should not necessarily be sought in other, currently observable languages like Icelandic, Hebrew, or Sanskrit, but it may be found in a hypothetical language for which we have no records. This insight had a profound effect and initiated an enormous outpouring of philological work; it gave birth to an independent discipline, which we now call linguistics, although it was left to Franz Bopp and Rasmus Rask to get the real work going.[2]

The historical record shows that the languages of the modern world, seen as external objects, evolved from earlier forms. People thought that we might be able to find out precisely how languages developed from one another. A central idea was that if we can understand the sound changes that transform words as they are transmitted from generation to generation, so we may understand the historical relationships among languages, how a language may have descended from some earlier language. There followed a century of research, which was to discover much about sound changes affecting the Indo-European languages.

Linguistics began as a HISTORICAL science and it turned out to be tremendously influential in the nineteenth century – in many ways at the center of the intellectual life of that century. Linguists, biologists, and historians talked to each other and read each other. The work of the linguists influenced major developments in biology and in history, outstandingly through the work of Charles Darwin and Karl Marx (Lightfoot 1999: ch. 2). And those nineteenth-century ideas have continued to influence the work of linguists into the twenty-first century. For better and for worse.

There are many questions one can ask about language: how it is acquired by children, how it is used by poets, how it varies sociologically, and so on. The central research question for the nineteenth century was: how did a language

---

[2] Robins (1967) gives an excellent account of work on language before the nineteenth century, and Pedersen (1931) describes the efflorescence in the nineteenth century, equipping his story with photographs of the major players and detailed accounts of individual contributions. Sampson (1980) has a good chapter on the nineteenth century, stressing the influence philologists and biologists had on each other. Davies (1998) offers a rich history of the century, which supersedes all earlier work on nineteenth-century linguistics.

get to be the way that it is? As far as Hermann Paul was concerned, this was the only possible question: "Es ist eingewendet, dass es noch eine andere wissenschaftliche Betrachtung der Sprache gäbe, als die geschichtliche. Ich muss das in Abrede stellen" (It has been objected that there is another scientific view of language possible besides the historical. I must contradict this) (1880: 20). Whether other views were possible or not, this historical question first became central in Germany, and it grew not only out of Sir William Jones' insight but also from a general intellectual movement of the late eighteenth century to mid-nineteenth century that today we call Romanticism. The Romantics focused on ethnic and cultural origins of various phenomena. Since race, language, and culture were seen as closely related, the reconstruction of the prehistory of Germanic was attractive to these Romantics. The links were quite clear in the work of the linguists Johann Gottfried Herder (1744–1803) and Jacob Grimm (1785–1863). Jones' publication also coincided with a new interest in Near Eastern and Indian studies by European scholars.

Linguistics was thus resolutely about change and, for nineteenth-century linguists, what changed was a "language," an entity in the outside world, essentially an inventory of words. There was more to language than just words, of course, but everything else was attributable either to a universal "logic" or to individually variable "habits," and these matters did not greatly interest linguists of the time. The job of the linguists was to write the history of words, their pronunciations and their meanings. This understanding of what linguistics is about still characterizes some parts of the field, though classical historical linguistics is a relatively small subdiscipline today.

2.3   Historical relationships

It is not an accident that the words for 'father' are so similar in the Romance languages: *père* in French, *padre* in Spanish, *padre* in Italian, *patre* in Sardinian, *pare* in Catalan, *pai* in Portuguese. These forms are all transmogrified versions of Latin *pater* and historical linguists view French, Spanish, Italian, Sardinian, Catalan, and Portuguese as historically related to each other, in the sense that they are descended from Latin. That is, they share many words that are COGNATE and have a common, Latin ancestor.

Words are transmitted from one generation to the next and they may change their form over time. I call a table a *table*, because that's what my models called it. By examining CORRESPONDENCES as in the Romance words for 'father,' linguists postulated that languages are historically related to each other to greater or lesser degrees, and that they cluster in "families." There are parent, daughter, and sister languages, and other relatives. Latin is the parent of Italian, Portuguese, and Spanish, which are sisters. English and Dutch have more cognate words and the cognate words are more similar to each other than English and Spanish, so English and Dutch are more closely related, in fact sisters . . . although they have plenty of words that are not cognate: English *bicycle* and Dutch *fiets* refer to the same object but do not have a common origin.

The word for 'father' in the Germanic languages is different from what we find in the Romance languages, but not very different: Gothic *fadar*, English *father*, Dutch *vader*, German *Vater*, Danish *fader*. Just as in most of the Romance words, we have a two-syllable word, and the initial segment is a labial consonant (/p/ in Romance and /f/ in Germanic), followed by an open vowel and an alveolar consonant, and then some kind of vocalic *r*. Compare the very different words for 'father' in languages from different families, where the words do not have a common ancestor (as far as we can tell): Chinese *fuqin*, Japanese *titi-oya*, Basque *aita*, Finnish *isä*, and Korean *apeci*. The degree of similarity between the Germanic and Romance forms and the degree of difference reflects the fact that the Germanic languages are historically related to each other; they are also historically related to the Romance languages, but more indirectly. English is related historically to Dutch, to Spanish, and to Armenian, but most closely to Dutch and least closely to Armenian.

Linguists believe that languages, seen as external objects, change over the course of time. They also believe that modern French, Italian, and Romanian evolved from some form of Latin, that Hindi and Urdu evolved from some form of Sanskrit . . . even if Hindi and Urdu hardly differ from each other and are labeled as distinct languages mostly because they are spoken in two (often warring) countries and have different writing systems. We suppose that Latin and Sanskrit evolved from some common source for which we have no records, and we call that source Proto-Indo-European.

This idea that languages are historically related to one another is not very ancient. It occurs in the writings of Dante but it was not generally accepted until the late eighteenth century. In effect, the idea began to be worked out in detail only in the nineteenth century. That century saw intellectual developments in several fields focusing on the nature of historical change, and the study of language change was a central component of that more general phenomenon: Darwin and his associates studied change among species, while Karl Marx and others studied change among political systems.

It is now commonplace to think of languages as historically related and these relationships are often expressed in cladistic models (figure 2.1). These models were introduced by August Schleicher in 1861. Schleicher (1821–1868) had a *Stammbaumtheorie* or geneological tree model, which reflects the methods of botanical classification by species and genera in the Linnaean system. In fact, the trees are quite similar to the cladograms of modern biologists, which is why we refer to Schleicher's trees as cladistic models; these cladograms express the varying degrees to which species are related, depending on the number of

SHARED DERIVED CHARACTERISTICS ("synapomorphies"). Schleicher regarded himself as a natural scientist and he regarded language as one of the natural organisms; he wrote a short book on Darwinian theory and linguistics, *Die darwinische Theorie und die Sprachwissenschaft*, 1863.

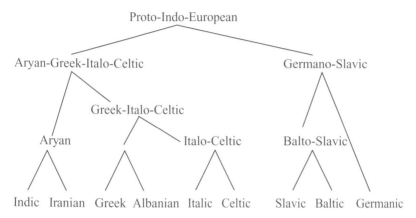

Figure 2.1 Schleicher's tree for the earliest stages of Indo-European languages

In these cladistic models, languages are grouped together in subfamilies, Romance, Celtic, Germanic, Indic, etc., according to the innovations that they share. For each subfamily, a parent *Grundsprache* (common language) is postulated, like some form of spoken Latin as the source of the Romance languages, or a language that is not recorded. The common ancestor of all the Indo-European languages, Proto-Indo-European (PIE), is not recorded and is reconstructed by comparing the corresponding forms in the various subfamilies.

Figure 2.1 is the tree for the earliest stages of the Indo-European languages proposed by Schleicher (1861–1862). I have anglicized and modernized some of his labels. The tree, of course, is incomplete: many languages that we have not specified fall under Germanic, and Celtic was subdivided into two groups, Brythonic and Goidelic; Brythonic consists of Cornish (which died out in the eighteenth century), Breton, and Welsh, and Goidelic embraces Manx (which died out in the twentieth century), Irish, and Scots Gaelic. The tree expresses the idea that, say, the Celtic languages are more closely related to the Latin-derived "Italic" languages (which we now call "Romance": Italian, French, Sardinian, Spanish, Galician, Catalan, Romanian, etc.) than the Slavic languages (Polish, Russian, etc.) are to either; and that the Baltic languages (Latvian, Lithuanian) are more closely related to Germanic than to Celtic, but not as closely related to Germanic as they are to the Slavic languages. And so on.

This was the first tree proposed for the Indo-European languages. We have no direct records for most of the *Grundsprachen* postulated, Aryan-Greek-Italo-Celtic, Balto-Slavic, etc., and we now doubt that Albanian and Greek represent any kind of unity. Cal Watkins has argued that there was no Italo-Celtic language. On the other hand, some features of Schleicher's tree remain undisputed today and many relationships not specified in Schleicher's tree have come to be established convincingly.

A great deal of work by many linguists over many generations has been devoted to articulating the details of the Indo-European family relationships. Cladograms like those of figure 2.1 are a somewhat misleading shorthand for something more complex. To say that two languages are historically related means that they share similarities that are not due to chance, borrowing, or universal features of all languages. Words may be cognate: spelling out the parent form of the word and the changes that produced the forms in the daughter languages constitutes the precise relationship between the languages. The cladograms are a very rough quantification of shared innovations. Putting Greek and Albanian under a single node indicates that there are innovations that the two languages share, but which are not shared by other languages in the tree.

Varying amounts of attention have been devoted to other families. There is a lively dispute about whether Japanese, or, more accurately, the various Japanese languages are historically related to the Korean languages, and, if so, how. There has also been a vigorous dispute about how many language families there are in Africa and among the indigenous, native American languages; much of this has been triggered by the ambitious work of Joseph Greenberg, who tried to establish very ancient historical relationships. Others argue for super-families like the famous Nostratic, which covers most of the languages of Europe, Africa, India, Asia, and, in some versions, even some North American languages.

There is only one kind of scientific evidence involved here: the comparative method. By the comparative method, one postulates a common source for corresponding forms in different languages; the corresponding forms are derived from the common source by regular sound changes. If the postulated sound changes are general and phonetically plausible, one has a productive account; if they are ad hoc and phonetically implausible, one has an ad hoc account. If a relationship cannot be demonstrated by the comparative method, there simply is no basis for asserting it as a matter of science. Because the comparative method involves comparison of words and morphology, and because these things change and are somewhat evanescent, there is an unavoidable temporal horizon. Proto-Indo-European is generally reckoned to date from around 3,000 BCE, about 5,000 years ago. Any linguistic relationship that implies a time depth of more than 7,000–10,000 years has to be very conjectural. And so, Nostratic (much more so, proto-World) involves much speculation, because such distant relationships are intrinsically unprovable by the only existing scientific method for these things.

Whatever the scale of our ambitions, we may think of external languages and their relationships as expressed in figure 2.1, but we should recognize some of the idealizations involved. *Stammbäume* of this kind idealize away from the fact that languages do not split sharply at some specific point and suddenly emerge in their full individuality. The splitting process is more gradual, initiated with relatively minor divergences. We might say that the first change that affected, say, Latin and not any of the other languages is the bifurcation point, the point at which Latin suddenly splits away. But that is not enough. Saying that French and Italian are descended from Latin glosses over the fact that they descended from different forms of Latin, and that "Latin" is a cover term for many different forms of speech. French descended from the Latin spoken in Gaul, Spanish and Portuguese from the Latin spoken in Iberia, and Sardinian from yet another form of Latin spoken on the island. As a result, the conventional tree models of the historical linguists would require vast elaboration to be equivalent to modern, biological cladograms, which are usually based strictly on the molecular structure of organisms.

In addition, languages that are geographically adjacent sometimes influence each other in one way or another, even if they are not closely related historically. This kind of contact-influence was recognized in the nineteenth century and the STAMMBAUMTHEORIE was supplemented by the WELLENTHEORIE; this was a theory of waves of changes that could spread over a geographical area through linguistic contact, affecting geographically contiguous languages that may not be closely related historically. So there may be common innovations that have nothing to do with a common history. To take a trivial example, many historically unrelated languages have a word for 'television' which sounds pretty much like the English *television*. During the period of the Scandinavian settlements, English drew many common words directly from the language of the settlers: *bait, bull, egg, fellow, give, hit, husband, law, low, loose, meek, oar, sister, skin, sky, take, wrong*. English drew much from French during the period of the Norman occupation, musical terms from Italian, *pundit, thug, calico* from India, and *moccasin, toboggan, tomahawk* from American Indian languages. This kind of commonality, due to factors other than a common history, is not expressed by the cladograms, linguistic or biological.

The cladograms of evolutionary biologists deal with branching order alone and exclude any other notion of similarity, such as similarity of form, function, or biological role. The lungfish and coelacanth are vertebrates with scales and fins, fish to you and me. However, they are genealogically more closely related to creatures that crawled out on to land to become amphibians, reptiles, mammals, and birds. The cladogram ignores the fact that the coelacanth looks and acts like a fish, and puts it in a sister group with birds and mammals.

Biologists recognize two very different reasons for similarities between organisms: the similarities might arise because they inherited the same features from a common ancestor (homologies) or because they evolved the features independently in response to life in similar environments (analogies). So humans share hair and a warm-blooded physiology with chimpanzees and mice by evolutionary history, or homology. Birds and bats both fly by analogy, and they have a very different evolutionary history, bats being mammals. Similarly, languages may share features because of a common ancestry or because of common developments. Distinguishing common ancestral features from common developments is often a tricky business for both biologists and for linguists, but the linguists' tree models and the biologists' cladograms are historical models only and determine relatedness only on the basis of homologies.[3]

2.4   Sound laws

As the nineteenth century progressed, linguists formulated historical "laws" with ever greater precision. They studied the similarities among cognate words, words derived from the same historical source; this was the basis for establishing historical relationships and then for establishing the sound changes that derived one form from another historically. To get a flavor of the general enterprise, it will be useful to track one matter in some detail: the shift in the Germanic consonant system, which became famous as "Grimm's Law."

Early in the century, the great Dane, Rasmus Rask, postulated general correspondences between the consonants of German and the ancient Indo-European languages, Greek, Latin, and Sanskrit. He compared words in different languages that seemed to correspond with each other and to be cognate, descended from some common ancestor word. Lining up these correspondences, he noted that where the ancient languages showed a *p* sound, in the corresponding words the Germanic languages showed a fricative *f*.

In 1822 Jacob Grimm, one of the brothers who collected fairy stories, revised his *Deutsche Grammatik* by adding a 595-page account of the phonology of some fifteen different languages and stages of languages. He built on the work of Rask and gave a detailed exposition of the Germanic consonant shift (*Lautverschiebung*), formulating a historical cycle (*Kreislauf* 'rotation') that came to be known as Grimm's Law. He observed that the ancient languages showed a

---

[3] Gould (1985) offers a fascinating and accessible account of how recent work on DNA hybridization has made it easier for biologists to distinguish homologies from analogies, by examining the molecular structure of organisms.

voiceless stop (*p, t, k*) where Germanic languages such as Gothic and English showed a corresponding fricative (*f, th, h*).

	Sanskrit	Greek	Latin	Gothic	English
p		**p**od-	**p**ed-	**f**otus	**f**oot
t	**t**rayas	**t**reis	**t**res	**th**reis	**th**ree
k		**k**ardia	**k**or	**h**airto	**h**eart

Similarly, where the ancient languages showed a voiced stop, Germanic showed a voiceless stop.

b		tur**b**e	tur**b**a	thaur**p**	thor**p**
d	**d**aśa	**d**eka	**d**ecem		**t**en
g		a**g**ros	a**g**er	a**k**rs	a**c**re

And where the ancient languages showed an aspirate (a stop pronounced with a puff of air and written b^h, etc.), Germanic showed an unaspirated voiced stop.

b^h	**b**^harāmi	**p**^hero	**f**ero	**b**aira	**b**ear
d^h	**d**^hā-	ti**t**^hēmi	**f**acio		**d**o
g^h	sti**g**^h-	stei**k**^ho		stei**g**a	**g**o

He took the ancient languages to manifest the consonants of the hypothetical parent language, Proto-Indo-European, more or less directly. The manifestation was not always direct: so the PIE voiced aspirates d^h and g^h were realized as voiceless t^h (written θ, theta) and k^h (χ, chi) in Greek, the aspirates b^h and d^h as a voiceless fricative *f* in Latin. This meant that there were some changes between PIE and the ancient languages. Grimm was interested mostly in the changes between PIE and early Germanic. One can view these changes as a cycle.

There were several exceptions, cases where the correspondences that Grimm hypothesized did not hold, and he showed no interest in them. Others were more interested, however. Many people soon noticed that a voiceless stop in the ancient languages corresponded to a voiceless stop in Germanic, when it was preceded by a fricative. So, while the third person singular of the verb 'to be' was *asti* in Sanskrit, *esti* in Greek, and *est* in Latin, Germanic also showed a *t* in the equivalent position: *ist*, where Grimm's Law would expect *isth*. Similarly Latin has *captus* 'taken' and *noctis* 'night,' while Gothic has *hafts* and *nahts*. In each case, the *t* does not change when it is preceded by a fricative like *s, f* and *h* in Germanic.

In the nineteenth century people were often active in more than one field, and next, in 1863, the ingenious mathematician/linguist Hermann Grassmann (1809–1877) noticed that certain voiced consonants seemed to be preserved in Germanic, not changing to a fricative, as Grimm's cycle would lead one to expect. So, while Sanskrit had *duhitā* 'daughter' and *bodhāmi* 'offer,' Gothic had *dauhtor* and *-biudan*, where the initial *d* and *b* are preserved. Grassmann showed that these are not really counterexamples to Grimm's Law, but just cases where Sanskrit does not manifest the proto-language, PIE, directly. He demonstrated that the *d* of 'daughter' and the *b* of 'offer' must have been the aspirates *d^h* and *b^h* respectively in PIE, corresponding then, as Grimm would expect, to unaspirated, voiced stops *d* and *b* in Germanic. He examined the internal structure of Greek and Sanskrit and showed that they underwent a change: if a word contained two aspirated consonants, the first was de-aspirated. This operation, which came to be honored as "Grassmann's Law," explained some puzzling curiosities.

In general, Greek and Sanskrit nouns show different case markings in the suffixes attached to the end of the stem, and the stem is invariant. However, in some rare instances, the initial consonant of the stem may differ depending on the case form. So, the nominative case of 'hair' in Greek is *t^hriks* (written θρίξ) and the genitive is *trik^hós* (τριχός), with an unaspirated *t* initially. Grassmann explained this oddity by assuming that the most primitive form of the root was *t^hrik^h-*, with two aspirates. The nominative ending was *-s* and the genitive was *-os*. Because aspirates cannot stand immediately before a sibilant *s*, *k^h* was de-aspirated with the nominative *-s* ending, yielding *t^hriks*. On the other hand, the most primitive form of the genitive was *t^hrik^hos*, where the *k^h* was not immediately before an *s*. Now Grassmann's Law, a really ingenious and productive piece of analysis, explains why one finds *trik^hós*: the first of the two aspirates, *t^h*, must be de-aspirated, and we understand why we sometimes find alternating stem forms.

The final step for Grimm's Law came in 1875. Grimm's Law, revised first by the observations about the fricatives, then by Grassmann, worked well for initial consonants, but there were still many apparent exceptions in medial position, and they were now explained by Karl Verner (1846–1896). Certain voiceless stops in the ancient languages did not become voiced stops in Germanic, as Grimm's Law would lead us to suppose, but they became voiced fricatives. So Sanskrit *pitār*, Greek *patēr*, and Latin *pater* show two voiceless stops, presumably indicating that the consonants for the word for 'father' in PIE were *p-t-r*. The first of these stops behaved according to Grimm's Law and became a fricative *f* in Germanic: Gothic *fadar*, English *father*, etc. However, the second stop, the *t*, did not become a voiceless fricative as in English *thin*; unexpectedly, it became a voiced stop *d* in Gothic. On the other hand, the word for 'brother' worked as expected: Sanskrit shows a medial *t* (*b^hrātā*) that corresponds to a voiceless fricative in Gothic (*brōþar*). Verner showed that the different histories of the medial *t* in 'father' and 'brother' were a function of the phonetics of the words: in one case the ancient accent preceded the *t* (*b^hrátā*) and in the other case it followed (*pitá*). This observation, not surprisingly now, entered the canon as Verner's Law.

Verner's Law yielded a more or less complete understanding of the evolution of the Germanic consonantal system and led to the triumphant notion that this was the way things always were: sound change was always regular, exceptionless, and phonetically conditioned. Verner had found a phonetic conditioning factor, something in the pronunciation of the word itself, which would predict how the medial consonant would behave, namely the position of the accent. At the end of the century, people like Eduard Sievers made phonetics into more of an empirical, experimental science, which promised to provide explanations for the changes represented by sound laws (Sievers 1876). The laws were thought to be reducible to facts about speech articulation, along with some general principles (see below).

Those are the details of the consonant shifts in Germanic; now let's stand back from the details. 1876 brought a lot of productive work and is often referred to as the *annus mirabilis* of the nineteenth century (Hoenigswald 1978). The idea that sound change was regular and systematic was formulated in 1878 in the preface to Osthoff and Brugmann's *Morphologische Untersuchungen*, and the people who held the idea of exceptionless regularity were the *Junggrammatiker*, the "neogrammarians." Davies (1998) describes them as "the instigators of a sort of Kuhnian revolution in both technique and methodology," and Hockett (1965: 188) saw them as "a group of young Turks, armed with a vitally important idea and with enormous arrogance, winning converts and making enemies as much through charisma as by reasonable persuasion." Davies says that early on "they were covered with opprobrium but they were also revered with the sort of devotion which is more suitable for the followers of a religious sect than for members of a scholarly movement," and eventually they turned into members of the establishment and were accused of stuffiness, dogmatism, and inflexibility.

This nineteenth-century work on the Germanic consonant shift illustrates a more general point. The field of linguistics first identified itself by claiming that language history was LAW GOVERNED, even if the notion of law (Grimm's Law, Grassmann's Law, Verner's Law) was scarcely that of Boyle's Law or the law of gravity, which are timeless. The laws referred to specific sound changes or "correspondences" affecting specific languages at specific times. One could formulate precise correspondences of the form $a \rightarrow b$ *in some phonetically definable context*, where a and b were sounds in corresponding words at two stages of history. The inventory of words in some language (attested or reconstructed) was converted into the inventory of corresponding words at some later stage. Sound a became something else, b, systematically. Languages were seen as inventories of words and it was those inventories that changed. In any event, languages were supposed to change in systematic ways and historical linguists, perhaps more than other kinds of linguists, have always been concerned with issues of explanation. The question then arises of what kind of explanation could be offered for sound changes of this type.

2.5   Historical explanations

Work on language history at this time reflected the two dominant models of what a science should be: Newtonian mechanics and Darwin's theory of evolution. It also reflected the influence of Hegel, as was explicit in the work of Schleicher on the "*Sprachgeist*" 'spirit of the language'. Newton had all phenomena describable by deterministic laws of force and motion, in such a way that all future states were, in principle, predictable in a "straight-line," linear fashion from a complete knowledge of the present state. This inspired the notion of sound LAWS to describe the history of changes. The term *Lautgesetz* ('sound law') was first coined by Bopp in 1824, and he even offered a mechanical explanation for Ablaut alternations (i.e. alternations like English *fell-fall*, *take-took*, *swim-swam*, where the difference in the medial vowel determines the difference in meaning) by invoking a "law of gravity" and postulating that syllables had different "weights." As we just saw, the concept of the sound law became more rigorous as the century proceeded, until eventually in 1878 sound change was declared to be regular and exceptionless.

Darwin was inspired by work on language history, and he, in turn. inspired the linguists to view languages as natural organisms, on a par with plants and animals. He influenced Schleicher, as we have noted, Franz Bopp (1791–1867), and August Pott (1802–1877). The linguist's language families, languages, dialects, and idiolects were the biologist's genera, species, varieties, and individuals. Languages, like species, compete with each other in a struggle for survival, in the view of Schleicher, and there were inexorable laws of change to be discovered.

Nineteenth-century linguists treated languages as objects "out there," as noted, but some knew that they reflected psychological properties. Karl Brugmann wrote at the beginning of his career that "the human speech mechanism has a twofold aspect, a mental and a physical" (Lehmann 1967: 198), going on to talk about the "psychophysical mechanism." At the end of his career, he wrote a monograph entitled "Varieties of sentence formation according to the basic psychological functions in the Indo-European languages" (Brugmann 1918); many of the central ideas recur in Brugmann (1925: ch. 6). Heymann Steinthal (1823–1899), strongly influenced by Hegel, was a linguist who wrote extensively about psychology and its links with language. He, in turn, influenced Hermann Paul, who strikes us now as an early kindred spirit in the way he thought about psychology. Furthermore, there were psychologists who dealt with language and its acquisition, Wilhelm Wundt (1832–1920) and others. Wundt was known to and greatly admired by Leonard Bloomfield (1887–1947), when he was young, before he discovered Watson and the behaviorists.

The psychological notions of the time were problematic, partly because they were wrapped up in ideas of Hegel's. Grimm, for example, adopted a mystical belief in a Hegelian *Sprachgeist*, which had some existence above and beyond individuals (below). This idea was formulated as *Völkerpsychologie* by Wundt, Steinthal, and Moritz Lazarus and this group psychology was attacked by Paul as being incoherent (1880: 11):

Alle psychischen Prozesse vollziehen sich in den Einzelgeistern und nirgends sonst. Weder Volksgeist noch Elemente des Volksgeistes wie Kunst, Religion etc. haben eine konkrete Existenz, und folglich kann auch nichts in ihnen und zwischen ihnen vorgehen. Daher weg mit diesen Abstraktionen!

'All psychical processes come to their fulfillment in individual minds, and nowhere else. Neither the popular mind, nor elements of it, such as art, religion, etc., have any concrete existence, and therefore nothing can come to pass in them and between them. Away, then, with these abstractions!'

Whatever the problems, linguists separated this kind of psychologizing from their day-to-day work. Pedersen's (1931) survey of nineteenth-century work on language scarcely refers to the psychologists at all. William Dwight Whitney, professor of Sanskrit and comparative philology at Yale College, put the demarcation clearly:

The human capacity to which the production of language is most directly due is, as has been seen, the power of intelligently, and not by blind instinct alone, adapting means to ends. This is by no means a unitary capacity; on the contrary, it is a highly composite and intricate one. But it does not belong to the linguistic student to unravel and explain . . . it falls, rather, to the student of the human mind and its powers, to the psychologist. So with all the mental capacities involved in language. . . (1875: 303)

And this was the general view of linguists through Bloomfield and the structuralists: leave psychology to the psychologists.

Linguists generally did not appeal to psychology to explain historical changes. Instead, there were independent laws of history to be found. These historical laws operated on the sounds of the languages and were manifested in the relationship between corresponding words in different, historically related languages.

The end-of-the-century neogrammarians were the culmination of this research paradigm but they confronted two major problems. First, there were regularities of language change that could not be stated in purely phonetic terms, which suggested that it wasn't the language or the sounds that were changing but rather some kind of abstract system. This matter was dealt with by a terminological move: they were dealing with the law-governed regularities of "sound change," but there could be other kinds of change which worked differently, namely what was called "analogical change," which was not law-governed in the same way. Analogy was a different and somewhat more mysterious kind of regularity.

It may make sense to think of words being transmitted from one generation to another, and, if they are transmitted in different form, then change has taken place. But in this regard the nineteenth-century linguists were focusing on the products of human behavior rather than on the internal processes that underlie the behavior, on E-language rather than I-language. Not all aspects of language can be treated productively in this way, and sometimes one has to deal with the underlying processes and abstract systems. This is true for Grimm's Law, for example, which affected many consonants in a kind of cycle (figure 2.2); it is also true of more complex changes such as the famous Great English Vowel Shift, which changed all the long vowels of Middle English in another kind of cycle (raising all vowels by one step and diphthongizing the highest vowels: so /tiːm/ 'time' (rhyming with modern *team*) became /taim/, /sweːt/ 'sweet' (rhyming with modern *sweat*, modulo the difference in vowel length) became /swiːt/, and /huːs/ 'house' (with the vowel of modern *loose*) became /haus/. Grimm's Law and the Great Vowel Shift affect many sounds and represent changes in systems.[4] Individual words change but those changes only make sense in the context of the systematic change of figure 2.3 and of Grimm's *Kreislauf* (figure 2.2).

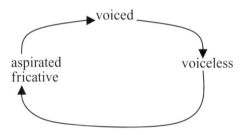

Figure 2.2 Grimm's *Kreislauf*

---

[4] The neogrammarians worked with the products of language rather than with the internal, underlying processes and abstract systems. Consequently, there were principled reasons why they did not extend their ideas of phonetic change to the domain of syntax, which requires some kind of abstract system (for discussion, see Lightfoot 1979). Brugmann & Delbrück (1886–1900) provide many sound laws to relate the words of languages but their discussion of syntax is quite different: no comparable historical developments are postulated. Instead, their discussion of syntax is confined to catalogs of clause types in various languages with no diachronic links specified.

It makes no sense to think of (sets of) sentences, products of behavior, being transmitted from one generation to another, because language acquisition is clearly not just a matter of acquiring sets of sentences, as will become clear in the next chapter. None of this bothered nineteenth-century linguists, because they thought of language as a collection of words, with everything else due either to universal "logic" or individually variable "habits." So there wasn't anything to have a history of except words, their pronunciations, and their meanings.

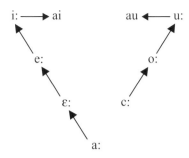

Figure 2.3 The Great Vowel Shift

So, as far as one can tell, the first problem and the matter of abstract systems assumed very little, if any, importance at the time. Rather, there was much debate about the second problem, the causes of sound change.

Grimm's, Grassmann's, and Verner's Laws were not general laws like Boyle's Law and therefore they required a deeper explanation. Changes were taken to be DIRECTIONAL ... as in biology, where the replacement of one species by another was taken to result from a mutation that yields an organism that is more successful in the struggle for survival in a particular environment. Rask (1818) held that languages became simpler. Schleicher (1848) identified a progression from isolating to agglutinating to inflectional types, although this was said to hold for preliterate societies and Rask's drive to simplicity was relevant for postliterate societies. There was widespread agreement that language change followed fixed developmental laws and that there was a direction to change, but there was active disagreement about WHICH direction that was. This was a matter of live dispute. By the end of the nineteenth century there was an enormous body of work on sound correspondences between historically related languages and vast compendia of changes that had taken place in many Indo-European languages. The great monument was Karl Brugmann and Berthold Delbrück's multivolume *Grundriss der vergleichenden Grammatik der indogermanischen Sprachen*, published between 1886 and 1900. But alongside such compendia there were few sustainable ideas of why those changes had happened. Eventually the directionality view crumbled.

The notion that languages became simpler/more natural/easier to pronounce was, first, circular. "Simpler" etc. is what languages change to and there was no independent definition in a framework dealing entirely with historical change. Since linguists regarded their work as essentially concerned with language change, they sealed it off from other concerns, and did not work on language acquisition in an integrated way. Consequently, they had no independent way to define their central notions. Once we move beyond the nineteenth century, we find less restricted approaches; linguists like Jespersen broke out of the circle by developing independent notions of simplicity. Even in the late nineteenth century, the beginning of instrumental phonetics enabled people like Sievers to link changes to possible assimilation patterns that change sounds in certain phonetic environments.

Second, the idea that languages change towards greater simplicity (or whatever) gives no account of why a given change should take place when it does – unlike the laws of gravity, which apply to all objects at all times. To that extent, invoking notions of directionality was no more lawlike than the laws of Grimm, Grassmann, and Verner, which directionality was intended to explain.

There was much discussion of the causes of sound change in the contemporary literature, and this was where the problems were perceived to lie. There were occasional attempts to break out of the circle by invoking psychology, but the psychology was implausible. So Grimm (1848: 417, 437) explained his law of consonant shifts as

connected with the German's mighty progress and struggle for freedom . . . the invincible German race was becoming ever more vividly aware of the unstoppability of its advance into all parts of Europe . . . How could such a forceful mobilization of the race have failed to stir up its language at the same time, jolting it out of its traditional rut and exalting it? Does there not lie a certain courage and pride in the strengthening of voiced stop into voiceless stop and voiceless stop into fricative?

Of course, Grimm's contemporaries did not accept such explanations uniformly, but this style of explanation was not unique. If this seems a bit wild and far-fetched, it is not substantially different from a claim made by Otto Jespersen. The verb *like* shifted its meaning in the fifteenth century and ceased to mean 'cause pleasure for' or 'please.' One could no longer say things like *The pears like the king*, meaning 'the pears please the king,' as was possible in earlier English. Jespersen claimed that this shift was due to the "greater interest taken in persons than in things."

Explanations of this kind may never have had much going for them, but they were curiously resistant and were never decisively and explicitly refuted. One has to see them for what they are: psychological elements introduced into essentially a historicist and a-psychological theory, based crucially on an external notion of languages, as an attempt to break out of a narrow circle and reach some level of explanation. The psychology invoked was never convincing.

By the early twentieth century the data of linguistics seemed to be an inventory of sound changes occurring for no good reason and tending in no particular direction. The historical approach had not brought a scientific, Newtonian-style analysis of language, of the kind that had been hoped for, and there was no predictability about changes. The psychological moves of Paul, Jespersen, et al.

could not provide the necessary underpinning. Consequently, the program was not viable; no sustainable explanations were available for the observed phenomena, i.e. historical changes, and there was no science of history which met nineteenth-century demands. The main problem here is that the demands were misconceived and too ambitious for the externalist notion of language employed.

Another way of looking at this is to note that some changes in language may be brought about by contact with other languages (there are very few well-established cases in the literature, but let us agree that they may exist) or by novel expressions taking root in the language as speakers strive for unusual or striking forms. Also, the use of some constructions may change in frequency of occurrence. In that case, one cannot predict the development of Portuguese unless one is able to show which foreign influences will succeed and which novel expressions, once adopted, will survive. So linguistic history cannot be determined by structural factors alone. One cannot give a good description of the current state of one's favorite language and expect the historians to engage in a kind of Newtonian determinism and to provide a computer program that will predict the state of the language in, say, 200 years. For all the talk of directionality, the evidence is that nineteenth-century linguists were not altogether at ease with it; certainly their analyses allowed for particular, contingent factors. After all, in certain circumstances some forms of spoken Latin developed into some form of French, and in other circumstances other forms of Latin developed into Spanish and Sardinian; there was nothing intrinsic to Latin that forced it to develop into French.

The historicist paradigm was largely abandoned in the 1920s, i.e. the notion that there are principles of history to be discovered that would account for a language's development. Indeed, there was a virulent anti-historicism in the writing of the structuralists Franz Boas, Leonard Bloomfield, and Edward Sapir. They worked on language change to their deaths, showing that the traditional methods of historical and comparative linguistics were as applicable to the unwritten, indigenous languages of North America as they were to Indo-European; Bloomfield worked on the reconstruction of proto-Algonquian for most of his career. They also perpetuated many of the analytical procedures of the historical linguists in their own synchronic work. However, they abandoned HISTORICISM; they abandoned the earlier program of seeking to explain how it was that languages came to be the way they are.

The perceived problems related to the circularity of invoking historical principles and to the psychological claims. Sapir (1929) wrote that the psychological interpretation of language change was "desirable and even necessary" but the existing psychological explanations were unhelpful and "do not immediately tie up with what we actually know about the historical behavior of language." Bloomfield (1933: 17) complained about the circularity of Paul's psychologizing, saying that there was no independent evidence for the mental processes other than the linguistic processes they were supposed to explain. The historicist paradigm was not really refuted or shown to be seriously inadequate by Bloomfield, Boas, Sapir, and the structuralists; rather, it was just abandoned as yielding diminishing returns. The paradigm had turned to psychology to avoid an inbuilt circularity and then collapsed because of the inadequacy of the psychology invoked. Work on language change flourished, but twentieth-century structuralists, by and large, did not appeal to historicist explanations.

The highly deterministic view of history that the linguists sometimes articulated, the idea that there are laws which determine the way that history proceeds, is a hallmark of the nineteenth century. We have seen how it guided the systematic study of language in the nineteenth century, and it played a role in the development of Darwinian ideas and in the domain of political history.

We know that Darwin read the linguists and vice versa, and Marx dedicated *Das Kapital* to Darwin. Darwin was too much of a Victorian not to appeal to notions of progress, but he was critical of the notion and modulated in his appeals to it. Marx too had an interesting theory of change in which ideas are socially embedded and are amended through conflict, through the clash of theses and antitheses. One changes by negating some previous idea, and then one negates that negation without going back to the first idea, having already moved on somewhere else. Marx's view of social change and revolution, in which small insults to the system build up until the system itself breaks, is a very sensible approach and quite compatible with what we shall sketch in later chapters. However, Marx was very much a nineteenth-century thinker in that he was caught up in notions of predestiny and determinism, particularly in theories of history, developing historical laws prescribing that a feudal society must necessarily develop into a mercantilist society, a mercantilist into a capitalist society, capitalism into socialism, and socialism into communism (Cohen 1978). For Marx, the real task of economics was to explain how society evolved over time. At his funeral, Engels eulogized him in a way that he would have liked: "Just as Darwin discovered the law of evolution in organic nature, so Marx discovered the law of evolution in human history."

The nineteenth-century search for deterministic laws for the history of languages failed. Linguists had focused entirely on external languages, on products rather than internal processes, and were unable to find explanations for the sound changes they were describing, and they had no account for why new languages should emerge in the way and at the time that they did.

2.6   Drift, typologists, and grammaticalization

Languages were seen as external objects floating smoothly through time and space, and that nineteenth-century image survived the twentieth century. Despite the move away from historicism in the 1920s, linguists resumed the search for historical principles in the latter decades of the twentieth century. In the 1970s much work recast the notion of "drift," originated by Sapir (1921: ch. 7).[5] The "typologists," working from Greenberg's (1966) word-order harmonies, claimed that languages changed along universal diachronic continua, moving from one pure type to another via universally defined transitional stages. Languages change from one pure type to another by losing/acquiring the relevant orders in the sequence specified by the hierarchies. A pure subject–verb–object language, for example, has verb–object order, auxiliary–verb, noun–adjective, and preposition–noun phrase, and these orders are ranked in a hierarchy. A subject–object–verb language is essentially the mirror image and has the opposite orders: object–verb, verb–auxiliary, adjective–noun, and noun phrase–preposition, etc. If a language changes from the object–verb type to the verb–object type, it acquires all of the new orders in the sequence prescribed by the hierarchy: first verb–object, then auxiliary–verb, and so on. The hierarchy is the substance of a historical law that stipulates how a language of one type changes to a language of a different type. The typologists argued that notions like the continua of subject–object–verb to subject–verb–object constituted diachronic explanations (Vennemann 1975); for them, the drift was the explanatory force, rather than being something that required explanation, and no local causes were needed. The typologists remained faithful to the methods of the nineteenth century. They dealt with the products of the language capacity rather than with the capacity itself, and they retained the same kind of historical determinism, believing that languages of one type change inexorably to a language of another type, like their nineteenth-century predecessors. The goal remained one of finding "straight-line explanations for language change" (Lass 1980), generalizations which would hold for history. And they were no more successful.

A more recent line of work has emphasized the alleged unidirectionality of change, also treating languages as external objects "out there," subject to change in certain inevitable ways. GRAMMATICALIZATION, a notion first introduced by Antoine Meillet in the 1930s, is taken to be a semantic tendency for an item with a full lexical meaning to be bleached over time and to come to be used as a grammatical function. So the Old English verb *willan* 'wish,'

---

[5]   An important difference is that Sapir regarded drift as an explanandum, something to be explained, while modern work has taken drift as an explanatory force, an explanans (see Lightfoot 1999: ch. 8).

became an Inflectional marker of future tense (chapter 5); verbs meaning 'say' have become sentence introducers in some languages, equivalent to English *that* in a sentence like *I think that it is hot*. Such changes are said to be quite general and unidirectional; one does not find changes proceeding in the reverse direction, so it is said. We shall discuss an instance of grammaticalization in chapter 6 and there are many examples (Hopper & Traugott 2003). Grammaticalization is a real phenomenon but it is quite a different matter to claim that it is general, unidirectional, or an explanatory force. If there were a universal tendency to grammaticalize, there would be no counterdevelopments, when bound forms become independent lexical items (affixes becoming clitics or independent words – an example of this, to be discussed in chapter 6, is genitive endings in -*es* in Middle English being reanalyzed as *his*, yielding genitives like *Christ his sake, Mrs. Sands his maid*); for further examples and discussion, see van Gelderen (1997), Janda (2001), Joseph (2001), Newmeyer (1998: ch. 5). When grammaticalization takes place, it is explained when one points to local factors that promoted the new grammar, new triggering experiences, changes in cues, or what Kiparsky (1996) called the "enabling causes." Grammaticalization, interesting as a PHENOMENON, is not an explanatory force.[6]

2.7   Conclusion

We have seen that much of traditional historical linguistics is predicated on E-language conceptions, taking languages to be objects out there, asking how a language with certain properties can change into a different language, and appealing to historical principles for explanations. Languages are taken as givens and linguists debate the rate at which languages change, assuming that they can specify when Latin became French and then, much more speculatively, when Proto-Indo-European became Proto-Germanic. Theories have been developed about what drives linguistic diversification and why languages spread. One theory keys the distribution and areal extent of many of the world's languages to the expansion of farming (Renfrew 2000). Dixon (1997) divides linguistic development into periods of equilibrium, when "languages in contact will diffuse features between each other, becoming more and more similar" (1997: 70–71), and periods of cataclysmic events which trigger "split and expansion" (1997: 67). The *Stammbaum* model of languages splitting (figure 2.1) is relevant, he says, only for the cataclysmic periods of punctuation and not for the longer periods of equilibrium. This presupposes that there was a definable point at which, say, Latin changed into French, but he does not say when that was or how we can determine such points. Nichols (1992) undertakes population

---

[6] For more discussion, see Lightfoot (1999: ch. 8). For an attempt to understand grammaticalization through Minimalist approaches to grammatical theory, see Roberts & Roussou (2003).

studies, seeking links among language populations, establishing the relative age of linguistic features, trying to show how these features have spread and how languages came to have their geographical distributions. These approaches are based on detailed assumptions about the divisions between languages that are not justified or examined or even articulated.

Languages, seen as external objects, have been the stock-in-trade of traditional historical linguistics. Efforts to establish principles that languages tend to change in certain directions have not generalized well and have yielded no understanding of how new languages have emerged when they have. I intend to investigate an alternative approach that does not focus exclusively on external languages but incorporates individual linguistic capacities, people's language organs.

3   Some properties of language organs

3.1   Recursive and compositional

English, Dutch, etc., are external languages and such "languages" have no biological reality and cannot even be defined in any precise way, as we saw in the last chapter. Certainly children do not acquire one of those external objects, as if selecting from a supermarket aisle. In this chapter I shall begin to examine a different approach, where we view languages as private, internal, individual entities. A person has a linguistic capacity, acquired under the conditions of childhood, and represented in his/her brain. No two people speak absolutely alike and, personally, I speak David Lightfoot, slightly different from my brothers' speech, and our mother can tell us apart on the telephone. We shall investigate some of the properties that a person's individual language must have, what we are calling her I-language, and the way that it is acquired in childhood.

First, as we noted in chapter 1, a person's language capacity ranges over an infinitude of data. One can appreciate this on an intuitive level. One expresses and encounters new sentences all the time. Take any random sentence from the last chapter and it is likely that you have not said it or heard it in just that form, but there is no difficulty in understanding what it means, or so I hope. Similarly the next complete sentence that you utter is likely to be novel. It may be quite banal, perhaps something along the lines of *I wonder whether Manchester United can beat Real Madrid next week*, but you will say it if that is the thought you want to express and not because you are imitating somebody who said just that sometime previously. Always novelty.

One can also appreciate the infinitude of the language capacity at a more precise level. We all have the capacity to produce sentences of indefinite length. I gave an example in chapter 1 of a long, complex sentence that many children are exposed to and is completely straightforward to understand: *This is the cow that kicked the dog that chased the cat that killed the rat that caught the mouse that nibbled the cheese that lay in the house that Jack built.* That sentence involves a sequence of seven relative clauses, each introduced by *that*, and one could make it longer by inserting *the snake that stung* and *the farmer that shot*, etc. In fact, one could lengthen the sentence in that way for ten minutes, or twenty, ad nauseam, or ad mortem. Everybody has a language capacity that would enable us to keep a sentence going indefinitely, if we were so inclined. We don't do that, but the reason lies in our attention span and in the fact that all of us have better things to do than to produce a single, unending sentence. Our language CAPACITY permits any sentence to be extended indefinitely, and therefore there is an indefinite number of sentences and everybody's language capacity ranges over an infinitude of data.

Regardless of where we were raised and whether we grew up in some form of English-speaking community or in Tokyo or Tegucigalpa, we all have three RECURSIVE devices enabling us to produce sentences of indefinite length. One, the one just illustrated, is the relative clause or what linguists call RELATIVIZATION, where the clause modifies the head noun as an adjective modifies a noun or an adverb modifies a verb.

A second device is COMPLEMENTATION, where we use a verb followed by a complement clause (again introduced each time by *that* in this example): *Gerry said that Jim said that Sheila thought that Darryl said that Mieke told . . .* and so on until patience runs out.

The third recursive device is COORDINATION, introduced by words like *and*, *but*, and *while*: *Rick and Jennifer went to the movie and Hillary and Stacey to the store, while Stuart and Karin and Julie worked where Mary and Daniel were watching, but Liam and Ellen and Chris slept.* So three recursive devices and, of course, we are free to combine those devices in any one expression (*Fred and the woman I met in Hamburg thought that Chicago was hot*); that's what yields the infinite capacity.

So a person's language capacity ranges over infinity, but if grammars are represented in the brain, they need to be finite. That means that grammars need to specify that any noun may be modified by a relative clause (*farmer who mowed the grass*), that certain verbs may be followed by a clause (that may contain another verb that may, in turn, be followed by a clause: *said that Fred thought that Chicago was hot*), and that any category may be linked with a coordinator, which may, in turn, be linked with another coordinator (*John and Susan and Mary*). That information is finite but may be used indefinitely. In sum, we have three recursive devices that enable us to utter a sentence of indefinite length, and that is a fundamental property of people's language organs, their grammars, their I-languages.

Furthermore, nobody has ever heard a sentence of indefinite length; everything you or I have ever heard has ended at some point. Therefore the indefinitely recursive nature of these three devices is not learned from experience but must be an intrinsic property of our grammars, independent of experience. So the first property of language organs turns out not to be learnable.

A second fundamental property of everybody's grammar is that it is COMPOSITIONAL: expressions are made of units, made up of smaller units, each made up of still smaller units. This compositionality of language can be illustrated by the ambiguity of phrases like *I saw old men and women* or *I saw a man with a telescope*. In the first case, I may have seen old men and old women or old men and women of whom some were young. The adjective *old* may modify *men* or *men and women*. Put differently, *and women* may be linked with *old men* or just with *men*; the complement of *saw* may be [[old men] and women] or [old [men and women]] and the subunits are different, corresponding to the two possible meanings. Similarly, I may have seen a man who had a telescope or perhaps I saw a man when I was using a telescope, and the complement of *saw* may be [a man with a telescope] or just [a man]; if the latter, then *with a telescope* modifies the verb phrase unit VP[saw a man]. Not all such sentences are ambiguous: *I saw a man with curly hair* would most naturally have a constituent structure VP[saw [a man with curly hair]], because one doesn't see with curly hair, and *I saw a man in Chicago* would most naturally be [VP[saw [a man]] PP[in Chicago]]. Different units. People's grammars make both possibilities available. Each structure correlates with a certain function, which will be more or less appropriate under different circumstances, and that is a matter of the USE of the system.

Linguists analyze this by saying that words belong to categories like noun, verb, preposition, adjective, determiner, and inflection, and that such categories head phrases. *Saw a man* is a verb phrase headed by the verb *saw*, *a man with curly hair* is a determiner phrase headed by the determiner *a*, which is followed by a noun phrase *man with curly hair*, headed by the noun *man*. This yields constituent structures along the lines of (1), where VP is a verb phrase, DP a determiner phrase, NP a noun phrase, PP a preposition phrase, and A an adjective.

(1)

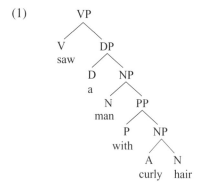

This kind of compositionality is another fundamental property of people's grammars, regardless of their childhood experience. However, the fact that grammars are compositional, having hierarchical structures of this type, is a universal property of everybody's system and not a response to particular childhood experiences. It is part of what children bring to the analysis of what they hear. There are aspects of phrase structure which do not depend on initial experiences and some that do. For example, some grammars have structures like that of (1), where the verb precedes its complement, while other grammars (e.g. those of German, Dutch, Japanese, and Korean speakers) have complements preceding verbs. This may be a matter of differing phrase structure (or perhaps not; it might be handled differently) but, in any case, it is an example of what linguists have called parametric variation.

Linguists have theories of phrase structure. A head may have one complement (e.g. the DP [a man with curly hair] is the complement of the verb *saw* in (1)), a number of adjuncts (the PP [with curly hair] is an adjunct to *man* in (1)), and a Specifier (*John* in *John's book*). The phrase structure for any expression needs to provide the units to which the grammar's computational operations apply. That will make sense in a few pages.

So a person's grammar is represented in his/her brain and characterizes his/her linguistic capacity. It is finite, ranges over infinity, and is compositional. We know more about grammars: for example, they are used in speech production and comprehension. That is to say, when you listen to somebody speak, you interpret what they say by accessing your own grammar. If you are a speaker of Icelandic and the speaker speaks some form of Japanese, your grammar won't be of any help and you won't understand. Similarly, when we speak, we utilize our particular grammar. We also know that grammars are acquired in the first few years of life and that is the fact that has had greatest influence on what we have learned about grammars over the last fifty years. We might have learned more from studying how grammars are used in speech comprehension, but that's not the way it has been.

The reality is that we have learned most about grammars so far from the fact that they distinguish well-formed from ill-formed structures, matching well-formed structures to appropriate meanings (logical forms), and from the fact that they are acquired by children in the first few years of life on exposure to some initial experiences. We have already seen two general properties of grammars that are not learned from environmental input, namely the recursive property manifested by the devices of relativization, complementation, and coordination, and the nature of phrase structure. We shall now see more specific properties of grammars and I shall focus on these poverty-of-stimulus problems relentlessly.

3.2   Poverty of the stimulus

Linguists have been impressed with poverty-of-stimulus problems: children
come to have a system that is not fully determined by their initial experiences. This was discussed briefly in chapter 1 but I will now work up some
poverty-of-stimulus problems in more detail, because poverty-of-stimulus problems are fundamental to our approach. I will point to some things that children learn from their environment, contrasting it with information prescribed
internally.

I noted in chapter 1 that children might hear (2a) or (2b) and thereby learn
that *is* may be pronounced in a reduced form as *'s*. That is, there is an operation
(2c).

(2)   a. Kim is taller.
       b. Kim's taller.
       c. is → 's

However, nobody would reduce the second *is* in (3a) to say **Kim's taller than
Jim's*, nor the other instances of *is* in (3b–e): **I don't know what the problem's
with this solution, *I wonder where the concert's on Wednesday, *She asked
what that's up there, *Sit raining?*

(3)   a. Kim's taller than Jim is.
       b. I don't know what the problem is with this solution.
       c. I wonder where the concert is on Wednesday.
       d. She asked what that is up there.
       e. Is it raining?

In other words, the operation (2c), learned by hearing expressions like (2a)
and (2b), does not apply in these cases and the problem is that this restriction
is not learnable: there are no data available to the child that demonstrate the
restriction, on the assumption that children are exposed to things they hear and
not systematically to information about what does not occur. This is the poverty-
of-stimulus problem. The stimulus that children have, their initial experience,
is not rich enough to determine the restriction on (2c) and a host of other
things that characterize their mature capacity. Somehow children know from
something like (2b) that *is* may be reduced but they also know not to reduce *is*
in other contexts, even though they have no evidence to that effect – remember
that children are not conservative and do not say only what they have heard;
they innovate in the same way that adults use novel expressions every waking
minute.

Linguists have postulated that children must have certain information independently of experience, available generally to the species innately and enabling
them to develop the kinds of grammars they have on the basis of their

rudimentary experience in the first few years of life. As noted in chapter 1, we have worked with the explanatory schema of (4).

(4)   a. Primary Linguistic Data (UG → grammar)
         b. Triggering experience (genotype → phenotype)

Children are exposed to primary data. The primary data are the kinds of things that any child could be expected to hear; they do not include negative data about what does not occur, nor information about paraphrase relations, entailments, and certainly not comparative data from other languages. That kind of "secondary data" is available to researchers, linguists, and features in books, articles, and argumentation generally, but is not available to young children. On the basis of exposure only to primary data and endowed with certain properties encoded somehow in the genetic material (Universal Grammar), children acquire a mature grammar, part of their phenotype that varies depending on whether their initial experiences were in Tokyo or Toronto. This grammar is their language organ, it develops in accordance with the prescriptions of UG, and it accounts also for secondary data. Put differently, children have triggering experiences that stimulate their genetic properties to develop into their phenotypic properties, perhaps being able to understand Japanese speakers and speak some form of Japanese.

Under this view, linguists have sought to tease apart what can plausibly be learned and which aspects of a person's mature linguistic capacity cannot be learned. The capacity to form sentences of indefinite length is not learned. Every sentence or expression that you have heard has ended; nobody ever heard a sentence of indefinite length, and therefore that property of people's linguistic capacity is not learned from experience but must be part of what the human brain brings to language acquisition.

3.3   Deletion

Here is another example of a poverty-of-stimulus problem and we will work out some of the details over the next several pages: for English speakers, sentence introducers like *that* (which linguists call "complementizers") may generally be omitted, unlike equivalent words in Dutch, French, Spanish, Italian, and various other languages. If *that* is a complementizer, C, then the phrase it heads is a complementizer phrase, CP, which I indicate in (5). A child might hear the sentences of (5a–c) pronounced with or without the complementizer *that*. Such experiences would license a computational operation (5d) whereby *that* may delete – the operation changes the structure, deleting an element; the operation is learnable on exposure to sentences like those corresponding to (5a–c): *Peter said Kay left*, *The book Kay wrote arrived*, *It was obvious Kay left*. French and

Dutch children have no such comparable experiences and hence no grounds to postulate a comparable device in their grammars; nothing like (5d) would be triggered.

(5)   a. Peter said cp[that/0 Kay left].
        b. The book cp[that/0 Kay wrote] arrived.
        c. It was obvious cp[that/0 Kay left].
        d. That → 0.

In this chapter I will formulate things consistently as poverty-of-stimulus problems. A linguist may observe that the generalization (5d) breaks down at certain points and *that* may NOT be omitted in the contexts of (6). Nobody would say *Kay left was obvious to all of us* (6c). The crucial data here are negative data, data about what does NOT occur, and hence not available to children; that is the poverty of the stimulus. UG must be playing some role.

(6)   a. Peter said yesterday in Chicago cp[that/*0 Kay had left].
        b. The book arrived yesterday cp[that/*0 Kay wrote].
        c. cp[that/*0 Kay left] was obvious to all of us.
        d. Fay believes, but Kay doesn't, cp[that/*0 Ray is smart].
        e. Fay said Ray left and Tim ve cp[that/*0 Jim stayed].

Researchers can see that *that* is omitted if its clause is the COMPLEMENT of an overt, adjacent word, completing the meaning of that adjacent word.[1] In (5) the clause indicated in square brackets (CP) is the complement of the word immediately preceding it. In (6a,b), on the other hand, the clause is the complement of *said* and *book* respectively, neither adjacent; it does not complete the meaning of the adjacent *Chicago* or of *yesterday* and is not its complement. In (6c), the clause is the complement of nothing, in (6d) the complement of *believes*, which is not adjacent, and in (6e) the complement of a verb that is understood but not overt ("e" for empty). Children cannot learn this, because the relevant data are non-primary data, data about what does not occur, and children do not experience such data.

If we just look at this narrow range of facts, it seems that we need to postulate as part of Universal Grammar, the linguistic genotype, that complementizers, if they are deletable, may only be deleted from clauses that are complements of an adjacent, overt word and we solve this particular poverty-of-stimulus problem. Deletability is a learned property of English speakers but not of typical French speakers, but the CONDITIONS of deletability are not learned. The unlearned restriction on deletability looks very specific, perhaps too specialized, but it solves our immediate problem and things get more interesting, if we look further.

---

[1] In (5a,c) the clause completes the meaning of *said* and *was obvious*, respectively, which would mean nothing if the clause were not present.

The data are complex but there is a simple analysis. Keep your eye on the analysis, particularly the single condition of (10), and the apparent complexity of data will be understandable.

In the last section I discussed the compositionality of language, the fact that expressions consist of subunits hierarchically organized. That feature of everybody's language capacity also cannot be learned from a typical child's initial experience and must also be provided by UG, but I won't pursue that here.

Current work assumes a bottom-up approach to phrase structure: structures are built up word by word. Elements drawn from the lexicon are M E R G E D into structures one-by-one. So the verb *visit* may be merged with the noun *London* to yield a verb phrase, VP (7a). Then the inflectional element *will* is merged with that VP to yield an inflection phrase, IP (7b), and the (pro)noun *you* is merged with that IP to yield (7c).

(7)   a. $_{VP}[_V visit \,_N London]$
        b. $_{IP}[_I will \,_{VP}[_V visit \,_N London]]$
        c. $_{IP}[_N you \,_{IP}[_I will \,_{VP}[_V visit \,_N London]]$

An expression like (8a) is built bottom-up in the same way, but it involves copying, another computational operation. It contains the word *what*, which is displaced: understood in one position (the complement of *buy*) and pronounced elsewhere (at the front of the expression). At a certain point the IP *you did buy what* is built (8b) and then *did* is copied and merged, *Did you did buy what?*, and then *what*, yielding *What did you did buy what?* In each case the copied element is later deleted (8c), *What did you buy?* This is crucial for everything that follows.

(8)   a. What did you buy?
        b. $_{IP}[you \, did \,_{VP}[buy \, what]]$
        c. $[what_i \, [did_j \,_{IP}[you \, \text{did}_j \, buy \, \text{what}_i]]]$

There is good reason to believe that UG requires that copied elements must be deleted and that children know that in advance of experience and don't have to learn it.[2] But here I shall simply assume that copied elements must be deleted and now the question is how *what* is deleted.

The condition we just postulated for the deletion of complementizers seems to be relevant for the deletion of copies. A copy may be deleted if it is the complement or in the complement of an adjacent, overt word. English-speaking children learn that wh- elements are displaced, pronounced in a position other

---

[2] Jairo Nunes (1995, 2004) argues elegantly that deletion of copied elements follows from the linearization of chains – words must be pronounced in sequence. Given the way that chains get linearized, copied items must delete, but you will need to read Nunes to understand this.

than where they are understood, on hearing and understanding a sentence like *Who did Jay see?* In (9a) the copied element is the complement of the adjacent verb, and in (9b) the lowest *who* is the complement of *saw* and the intermediate *who* is contained in the complement of *say* and is adjacent to it.[3]

(9)   a. Who$_i$ did Jay see ~~who$_i$~~?
        b. Who$_i$ did Jay say $_{CP}$[~~who$_i$~~ that Fay saw ~~who$_i$~~]?

This suggests a UG condition (10).

(10)   Something is deleted if it is (in) the complement of an adjacent, overt word.

Assuming the structures of (9a,b), *who$_i$* is deleted when it is adjacent to an overt word and is its complement (9a) or in its complement (9b). In (9b) the lowest *who* is the complement of *saw* and the middle *who* is in the complement of *say* and adjacent to it. If (10) is the condition, it will predict, with no further learning, that (11a) is ill-formed, because the boldface **who** is undeletable (henceforth boldface will indicate elements that may not be deleted); it is in a clause (CP) that is the complement of a verb, but an understood, not overt verb, "e" for empty again. In general, verbs may be understood in the second conjunct, through an operation called "Gapping": *Jim kissed Tim and Kay Ray, Jim visited Hamburg and Tim Dresden.* In the second part of (11a), the lowest *who* is the complement of the adjacent, overt *hit*, hence deletable. If the higher verb were overt in the second conjunct (11b), then *who* WOULD be in the complement of an overt verb, and therefore deletable, and (11b) is well-formed; the only difference between the structures is that, in the second conjunct, (11a) has a gapped verb and (11b) has an overt verb, *think*.

(11)   a. *Who$_i$ did Jay think [~~who$_i$~~ Kay hit ~~who$_i$~~] and who$_j$ did Jim $_{VE}$ $_{CP}$[**who$_j$** [Kim hit ~~who$_j$~~]]?
            Who did Jay think Kay hit and who did Jim Kim hit?
        b. Who$_i$ did Jay think [~~who$_i$~~ Kay hit ~~who$_i$~~] and who$_j$ did Jim $_V$think $_{CP}$[~~who$_j$~~ [Kim hit ~~who$_j$~~]]?
            Who did Jay think Kay hit and who did Jim think Kim hit?

We solve the poverty-of-stimulus problem posed by (11a): children learn simply that wh- items may be displaced and that verbs may be gapped in a conjunct clause; then the UG condition (10) causes the derivation of (11a) to crash with no further learning.

---

[3] On hearing something like *Who did Jay see?*, children learn that wh- elements may be displaced to the front of their clause, it seems. This entails that in a complex, two-clause expression like (9b), *who* is displaced first to the front of its own clause and then to the front of the next clause, successively.

Let's take stock of where we are. We postulated that children can learn from their environment that complementizers may be omitted and that wh- phrases may be displaced. This much is learned, because it is not true of all languages. French and Dutch speakers do not omit complementizers and "wh- phrases" (their equivalents *shei* 'who,' *sheme* 'what,' etc. in Chinese) are not displaced in Chinese, Japanese, and Korean – rather, they are pronounced where they are understood and people say, in Chinese, "He teaches who?" or *Ta jiao shi?* However, children do not learn the restrictions, that complementizers are not omitted in (6), that *who* may not be displaced in (11a). They do not learn this, because it is unlearnable: there are no relevant data among the primary data that children have access to, the things they hear. Furthermore, they do not need to learn the restrictions, if we postulate a UG condition (10) available independently of experience. Postulating the simple UG condition of (10) permits us to say that children learn a few simple things from their experience and, as a result, gain a complex capacity enabling them to omit complementizers and displace wh- phrases appropriately, in certain contexts and not in others. And much more, as we shall see. The single, simple condition (10) explains a large range of apparently complex data.

Remember the point made earlier, that a person's language capacity ranges over infinity and that everybody uses novel expressions every waking hour. That entails that we cannot say that children don't say **Kay left was obvious to all of us* (6c) and **Who did Jay think Kay hit and who did Jim Kim hit?* (11a) because they don't hear such things, as if children were so conservative as only to say what they hear. Children aren't like that and constantly say things they haven't heard, just like adults. We need to DEDUCE why children don't say (6c) and (11a), because it doesn't follow merely from the data they are exposed to.

Consider something else that children learn, which will yield more evidence that an item may be deleted if it is the complement or in the complement of an overt, adjacent word: verbs may be "gapped" and be empty ("e") in a conjunct clause (12a,b), as we saw with (11a). The operation appears to be readily learnable from exposure to something like (12b), where the verb is missing, understood but not pronounced. Now we see that this operation interacts interestingly with the wh- displacement operation. *Which man* is deletable in the leftmost conjunct of (12c) (the complement of the adjacent *introduce*: *Which man did Jay introduce to Ray?*) but not the boldface **which woman** in the rightmost conjunct (the complement of a non-overt verb). So the corresponding sentence (12c) is ill-formed. Similarly in (12d,e, and g), where the boldface element fails to meet the condition for deletion because the adjacent verb is not overt. These structures involve wh- displacement (12c,d), readily learnable as noted above, and gapping (12b,c,d,e,f,g), learnable on exposure to something like (12b,f). They also involve heavy DP shift in (12e,g), learnable on exposure to simple expressions like *John gave to Ray his favorite racket*; this operation moves a "heavy" DP, for example *his favorite racket*, away from its underlying position, here the complement of *gave* (only "heavy" DPs are displaced in this way and one does not find **John gave to Ray it* or even **John gave to Ray the racket*, where *it* and *the racket* are not heavy enough). Given these simple, learned operations, the UG principle (10) then solves the poverty-of-stimulus problems of (12c,d,e,g), explaining why they don't occur.

(12)   a. Jay introduced Kay to Ray and Jim introduced Kim to Tim.
       b. Jay introduced Kay to Ray and Jim ᵥe Kim to Tim.
          Jay introduced Kay to Ray and Jim Kim to Tim.
       c. *Which man$_i$ did Jay introduce ~~which man$_i$~~ to Ray and which woman$_j$ did Jim ᵥe **which woman$_j$** to Tim?
          *Which man did Jay introduce to Ray and which woman did Jim to Tim?
       d. *Jay wondered what$_i$ Kay gave ~~what$_i$~~ to Ray and what$_j$ Jim ᵥe **what$_j$** to Tim.
          *Jay wondered what Kay gave to Ray and what Jim to Tim.
       e. *Jay admired [~~his uncle from Paramus~~]$_i$ greatly [his uncle from Paramus]$_i$ but Jim ᵥe **[his uncle from New York]$_j$** only moderately [his uncle from New York]$_j$.
          *Jay admired greatly his uncle from Paramus but Jim only moderately his uncle from New York.
       f. Jay gave his favorite racket to Ray and Jim ᵥe his favorite plant to Tim.
       g. *Jay gave [~~his favorite racket~~]$_i$ to Ray [his favorite racket]$_i$ and Jim ᵥe **[his favorite plant]$_j$** to Tim [his favorite plant]$_j$.
          *Jay gave to Ray his favorite racket and Jim to Tim his favorite plant.

Things get more complex and more interesting as we see more effects of our UG condition. This condition (10) explains why a complementizer may not be null if it occurs to the right of a gapped (non-overt) verb (13b); nor does one find a deleted copy in the same position (the boldface **who** in (13c), which is similar to (11a), now with complementizers present).

(13)   a. Jay thought Kay hit Ray and Jim ᵥe $_{CP}$[that Kim hit Tim].
       b. *Jay thought Kay hit Ray and Jim ᵥe $_{CP}$[**0** Kim hit Tim].
          *Jay thought Kay hit Ray and Jim Kim hit Tim.
       c. *Who$_i$ did Jay think [~~who$_i$~~ that Kay hit ~~who$_i$~~] and who$_j$ did Jim ᵥe $_{CP}$[**who$_j$** that [Kim hit ~~who$_j$~~]]?
          *Who did Jay think that Kay hit and who did Jim that Kim hit?

So children exposed to some form of English have plenty of evidence that a *that* complementizer is deletable (5d), that wh- phrases may be displaced (copied), that verbs may be gapped (12b), and that heavy DPs may be copied to the end of a clause (12e,g), but they also know WITHOUT EVIDENCE that complementizers and copies may not be deleted unless they are the complement or in the complement of an adjacent, overt word. And the data of (5–13) suggest that this is the information that UG needs to provide, and head–complement relations are crucial. The convergence of that information with the grammar-specific devices that delete a *that* complementizer and allow a wh- phrase and a heavy DP to be copied yields the distinctions noted and solves the poverty-of-stimulus problems. However, postulating that information at the level of UG leaves open the FORM that it must take, and we turn now to that matter.

Grammarians know that languages have CLITICS, little words that do not occur independently but "lean" against bigger words. We know that elements may cliticize to the left and become an indissoluble part of their host, clitics. When *is* reduces, its pronunciation is determined by the last segment of the word to which it attaches: voiceless if the last segment is a voiceless stop, voiced if the last segment is voiced, and syllabic elsewhere (14a). Precisely the same is true of the plural marker (14b), the possessive (14c), and the third person singular ending on a verb (14d).

(14)   a. Pat's happy, Doug's happy, and Alice's here.
        b. Cats, dogs, and chalices.
        c. Pat's dog, Doug's cat, and Alice's crocodile.
        d. Commits, digs, and misses.

Children understand *Pat's happy* as 'Pat is happy,' *Pat* being the subject of the phrase *is happy*. However, *is* is pronounced indissolubly with *Pat*, and children analyze what they hear as (15a), i.e. with reduced *is* attached to the noun, with normal pronunciation applying. So from hearing and understanding an expression like *Pat's happy*, children learn that *is* may be reduced and absorbed like a clitic into the preceding word (15b).

(15)   a. $_N$Pat+'s
        b. noun+clitic

Similar factors affect the pronunciation of *to* in reduced *wanna*: the *to* cliti-cizes to *want*, to form an indissoluble word, but here the cliticization affects an element within the IP that is the complement of an adjacent *want*, reminiscent of the phenomena just discussed. In (16b,c) *to* does not meet this condition and is not reducible: nobody would say **Who do you wanna visit Rio?* or **I don't wanna win games to be our only goal*. In (16b) *to* is not adjacent to *want* and in (16c) the lower IP containing *to* is not the complement of the adjacent *want*.[4]

---

[4] (16a) also has an understood element as the subject of *to go*, namely a subject *you*, but it has long been known that this element doesn't "count" as a real element intervening between *want*

(16)   a. Where do you want to go?
       b. Who$_i$ do you want $_{IP}$[~~who~~$_i$ to visit Rio]?
       c. I don't want $_{IP}$[$_{IP}$[to win games] to be our only goal].

So our complement condition affects the formation of *wanna* reductions.

If we draw (14) together with the material of (3), elaborated here as (17), we now find something interesting: copies do not delete if they are right-adjacent to a cliticized verb. In (17a,c,d) the copied wh- phrases may be deleted if *is* is in its full form, but not if it is reduced to its clitic form; the corresponding sentences with *'s* do not occur (**Kim is happer than Tim's, *I wonder what that's up there, *I wonder where the concert's on Wednesday*).

(17)   a. Kim is happier$_i$ than Tim is ~~what~~$_i$.
         Kim is happier than Tim is/*'s.
       b. That is a fan up there.
       c. I wonder what$_i$ that is ~~what~~$_i$ up there.
         I wonder what that is/*'s up there.
       d. I wonder where$_i$ the concert is ~~where~~$_i$ on Wednesday.
         I wonder where the concert is/*'s on Wednesday.

This suggests that a deleted copy is INCORPORATED into the element of which it is the complement. In (17), if *is* cliticizes on to the subject noun and becomes part of that noun, it has been moved from one unit to another and no longer heads a phrase of which *what/where* is the complement and no incorporation is possible.

That idea enables us to capture another subtle and interesting distinction. The sentence (18a) is ambiguous: it may mean that Mary is dancing in New York or just that she is in New York, but working on Wall Street and not dancing. The former interpretation has a structure with an empty verb, understood as 'dancing' (18b). If empty elements (like an understood verb) are incorporated, there must be an appropriate host. There is an appropriate host in (18b), where the structure has [is $_{VP}$[~~dancing~~ in NY]], where the VP is the complement of *is*, and the deleted verb *dancing* incorporates into an adjacent full verb, *is*. However, in (18c) *is* is cliticized on to *Mary*, the VP *dancing in NY* isn't the complement of *Mary's*, and the boldface empty verb has no appropriate host. Consequently (18d) unambiguously means that Mary is in New York, occupation unspecified, because there is no empty, understood verb. Again, it is inconceivable that children LEARN such distinctions purely on the basis of external evidence.

---

and *to*, unlike the copied *who* in (16b). This has had various treatments in the technical literature, none of them entirely satisfying. For sophisticates, I should point out that Lightfoot (2006) gives a more technical and more comprehensive version of section 3.3 here.

(18) a. Max is dancing in London and Mary is in New York.
      b. Max is dancing in London and Mary is $_V$e in New York.
      c. *Max is dancing in London and Mary's $_V$**e** in New York.
      d. Max is dancing in London and Mary's in New York.

Further distinctions follow. English speakers allow ellipsed VPs and children have plenty of evidence to that effect (19a). In (19a) the empty VP ("e" for empty or ellipsed) is the complement of *did*. In fact, there must be an overt inflectional element to license the empty VP, suggesting that empty VPs occur only where they are incorporated into a host, like omitted complementizers and deleted copies. (19b) is ill-formed because part of the VP remains, *to Naples*, and there is no empty VP. In the ungrammatical structures of (19c,d) the empty VP is separated from its potential host, hence failure to incorporate. An ellipsed VP may occur in a subordinate clause (19e), to the left of its antecedent (19f), in a separate sentence from its antecedent (19g), or within a complex DP (19h), or even without any overt antecedent (19i), but it always requires an overt inflectional element immediately to the left.

(19) a. Max left on Wednesday but Mary did $_{VP}$e as well.
      b. *Max left for Rio but Mary didn't $_{VP}$[e for Naples].
      c. They denied reading it, although they all had $_{VP}$e.
        vs. *They denied reading it, although they had all $_{VP}$e.
      d. They denied reading it, although they often/certainly had $_{VP}$e.
        vs. *They denied reading it, although they had often/certainly $_{VP}$e.
      e. Max left for Rio, although Mary didn't $_{VP}$e.
      f. Although Max couldn't $_{VP}$e, Mary was able to leave for Rio.
      g. Susan went to Rio.
        Yes, but Jane didn't $_{VP}$e.
      h. The man who speaks French knows $_{DP}$[the woman who doesn't $_{VP}$e].
      i. Don't $_{VP}$e!

This suggests that, like omitted complementizers, deleted copies and the empty verb of (18b), an ellipsed VP incorporates to the left, to an adjacent, overt item of which it is the complement (20).

(20) Max could visit Rio and Susan $_{INFL}$could+$_{VP}$e.

That, in turn, now explains the non-occurrence of (21a), noted by Zagona (1988): the ellipsed VP needs an appropriate host, a full phonological word, of which it is the complement, as in (21b); in (21a) *has* has become part of the noun *John* and no longer heads a phrase of which $_{VP}$e is the complement.

(21) a. *I haven't seen that movie, but John's $_{VP}$e.
      b. I haven't seen that movie, but John has+$_{VP}$e.

head compl.

So copies must be deleted and our analysis takes deleted items to be incorporated into a preceding host. In (22a) the complement incorporates into the adjacent *see* and in (22b) *Jay* is in the complement of the adjacent *expected* and accordingly incorporates into it.[5]

(22)   a. Who$_i$ did Jay see ~~who$_i$~~?
         b. Jay$_i$ was expected [~~Jay$_i$~~ to win].

This analysis captures many other distinctions. For example, English speakers' grammars typically have an operation whereby a "heavy" DP is displaced to the right, as we have noted. Under this approach, that now means copying and reducing the copied element to silence by absorbing it into a host. In (23a) the copied element is the complement of *introduced*, hence incorporated successfully; in (23b) it is in the complement of *expect* and adjacent to it; but in (23c) the element which needs to delete is neither the complement nor contained in the complement of anything and the derivation is ill-formed and crashes.

(23)   a. I introduced [~~all the students from Brazil~~]$_i$ to Mary [all the students from Brazil]$_i$
            I introduced to Mary all the students from Brazil.
         b. I expect [[~~all the students from Brazil~~]$_i$ to be at the party][all the students from Brazil]$_i$
            I expect to be at the party all the students from Brazil.
         c. *[[**all the students from Brazil**]$_i$ are unhappy] [all the students from Brazil]$_i$
            **Are unhappy all the students from Brazil.*

Our UG principle (10) that deletion is incorporation solves the poverty-of-stimulus problem of (23c): children simply learn that heavy DPs may be copied to the right and the UG condition accounts for the non-occurrence of (23c) with no further learning or experience needed.

We are beginning to see how children attain a complex mature capacity and that the apparent complexities arise from an interaction of one simple UG property and some simple operations that can be learned from exposure to simple utterances of a kind that any child hears.

Consider now "objective genitives" like (24). An expression like *Jay's picture* is three-ways ambiguous: Jay may be the owner of the picture, the painter, or the person portrayed. The latter reading is the so-called objective genitive; *Jay* is understood as the object complement of *picture*. It is usually analyzed as in

---

[5] The analysis appeals to complements and to adjacency. As a head merges, it may merge with a phrase which is its complement. If so, then that phrase and the first element contained in it are both adjacent to that head.

(24), where *Jay* is copied from the "object" position to the Specifier of the DP. The operation is specific to grammars of English speakers and does not occur in French, for example. This much is learnable: children hear expressions like *Jay's picture* in contexts where it is clear that Jay is pictured.

(24)   DP[Jayᵢ's NP[picture J̶a̶y̶ᵢ]]

A curious thing is that comparable expressions like *The picture of Jay's*, *The picture is Jay's*, and *The picture which is Jay's* (25) show only a two-way ambiguity, where Jay may be the owner or the painter but not the person portrayed. This is yet another poverty-of-stimulus problem, because it is inconceivable that children are systematically supplied with evidence that the objective interpretation is not available in these cases. We now have an explanation, because the structure of these expressions would need to be as in (25).

(25)   a. *the picture of DP[Jay's NP[e **Jay**]]   (*The picture of Jay's*)
        b. *the picture is DP[Jay's NP[e **Jay**]]   (*The picture is Jay's*)
        c. *the picture which is   (*The picture which is Jay's*)
           DP[Jay's NP[e **Jay**]]

A preposition like *of* is always followed by a DP, a possessive like *Jay's* occurs only as the Specifier and head of a DP (26), and Ds always have an NP complement, even if the noun is empty (e), as it is here (where it is understood as 'picture'). Now we can see why the structures are ill-formed: the lower *Jay* has no host to incorporate into, hence boldface and the derivation crashes. *Jay* is the complement of the adjacent noun but that noun is not overt, hence not an appropriate host.

(26)

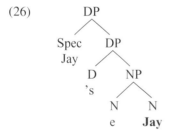

(27) reflects another distinction provided by this account. (27a) has a gapped verb, is well-formed, and involves no deletion of a copied element, whereas (27b) involves two instances of DP-copying and deletion (to yield the passive constructions). The leftmost instance is well-formed (*Jay is known to have left*), because the copied *Jay* is in the complement of the adjacent *known* and therefore deletes; however, in the rightmost conjunct, the copied *he* has no overt host to

incorporate into and therefore cannot delete, hence boldface and leading the derivation to crash.[6]

(27)   a. It is known that Jay left but it isn't $_∨$e that he went to the movies.
        b. *Jay$_i$ is known [J̶a̶y̶$_i$ to have left] but he$_i$ isn't $_∨$e [**he$_i$** to have gone to the movies].
           *Jay is known to have left but he isn't to have gone to the movies.

Innateness claims depend on detailed distinctions between what a child may be supposed to garner from his/her environment and what needs to be specified internally, innately. I have argued that English speakers L E A R N that verbs like *is* and *has* may be phonologically reduced, that complementizers may be null, that wh- phrases may be displaced (pronounced in positions other than where they are understood), that verbs may be gapped, that heavy DPs may be displaced to the right, VPs may be ellipsed, possessive noun phrases may have objective interpretations. These seven properties reflect the computational operations of (28); they are readily learnable from the linguistic environment and we can point to plausible primary linguistic data (PLD): all English-speaking children hear sentences like *Peter said Kay left* (5a), manifesting a null complementizer (28a); *Who did Jay see?* (9a), a displaced wh- phrase (28b); *Jay introduced Kay to Ray and Jim Kim to Tim* (12b), gapping (28c); *Kim's happy*, reduction (28d); *Max left for Rio although Mary didn't* (19f), an ellipsed VP (28e); *Jay gave to Ray his favorite racket* (12g), heavy DP shift (28f); and *Jay's picture*, meaning 'picture of Jay' (24; 28g).

(28)   a. *that* → 0
        b. copy wh-
        c. gap V
        d. *is* → *'s*
        e. ellipse VP
        f. copy heavy DP to right
        g. copy DP to leftward Specifier

An empty element (a deleted phrasal copy, null complementizer, ellipsed VP, the empty *dancing* in (18b,c)) is incorporated into an adjacent phonological head (N, V, I) of which it is its complement or in its complement. One simple idea at the level of UG interacts with seven grammar-specific devices, all demonstrably learnable, and that interaction yields a complex range of phenomena.

---

[6] There is much more to be said about what this analysis predicts, but we could also ask about the F O R M of the UG information. So far we have been talking about deletion sites as involving incorporation into a host, and Lightfoot (2006) goes on to argue that the incorporated element is a kind of clitic, which yields further predictions that I will not discuss here.

We seek a single object: the genetic properties of the language organ. They permit language acquisition to take place in the way that it does. What we postulate must solve the poverty-of-stimulus problems that we identify and solve them for ALL languages. In addition, the grammars that our theory of UG permits must meet other demands.

To take just one example (and to return to a point made earlier in the chapter), grammars must allow speech comprehension to take place in the way that it does. That means that considerations of parsing might drive proposals (parsing deals with how the brain analyzes incoming speech signals and assigns structure and meaning). That hasn't happened much yet, but there is no principled reason why not and the situation might change. Similarly for evidence drawn from brain imaging or even from brain damage. In fact, the proposals here look promising for studies of on-line parsing. When a person hears a displaced element, say a wh- phrase at the beginning of an expression, he/she needs to search for the deletion site, the position in which it needs to be understood. The ideas developed here restrict the places that the person can look. I cannot examine the consequences of this at this time, but they look potentially useful for parsing studies. In fact, perhaps somebody could have arrived at such proposals from the study of on-line parsing.

One uses what looks like the best evidence available at any given time, but that will vary as research progresses. There are many basic requirements that our hypotheses must meet, no shortage of empirical constraints, and therefore many angles one may take on what we aim for. In this section we have seen how a complex range of data can follow from a simple analysis, distinguishing what children may learn from experience and what they may not.

3.4   Binding Theory

In the next two sections I shall consider two other areas where we now have vastly simpler descriptions than were used earlier, and in these areas, too, the driving force has been arguments from the poverty of the stimulus. One deals with the way that pronouns and reflexives refer to other nouns and the other deals with the pronunciation of sentences – one deals with meaning and the other with sound.

There are plenty of poverty-of-stimulus problems in the interconnectedness of words. For example, the pronouns *she*, *her* may refer to Kim in (29a,b,c) but not in (29d,e,f). We may express this by using indices: in (29a,b,c) *Kim* may have the same index as *her* and *she*, referring to the same person, but in (29d,e,f) *Kim* has a different index from *her/she*, necessarily referring to somebody else.

(29)   a. Kim_i loves her_i mother.
          b. Kim_i expected she_i would win.
          c. Her_i mother loves Kim_i.

    d. Kim$_i$ expected her$_j$ to win.
    e. Kim$_i$ loves her$_j$.
    f. She$_i$ said that Kim$_j$ left.

Sentences (30a,b) may be statements about one person Kim (so the same index), but (30c,d,e) may only be interpreted as a statement about two women of the same name (distinct indices). We know this independently of context or of any aspect of the speech situation; in fact, we know this simply from the form of the expression.

(30)   a. Kim$_i$'s father says Kim$_i$ is happy.
          b. Kim$_i$'s father loves Kim$_i$'s mother.
          c. Kim$_i$ loves Kim$_j$'s mother.
          d. Kim$_i$ says Kim$_j$ is happy.
          e. Kim$_i$ says Kim$_j$'s mother is happy.

How does the form of the expression convey all this information? Why, for example, may *her* refer to Kim in (29a) but the two *Kim*s in (30c) may not refer to the same woman? Why may *she* refer to Kim in (29b) but not *her* in (29d)? Here is another area where children acquire a system which goes far beyond the input they receive. Again we have elaborate subconscious knowledge, which is not acquired through instruction of any kind – most readers would have been unaware of these distinctions until they read the last paragraphs, therefore unable to provide the necessary instruction. A child may hear (29a) in a context where *her* clearly refers to Kim or in a context where *her* refers to another woman unnamed in this expression, perhaps the queen of England. On the other hand, a sentence (29e) is heard only in a context where *her* refers to another woman, in fact to any woman other than Kim, but children are not supplied with evidence or told that *her* cannot refer to Kim, unlike in (29a). This is the poverty-of-stimulus problem and children's behavior does not differ much from adults' (except in some narrow ways with regard to pronouns). If there is no learning here, then that would explain why we do not observe children making errors in the reference of names and pronouns (except in that narrow domain, which I will not discuss; see Thornton & Wexler 1999) – they show no signs of learning by trial-and-error. But how can we say that there is no learning? Is there an alternative to learning?

Twenty-five years ago Noam Chomsky proposed the Binding Theory as a solution to these poverty-of-stimulus problems (Chomsky 1981a). Before that, linguists had offered complex indexing procedures to yield the right results – for a sense of the complexity, and for some self-torture, see the appendix to Chomsky (1980), written just before the introduction of the Binding Theory. The Binding Theory (31) permitted a dramatic simplification of descriptions and constitutes a component of UG, available to humans in advance of experience, in fact enabling us to interpret our experience, and it divides nominals into three types: ANAPHORS like reflexive pronouns, *himself*, *themselves* in English, PRONOUNS like *she*, *her*, *their*, and NAMES (everything else).

(31)   Binding Theory
        A. anaphors are coindexed within their Domain.
        B. pronouns are free within their Domain.
        C. names are free.

Each nominal is contained inside a Domain, roughly its clause or a larger DP, and it is either coindexed with another, higher DP or not; if not, then it is free. One can think of this in the following way: if one starts from a word, one proceeds up the structure until one comes to a sister DP. If the starting point was an anaphor, that sister DP needs to be local (contained within the same Domain) and to bear the same index; if the starting point was a pronoun, any sister DP within the Domain needs to bear a different index; and if one starts from a name, any sister DP anywhere needs to bear a different index.

   So (32a) has the structure (33). One starts from *herself*, an anaphor, and proceeds up the structure until the lower IP, at which point there is a sister DP, *Kim's mother*. *Herself* must be coindexed with (and refer to) that maximal DP *Kim's mother*; it may not refer just to the DP *Kim*, because that DP is not a sister to the IP – it is contained within the larger DP and is therefore inaccessible to the Binding Theory. (32b) has the same structure, just *her* in place of *herself* – and *her* may not be coindexed with the DP *Kim's mother*, because it needs to be free in its clause. *Her* may be coindexed with Kim, because the DP *Kim* is not a sister to the IP and is, therefore, inaccessible to the demands of the Binding Theory.

(32)   a. DP[DP[Kim]'s mother]i washed herselfi.
        b. DP[DP[Kim]'s mother]j washed heri.
        c. DP[DP[Kim]'s mother] said CP[that the doctori washed herj].
        d. DP[DP[Kim]'s mother] said that the doctor washed Kim.
        e. Kim said CP[that the doctori washed herj].
        f. Kimi said that the doctor washed Kimj.

(33)

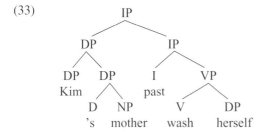

(32c) is ambiguous and *her* may refer to *Kim* or to *Kim's mother*. The Binding Theory stipulates only that *her*, a pronoun, be free within its own Domain, the clause (CP) indicated; beyond that, there is nothing systematic to be said and any indexing is possible. Similarly, in (32e) *her* may be coindexed with *Kim*, being free (not coindexed) within its own clause. (32d) may also be a statement about one Kim; the lower *Kim*, the complement of *washed*, may not be coindexed with a sister DP as we work up the tree structure, but is permitted to be coindexed with the DP *Kim*, which is not a sister to any node dominating the lower *Kim*, hence invisible to the Binding Theory. (32f), on the other hand, concerns two Kims; the lower *Kim* may not be coindexed with the higher *Kim*, whose DP is a sister to a node dominating the lower *Kim*.

Countless more distinctions follow from this Binding Theory. (34a) is well-formed, because the anaphor *themselves* is coindexed with a sister DP within its own Domain, when we move up the tree.

(34)   a. The students$_i$ washed themselves$_i$.
         b. $_{DP}$[The students'$_j$ brothers]$_i$ washed themselves$_i$.
         c. *The students said $_{CP}$[that Bob washed themselves].

In (34b) *themselves* may only refer to *the students' brothers* and not to *the students*, because only the larger DP is a sister to a node dominating *themselves*. And (34c) is ill-formed, because *themselves* is not coindexed within its Domain, the clause (CP) indicated.

The Binding Theory yields the necessary distinctions but itself cannot be learned from data available to young children. We therefore say that it is part of UG, part of what children bring to the analysis of initial experience. That means that children must learn which words are anaphors, which pronouns, and which are names. These are the three possibilities, for all languages, and they are defined in (31). Once a child has learned that *themselves* is an anaphor, *her* a pronoun, etc., all the appropriate indexing relations follow, with no further learning. Similarly for other languages, children learn which words are anaphors and which are pronouns and everything else follows. How, then, is this learned?

Exposure to a simple sentence like (35a), interpreted with *themselves* referring to *they* (coindexed), suffices to show that *themselves* is an anaphor and not a pronoun or name; pronouns and names may not be coindexed with a maximal element within its Domain.

(35)   a. They$_i$ washed themselves$_i$.
         b. Kim$_i$'s father loves her$_j$.
         c. Kim$_i$ heard $_{DP}$[Bill's speeches about her$_i$].
         d. Kim left.

(35b), interpreted with *her* referring to *Kim*, shows that *her* is no anaphor (not coindexed with a sister DP within its Domain, when we move up the tree structure), and (35c), with *her* referring to *Kim*, shows that *her* is not a name (names may not be coindexed with a sister DP anywhere); the Domain of *her* is the DP indicated and *her* is free within that DP. If neither an anaphor nor a name, then *her* is a pronoun.

A very simple expression like (35d) shows that *Kim* is not an anaphor, but there is no positive evidence available to a child showing that *Kim* is not a pronoun. Analysts know that *Kim* is not a pronoun, because one does not find sentences of the form *Kim said that Kim left*, with the two *Kim*s referring to the same person, but that is a negative fact concerning something which does not occur, hence unavailable to young children. That suggests a hierarchical organization.

The starting point for a child is that every word is a name, unless there is positive, refuting evidence. Under that view, sentences like (35a) show that *themselves* is an anaphor, and not a pronoun nor a name. And (35c) shows that *her* is not a name, because it is coindexed with a sister DP element ($_{DP}$Kim), and not an anaphor, because it is not locally coindexed. This yields a satisfactory account. We have a theory of mature capacity that provides the appropriate distinctions and one can show how children learn from environmental data which elements are anaphors and which are pronouns; everything else is a name.

We have just seen how syntactic structure underlies a simple algorithm that characterizes our capacity to use nouns to refer to other nouns. We posit information at the level of UG, the Binding Theory (31), and children need to learn which nouns are anaphors and pronouns; everything else is a name. We can point to simple experiences, hearing sentences like (35a–c), which would yield a simple system that works over an infinite domain. That gives us the right kind of analysis.

3.5   Intonation

A person's language system provides a mapping between sound and meaning over an infinite range. The last section shows how syntactic structure yields the right semantic information. In this section we will see how syntactic structure yields the right sound properties and we will focus on intonation patterns.

The early synthesized speech of computers sounded unnatural because every word was pronounced with the same stress – it sounded like a list, a roll-call of separate words. In natural language, on the other hand, words tend to be pronounced with slightly different stress, each language has its own music, and the music depends on the syntactic structure. Consider a system that generates much of this music. The system works in the now familiar bottom-up fashion, as we have seen for syntactic structure and for the operation of the Binding Theory. Each word is merged into its structure with a primary stress, which we will indicate with "1." Recall example (7), *You will visit London. Visit*-1 and *London*-1 are merged to form a VP. As the structure is formed, one of two computational operations applies (36).

(36)   a. In noun compounds, assign primary stress to the leftmost of two stress peaks.
        b. Otherwise, assign primary stress to the rightmost stress peak.

A word is a stress peak if there is no word more highly stressed. By convention, when primary stress is assigned to a word, all other stress levels are reduced by one degree. So we apply (36b) (there are no noun compounds and (36a) is not relevant) and our VP becomes (37a) and *visit* has less stress than *London*. Now we merge *will*-1 (37b) and we erase the inner brackets and make the rightmost stress peak primary (37c), weakening the other stresses by one degree.

(37)   a. [visit-2 London-1]
        b. [will-1 [visit-2 London-1]]
        c. [will-2 visit-3 London-1]
        d. [you-1 [will-2 visit-3 London-1]]
        e. [you-2 will-3 visit-4 London-1]

Finally we merge *you*-1 (37d), and (36b) yields (37e) and the stress contour 2 3 4 1: ⌐⌐⌐⌐ .
    Now let us derive the stress contour for *Kim's mother washed Tim*. We merge *Kim's*-1 with *mother*-1 to get (38a) and *washed*-1 with *Tim*-1 to get (38b). When these two units are merged, the rightmost stress peak, *Tim*, becomes primary and everything else is demoted one degree (38c) and we have the stress contour 3 2 3 1, where *Kim's* and *washed* have the same stress level: ⌐⌐⌐ .

(38)   a. $_{DP}$[Kim's-2 mother-1]
        b. $_{VP}$[washed-2 Tim-1]
        c. [Kim's-3 mother-2 washed-3 Tim-1]

    Now let us consider something more complex, with a noun compound, which will bring operation (36a) into play. In the phrase *Kim's blackboard eraser hit Tim*, first *black* is merged with *board* to yield the noun compound (39a) (through operation (36a)) and *hit* is merged with *Tim* to yield (39b) (through operation (36b)). A noun compound is a noun with an internal structure: *blackboard* is a noun consisting of *black* and *board* and *blackboard eraser* is also a noun compound, consisting of *blackboard* and *eraser*. Then (39a) is merged with *eraser*-1 to yield another noun compound (39c) (operation (36a) applies), which in turn is merged with *Kim's*-1 to yield (39d) (by operation 36b). Finally (39d) is merged with (39b) and the rightmost stress peak, *Tim*, becomes primary at the cost of everything else (39e): ⌐⌐⌐⌐ .

(39)   a. ₙ[black-1 board-2]
         b. ᵥₚ[hit-2 Tim-1]
         c. ₙ[black-1 board-3 eraser-2]
         d. ₙₚ[Kim's-2 black-1 board-4 eraser-3]
         e. [Kim's-3 black-2 board-5 eraser-4 hit-3 Tim-1]

Kim's black board eraser hit Tim, referring to a board eraser that is black, would be pronounced quite differently. Here there is no *blackboard* noun compound and the lowest units, the first to be merged, would be the noun compound *board eraser* (40a) and the VP *hit Tim* (40b). Then the adjective *black* would be merged with (40a) to yield the noun phrase (40c), and then *Kim's* would merge with (40c) to yield the DP (40d). (40d) would merge with (40b) to give (40e), with a very different stress contour from (39e), 3 4 2 5 3 1: ⌐⌐⌐ .

(40)   a. ₙ[board-1 eraser-2]
         b. ᵥₚ[hit-2 Tim-1]
         c. ₙₚ[black-2 board-1 eraser-3]
         d. ₙₚ[Kim's-2 black-3 board-1 eraser-4]
         e. [Kim's-3 black-4 board-2 eraser-5 hit-3 Tim-1]

With the operations of (36) applying bottom-up in this fashion, children know the appropriate stress contour for *Kim's blackboard eraser*, *Kim's black board eraser*, and countless other expressions they have never heard before. Other examples of noun compounds are *saxophone player*, *car wash*, *peanut vendor*, *girlfriend*, *football player*, *sex maniac*, *bank teller*, and *the White House*, where the president lives, but not *the white house* on the corner of my street. They are all recognizable from their 1–2 intonation pattern, whereas the white house on the corner of my street is 2–1.

There is more to sentence intonation than this; for example, I have said nothing about little words like the determiners *a* and *the*, or prepositions, or pronouns, which have different intonational properties, nor have I said anything about the contrastive stress of expressions like *Kim's MOTHER washed Tim*, where there is contrastive stress on *mother*, as if the speaker was contrasting the actions of Kim's mother as opposed to her father or sister. Nonetheless I have outlined a central part of any English speaker's knowledge.

We have a simple system that generates appropriate stress contours for an infinite range of expressions. The system works in a bottom-up fashion but that could not be deduced by even the most ingenious child from the unorganized, positive data available in the environment. In the examples of this section five levels of stress have been postulated. More complex examples involve still more levels. Trained phoneticians can recognize many distinctions, but probably not all these contours represent a physical reality detectable by the untrained human ear. How then could a child attain such a system without access to a phonetics laboratory, good training, or a carefully organized and "complete" set of facts?

The physical signal distinguishes clearly two degrees of stress and children can hear the difference between *blackboard* and *black board*, the first being 1–2, the second 2–1; similarly *girlfriend* and *girl friend*. This is sufficient to trigger the development of the two operations of (36), assuming a parallel syntactic analysis labeling *blackboard* and *girlfriend* an N and *black board* and *girl friend* an NP. That is the learning involved. If children also have the bottom-up analysis, given as a property of the genotype, they will then be able to perceive the proper stress contour of *Kim's blackboard eraser* and countless other phrases without further instruction, even if it is not always manifested clearly in the physical signal.

Under this account, the child correlates the different stress contours of *blackboard* and *black board* with their different syntactic and semantic properties and this triggers the two operations of (36) and thus a system that generates appropriate stress contours for an infinite range of expressions. *Blackboard* means what it means, a board for writing on that isn't necessarily black, and is pronounced accordingly. The structure of language partially determines what is linguistically relevant in the actual sound waves and this is a good example of the brain imposing structure on the world outside.

3.6   Conclusion

We have examined three areas of people's grammars and seen that we can account for complex arrays of distinctions between well-formed and ill-formed structures. We allow simple information at the level of UG to interact with simple, grammar-specific information that seems to be readily learnable from a child's linguistic experience. This illustrates how linguists can view the general properties of the human language capacity and some of the properties that are typically learned by young children acquiring particular systems.

Linguists' ideas about the language capacity have changed over the last fifty years and aficionados can identify three phases in the kinds of claims made about UG, the innateness claims of generative grammar. In the period of roughly 1955–1970, much energy was devoted to increasing the expressive power of grammars beyond that of the then-familiar phrase structure grammars, so that they might be adequate for the analysis of natural languages. This involved introducing distinct levels of representation and derivational operations mapping one to another (the key claim of Chomsky 1957) and a lexicon (the major technical innovation of Chomsky 1965). Then in the period from the late 1960s to roughly 1990, the emphasis lay on developing constraints on how computational operations apply, beginning with the A-over-A constraint of the early 1960s, through the conditions of Ross (1967), Chomsky (1973), and then the development of Government and Binding models and parameters of variation. Throughout that period, Ockham's methodological principles (entities may not be multiplied beyond necessity) minimized the elements invoked in analyses, but after about 1990 SUBSTANTIVE economy principles were introduced under the Minimalist Program and elements of grammars needed to be motivated by interface requirements. All of this influences the FORM of the innateness claims and they have differed significantly in each of these three periods.

In this chapter I have discussed three elements of the linguistic genotype, UG. They are some of the tools by which children analyze their experience, deleting elements in a certain way, seeking names, anaphors, and pronouns, and determining intonational structure in a bottom-up fashion. These common tools also explain how people, despite having quite different experiences, nonetheless converge on shared, uniform analyses and can communicate and understand each other.

I have aimed to give a sense of how we can think of grammars when we think of them as characterizing the linguistic capacity of an individual and when we take learnability concerns seriously and build on the fifty years of work on generative grammars. If grammars have these kinds of properties and if we can discover more about them by reasoning from poverty-of-stimulus problems of the kind illustrated here, then we can ask how such systems might be attained by children in the first few years of life, and that is what we will take up in the next chapter. That, in turn, will equip us to ask how they may change across time, a topic for later chapters.

4 Languages emerging in children

4.1 E-language perspectives

The central claim of this book is that if we view the human language capacity in terms of an I-language system, focusing on internal, individual properties, we will take different approaches to the study of language acquisition and therefore to the study of historical change. That, in turn, will enable us to understand how new languages may develop. Now that we have begun to explore I-language ideas, let's see how they might impinge on ideas about language acquisition and learnability. We shall adopt an approach quite different from what one finds in most of the generative literature.

Acquisition involves the study of children and LEARNABILITY represents its theoretical and computational aspect: learnability models portray how a natural language organ might emerge in a child under naturalistic boundary conditions. So far, I shall argue in this section, work on learnability has been dominated too much by E-language approaches. If children acquire I-languages with the properties discussed in the last chapter, one would expect acquisition to reflect their I-language nature. A simple example: if children acquire the kind of abstract systems just discussed, then one would expect those systems to permit deductions, to predict new phenomena. An English child may hear *Kim may have eaten* and *Kim has been eating*. At the point where the child's language organ analyzes *may* as an Inflection item and the perfective and progressive aspect markers as preceding the main verb, then it follows automatically that *Kim may have been eating* is also a sentence, and that sentence will automatically be part of a child's capacity even before he/she hears it.

Considering I-language approaches to acquisition will lead us to language change and new languages, which we will get to in the next chapter. But first some history of a different nature. I will go through this history because it illuminates a remarkable fact about modern work on learnability.

Chomsky's *Syntactic Structures* (1957) is often said to be the snowball that started the avalanche of the cognitive approach to language. But there is an irony: the book contains nothing about cognitive representations, nothing on grammars as mental systems triggered by childhood exposure to initial linguistic experiences. It has much to say about the methods of linguistic analysis and all of this can be translated and was translated very easily and early into claims about the psychological basis of language.[1]

For example, Chomsky (1957: 51) discussed the possible goals for a linguistic theory and distinguished a discovery procedure, a decision procedure, and an evaluation procedure.

(1)   a. corpus   →[   ]→ grammar

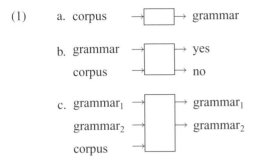

        b. grammar →[ ]→ yes
           corpus   →[ ]→ no

        c. grammar$_1$ →[   ]→ grammar$_1$
           grammar$_2$ →[   ]→ grammar$_2$
           corpus   →[   ]

A discovery procedure (1a) provides "a practical and mechanical method for constructing the grammar, given only a corpus of utterances." A weaker requirement would have a theory prescribe whether a certain grammar is the best one for a given corpus, a decision procedure (1b). Alternatively, a theory might provide an evaluation procedure, choosing which of two or more grammars is better for the language from which the corpus is drawn (1c). Chomsky argued that the latter, the weakest of the three alternatives, was the only realistic goal to set for linguistic theory.

The issue of selecting a grammar in this formulation was one for analysts comparing theories, not for children. Chomsky combated the structuralist goal of seeking a discovery method for grammars, whereby an analyst would follow mechanical procedures for the discovery of grammars and arrive at the correct description of some language. He argued, in contrast, that it was too ambitious to expect such a methodology and that the most realistic goal was to find a way of comparing hypotheses for generating a particular corpus of data. He was joining Popper (1959) in seeking to thwart the positivist notion that one could discover a predefined path to scientific truth: "One may arrive at a grammar by intuition, guess-work, all sorts of partial methodological hints, reliance on past experience, etc. . . . . Our ultimate aim is to provide an objective, non-intuitive way to evaluate a grammar once presented" (1957: 56).

---

[1] See my introduction to the second edition, Lightfoot (2002d).

In particular, there was no reason to expect a discovery method whereby a successful phonetic analysis would permit a successful phonemic analysis, which would allow a good morphological analysis and then a good syntactic analysis. "Once we have disclaimed any intention of finding a practical discovery procedure for grammars, certain problems that have been the subject of intense methodological controversy simply do not arise. Consider the problem of interdependence of levels" (Chomsky 1957: 56).

If units are defined by taxonomic procedures, then they need to be constructed on lower levels before higher-level units are constructed out of those lower-level units. However, once the goals are restricted to achieve an evaluation procedure, one may have independent levels of representation without circularity of definitions. Indeed, Chomsky argued that analysis at higher levels (of syntax) might influence lower (e.g. morphological) levels of analysis, and therefore that work on syntax could proceed even though there may be unresolved problems of phonemic or morphological analysis, perhaps to the advantage of the phonemic analysis.

This was the major METHODOLOGICAL innovation of *Syntactic Structures* and the claim to a genuinely scientific approach, pressed hardest by Robert Lees in his well-known review (Lees 1957), was based on the rigor of the formal, explicit, generative accounts and on the move away from seeking a discovery procedure in favor of an evaluation procedure for rating theories.[2]

Any scientific theory is based on a finite number of observations, and it seeks to relate the observed phenomena and to predict new phenomena by constructing general laws in terms of hypothetical constructs such as (in physics, for example) "mass" and "electron." Similarly, a grammar of English is based on a finite corpus of utterances (observations), and it will contain certain grammatical rules (laws) stated in terms of the particular phonemes, phrases, etc., of English (hypothetical constructs). (Chomsky 1957: 49)

What is remarkable about *Syntactic Structures* is how easily its claims were translatable into claims about human cognition, as Chomsky was to make explicit in his review of Skinner (Chomsky 1959) and then, famously, in the first chapter of *Aspects of the Theory of Syntax* (1965). There he redefined the field in more fundamental fashion and linked it to work on human psychology; from then on, matters of acquisition became central to linguistic theorizing, as I illustrated in chapter 3. The easy translation is the reason that the little book, having no discussion of matters of cognition, is nonetheless plausibly seen as the snowball that started it all.

The discussion about the goals of linguistic theory, for example, was straightforwardly translated point-for-point into criteria for a theory of language

---

[2] That was the major methodological innovation. The TECHNICAL innovation was to motivate different levels of analysis, which were related to each other formally by the device of a "transformational rule."

acquisition by children: the theory provides an evaluation metric by which children rate the success of candidate grammars for the purposes of understanding some finite corpus of data embodied in their initial linguistic experiences, converging ultimately on the most successful grammar. In fact, the celebrated discussion about the goals of linguistic theory, the distinction between discovery, decision, and evaluation procedures, is often cited as a discussion about what a child might be expected to do in the process of acquiring his/her grammar, as if Chomsky had actually been talking about children and the psychological interpretation of grammars: children compare competing grammars against a corpus, eventually converging on the correct grammar for a given corpus by a process of elimination.

Before he wrote the Introduction to *The Logical Structure of Linguistic Theory (LSLT)* – the text was written in 1955 and the introduction was written twenty years later, for the 1975 publication – Chomsky had come to view grammars as representations of fundamental aspects of the knowledge possessed by a speaker–hearer, i.e. as claims about psychology (*LSLT*: 5). Furthermore, there was a precise analog between the methodological claims of *Syntactic Structures* and *LSLT* and psychological claims about human cognition.

The construction of a grammar of a language by a linguist is in some respects analogous to the acquisition of language by a child. The linguist has a corpus of data; the child is presented with unanalyzed data of language use. (*LSLT*: 11)

The language learner (analogously, the linguist) approaches the problem of language acquisition (grammar construction) with a schematism that determines in advance the general properties of human language and the general properties of the grammars that may be constructed to account for linguistic phenomena. (*LSLT*: 12)

We thus have two variants of the fundamental problem of linguistics, as it was conceived in this work: under the methodological interpretation, the problem is taken to be the justification of grammars; under the psychological interpretation, the problem is to account for language acquisition . . . Under the methodogical interpretation, the selected grammar is the linguist's grammar, justified by the theory. Under the psychological interpretation, it is the speaker–hearer's grammar, chosen by the evaluation procedure from among the potential grammars permitted by the theory and compatible with the data as represented in terms of the preliminary analysis. (*LSLT*: 36)

The reason I have tracked this history is that most subsequent work on language learnability has followed *Syntactic Structures* in seeking theories that evaluate grammars relative to a corpus of utterances and this has led to too much reliance on E-language notions. Most modern work on learnability is essentially E-language based and therefore faces insuperable difficulties.

Chomsky (1965) viewed children as endowed with a metric evaluating grammars that can generate the primary data to which they are exposed (sets of sentences), along with appropriate structural descriptions for those data.[3] The evaluation metric picks the grammar that conforms to the invariant principles of UG and is most successful in generating those data and those structural descriptions. The child selects a grammar that matches his/her input as closely as possible – the output of the grammar matches the input that the child is exposed to. Again, if the data and the associated structural descriptions to which the child is exposed correspond fairly closely to the grammatical capacity of some older individual, one would expect the child's evaluation metric to select the same grammar as that older individual's. This expectation is reinforced if the space of available grammars has scattered peaks, as in the *Aspects* view, and if many aspects of the input have no effect on the mature system, for example, the order in which the child encounters sentences.

More recent models have also followed *Syntactic Structures* in appealing to E-language corpora. Grammars are evaluated according to their capacity to generate the corpus of sentences in the E-language that children are exposed to. The output of a child's grammar must match the input that he/she experiences. We shall examine two models.

Gibson & Wexler (1994) posited a Triggering Learning Algorithm (TLA), under which the child-learner uses grammars to analyze incoming sentences and eventually converges on the correct grammar, the grammar that generates the input data. If the child-learner cannot analyze a given sentence with the current grammar, then he/she follows a certain procedure, a learning algorithm, to change one of the current parameter settings and tries to reprocess the sentence using the new set of parameter values. The TLA guides the child to change certain parameter settings and, when analysis is possible for the sentence encountered, then the new parameter value is adopted, at least for a while. So the TLA is error-driven and the child changes one parameter setting at a time when the current grammar does not give the right results.

There is much to be said about the way that this model works and Fodor (1998) and Dresher (1999) have illuminating discussion, but what is crucial here is that the model has the child seeking grammars that permit analysis of incoming data, where the data consist of more or less unanalyzed sentences, elements of E-language: the target grammar generates the input data, the sentences that the child hears. Gibson & Wexler distinguish global and local triggers, but both are sentence-types (1994: 409). A global trigger would be a trigger, i.e. a sentence-type, that occurs in every language that has that parameter value. They note (1994: 425) that, because parameter values interact, parameter settings

---

[3] In fact, Chomsky takes the PLD to "consist of signals classified as sentences and nonsentences, and a partial and tentative pairing of signals with structural descriptions" (1965: 32). There is no reason to believe that children have access to systematic information about what does not occur.

manifest themselves differently in different languages and, therefore, global triggers are rare, in fact non-existent in their three-parameter system. Fodor (1998: 17) illustrates the point by considering the verb–object setting, which might be triggered by a subject–verb–object sentence in English, but by a verb–object–subject sentence in a subject-final, non-V2 language, and it would be a subject–auxiliary–verb–object sentence in a V2 language; each language needs its own "local" trigger.

Their table 3 (1994: 424), table 4.1 here, correlates sets of three parameter settings (Subject-final/initial,[4] Complement-final/initial, +/−verb-second) and S E T S of data (listed here in terms of primitives like Subject, Verb, First Object, Second Object). When exposed to some data set (right-hand column), the child selects the appropriate grammar (left-hand column) . . . although it would not be easy for the child to know which data set she is exposed to. Some of these grammars encompass familiar languages: grammar (e) encompasses English, (f) Swedish, (g) Japanese, and German is an example of grammar (h).

This selection proceeds in step-wise fashion and children are error driven. Suppose, for example, that a child has heard an SV sentence. That sentence is compatible with grammars (b, d, e, f, g, and h) – in general, short sentences are likely to be highly ambiguous structurally – and the child randomly picks grammar (e). Now the child encounters an OVS sentence, which cannot be parsed by grammar (e), and she must pick another grammar. Grammars (b, c, d, f, and h) will permit OVS, but if the child has access to the S E T of sentences encountered, she can look for a grammar that generates both SV and OVS and converge on either (b, d, f, or h), eliminating (a, c), because they do not generate SV, and eliminating (e, g), because they do not generate OVS. And so on, eliminating grammars as they fail to account for sentences encountered but not choosing grammars that fail to allow sentences previously encountered – hence the need to store data sets.

Fodor (1998: 25) points out that, in fact, there are silver bullets, sentence-types that uniquely require one of the eight grammars and that this is true for all eight grammars (boldface in table 4.1): a VOS sentence requires grammar (a) and is generated by no other of the eight grammars, O1AuxVO2S uniquely requires (b), an AdvOVS sentence indicates (c), an AdvAuxOVS points to (d), AdvSVO necessitates (e), AdvAuxSVO demands (f), SOV needs (g), and AdvAuxSOV requires (h). A different approach might exploit this, but that is not Gibson & Wexler's approach and, furthermore, the fact that there are silver bullets for these eight systems does not entail that, once we go beyond just three parameters, there will be similar silver bullets for all grammars; in fact, that is very unlikely.

---

[4] Somewhat misleadingly, Gibson & Wexler refer to this parameter as Specifier final/initial.

Table 4.1 *Correlation of parameter settings and data (Gibson & Wexler 1994)*

Parameter settings	Data in defined grammar
a. Spec-final Comp-final -V2 (VOS)	V S, **V O S**, V O1 O2 S Aux V S, Aux V O S, Aux V O1 O2 S, Adv V S Adv V O S, Adv V O1 O2 S, Adv Aux V S Adv Aux V O S, Adv Aux V O1 O2 S
b. Spec-final Comp-final +V2 (VOS + V2)	S V, S V O, O V S, S V O1 O2, O1 V O2 S, O2 V O1 S S Aux V, S Aux V O, O Aux V S S Aux V O1 O2, **O1 Aux V O2 S**, O2 Aux V O1 S Adv V S, Adv V O S, Adv V O1 O2 S Adv Aux V S, Adv Aux V O S, Adv Aux V O1 O2 S
c. Spec-final Comp-first -V2 (OVS)	V S, O V S, O2 O1 V S V Aux S, O V Aux S, O2 O1 V Aux S, Adv V S **Adv O V S**, Adv O2 O1 V S, Adv V Aux S Adv O V Aux S, Adv O2 O1 V Aux S
d. Spec-final Comp-first +V2 (OVS + V2)	S V, O V S, S V O, S V O2 O1, O1 V O2 S, O2 V O1 S S Aux V, S Aux O V, O Aux V S S Aux O2 O1 V, O1 Aux O2 V S, O2 Aux O1 V S Adv V S, Adv V O S, Adv V O2 O1 S Adv Aux V S, **Adv Aux O V S**, Adv Aux O2 O1 V S
e. Spec-first Comp-final -V2 (SVO)	S V, S V O, S V O1 O2 S Aux V, S Aux V O, S Aux V O1 O2, Adv S V **Adv S V O**, Adv S V O1 O2, Adv S Aux V Adv S Aux V O, Adv S Aux V O1 O2
f. Spec-first Comp-final +V2 (SVO + V2)	S V, S V O, O V S, S V O1 O2, O1 V S O2, O2 V S O1 S Aux V, S Aux V O, O Aux S V S Aux V O1 O2, O1 Aux S V O2, O2 Aux S V O1, Adv V S Adv V S O, Adv V S O1 O2, Adv Aux S V **Adv Aux S V O**, Adv Aux S V O1 O2
g. Spec-first Comp-first -V2 (SOV)	S V, **S O V**, S O2 O1 V S V Aux, S O V Aux, S O2 O1 V Aux, Adv S V Adv S O V, Adv S O2 O1 V, Adv S V Aux Adv S O V Aux, Adv S O2 O1 V Aux
h. Spec-first Comp-first +V2 (SOV + V2)	S V, S V O, O V S, S V O2 O1, O1 V S O2, O2 V S O1 S Aux V, S Aux O V, O Aux S V S Aux O2 O1 V, O1 Aux S O2 V, O2 Aux S O1 V Adv V S, Adv V S O, Adv V S O2 O1 Adv Aux S V, **Adv Aux S O V**, Adv Aux S O2 O1 V

Clark (1992) offers a similar kind of E-language-based model but one that differs from that of Gibson & Wexler in that the child cannot pinpoint the source of a grammar's failure, revising one particular parameter setting at a time. Clark's child takes a more global approach but has "an exquisite sense of the overall relative success of the grammar" (Dresher 1999: 54). Clark posits a Darwinian competition between grammars needed to parse sets of sentences. All grammars allowed by UG are available to each child and some grammars are used more than others in parsing what the child hears. A "genetic algorithm" picks those grammars whose elements are activated most often. A Fitness Metric compares with great precision how well each grammar fares, and the fittest grammars go on to reproduce in the next generation, while the least fit die out. Eventually the candidate grammars are narrowed to the most fit and the child converges on the correct grammar.

The Fitness Metric measures the fitness of grammars with respect to a set of sentences, with the exquisite precision pointed out by Dresher (2).

(2)   Fitness Metric

$$\frac{\left(\sum_{j=1}^{n} v_j + b \sum_{j=1}^{n} s_j + c \sum_{j=1}^{n} e_j\right) - (v_i + bs_i + ce_i)}{(n-1)\left(\sum_{j=1}^{n} v_j + b \sum_{j=1}^{n} s_j + c \sum_{j=1}^{n} e_j\right)}$$

where

v_i = the number of violations signaled by the parser associated with a given parameter setting;

s_i = the number of superset settings in the counter; b is a constant superset penalty <1;

e_i = the measure of elegance (= number of nodes) of counter i; $c < 1$ is a scaling factor

The central idea here is that grammars provide a means to understand certain sentences and not others; that is, they generate certain sentences but not others. The equation will be opaque to most readers but the Fitness Metric quantifies the failure of grammars to parse sentences, the "violations," v. The sum term, sigma, totals all the violations of all grammars under consideration, perhaps five grammars with a total of 50 failures or violations. One then subtracts the violations of any single grammar and divides by the total violations (multiplied by $n-1$). This provides a number that grades candidate grammars. For example, if one candidate grammar has 10 violations, its score is 50-10, divided by some number; if another candidate has 20 violations, its score is 50-20, divided by that number, a lower score. (There are two other factors involved in the equation, a superset penalty s, to which we shall return, and a measure of elegance e, which essentially prefers grammars with fewer nodes, but they are subject to a scaling condition and play only a very minor role, which I ignore here.) I have sketched Clark's Fitness Metric because it is the most sophisticated and precisely worked-out evaluation measure that I know. What it and other such evaluation measures do is rate grammars against a set of data, as outlined by Chomsky in 1957.

Clark's Fitness Metric has serious technical problems at its heart. First, there is no reason to suppose that a grammar with more parameters set correctly is more successful in parsing/generating incoming data. Dresher (1999) illustrates this by considering the settings needed to generate the phonological stress patterns of Selkup, computing the relative score the Fitness Metric would assign when the systems are applied to eight representative words. It isn't obvious what criterion the Fitness Metric should use, so he tried three different criteria: words correct, syllables correct, and main stress correct. Some results were as shown in (3).

(3)	Parameters correct		Words correct	Syllables correct		Main stress correct	
a.	4/10	40%	2/8 25%	7/20	35%	3/8	37.5%
b.	6/10	60%	1/8 12.5%	7/20	35%	5/8	62.5%
c.	7/10	70%	4/8 50%	12/20	60%	4/8	50%
d.	8/10	80%	5/8 62.5%	14/20	70%	5/8	62.5%
e.	9/10	90%	5/8 62.5%	14/20	70%	5/8	62.5%
f.	9/10	90%	3/8 37.5%	10/20	50%	3/8	37.5%

Candidates (e) and (f) are each correct in all but one (different) parameter, but they are very different in their apparent fitness. (e) scores high, but no higher than (d), which has fewer correct settings. Candidate (f), with only one parameter wrong, scores worse in every category than (c), which has three parameters wrong. And (a) does better than (b) in one category, despite having only four correct parameter settings. Dresher also points out that these results can be influenced in unpredictable ways by the chance occurrence of various types of words. As a result, there is no simple relationship between success and the number of parameters set correctly, which is a fundamental problem for the Fitness Metric.

The same is true, of course, in syntax: there is no reason to believe that changing any one parameter setting will have the same quantity of effects as changing another. One can see this by comparing the grammars provided by Gibson & Wexler. For example, grammar (a) differs from grammar (b) by one parameter setting and the set of sentence-types generated by the two grammars overlap by 40%. Grammar (a) also differs by one parameter setting from grammar (c), but the set of sentences generated by those two grammars overlap only by 16%. Grammar (f) (which has the properties of Swedish) overlaps 51%

with grammar (h) (German), but grammar (g) (Japanese) overlaps only 6% with grammar (h). Each of these pairs of grammars differs by only one of Gibson & Wexler's parameters but their degree of overlap in terms of the sentences generated varies between 6% and 51%.

A second technical problem is that the Fitness Metric also incorporates a version of Berwick's (1985) Subset Principle, whereby learners prefer those grammars that generate smaller sets of sentences, subsets of those generated by other grammars. These calculations are computed on hypothetical sets of sentences that MIGHT be generated by various grammars, not on actual sentences experienced. Again, the child is supposedly comparing sets of E-language elements generated by various grammars and ranking the grammars accordingly.

An example of this would be the very first parameters proposed, at least under that name (Chomsky 1981b: 55, citing Rizzi). Grammars are subject to a locality condition, restricting the distance over which an element may be copied, referred to in earlier work as a SUBJACENCY CONDITION, precluding movement over more than one BOUNDING NODE. In a celebrated footnote, Rizzi (1978: n25, reprinted as chapter 2 of Rizzi 1982) proposed that bounding nodes were parameterized: some grammars have DP, IP, and CP as bounding nodes (I modernize the terminology) and, as a result, wh- items may not be copied out of an embedded clause. In such languages one can say things like *What did Gerda drink?*, where copying crosses one bounding node (IP) (4a), but not *What do you think that Gerda drank?*, where *what* is copied outside the embedded clause where it is understood (4b). English grammars, on the other hand, have just DP and IP as bounding nodes and allow copying out of an embedded clause to yield (4b); there the second copying has both IP and CP intervening, which is fine if only IP is a bounding node and not both IP and CP, as in the more restricted languages. Italian, French, and Spanish grammars, however, have DP and CP as bounding nodes and allow copying from within a DP, along the lines of *Combien as-tu vu de personnes?* 'How many people have you seen?' (4c), where *combien* has been copied out of the containing DP and across an intervening IP node, which is not possible in English (**How many have you seen people?*). Other things being equal, these languages are in a subset relation: any wh- movement that can be used in the most restricted languages can be used in English, and any wh- extraction that can be used in English can be used in French, which also allows other possibilities not possible in English.

(4)   a. What did $_{IP}$[Gerda ~~did~~ drink ~~what~~]
       b. What do $_{IP}$[you ~~do~~ think $_{CP}$[~~what~~ that $_{IP}$[Gerda drank ~~what~~]]
       c. Combien as $_{IP}$[tu ~~as~~ vu $_{DP}$[~~combien~~ de personnes]

These are the major technical problems with the Fitness Metric but what all these models have in common is that learners eventually match their input, in the sense that they select grammars that generate the sentences of the input most effectively. It is only accurate grammars of this type that are submitted to Chomsky's (1965) evaluation metric, and Gibson & Wexler's error-driven children react to inaccurate grammars by seeking new parameter settings until a sufficient degree of accuracy is achieved. Similarly, Clark's genetic algorithm selects the grammar with the greatest fit with the set of sentences available to the child and furthermore ranks grammars according to hypothetical sets of sentences that C O U L D be generated. To the extent that they compare grammars according to the set of sentences that they generate or could generate, these approaches are E-language based. Furthermore, the models need to store sets of sentences and thereby they involve "batch learning."

In being E-language based, these models face huge feasibility problems. One can see those problems emerging with the system of Gibson & Wexler (1994). It is a toy system in the sense that it involves only three parameters and only eight competing grammars. Nonetheless the child needs to determine which of the eight data sets his/her language falls into. That cannot be determined from a single sentence, given the way their system works, but rather the child needs to store the set of sentences experienced and to compare that set with each of the eight possible sets, not a trivial task and one that requires memory banks incorporating the data sets illustrated in the right-hand column of table 4.1. The problem explodes when one considers more comprehensive systems. If there are thirty binary parameters (and even that seems far too parsimonious to be able to characterize the extent of variation among languages), then there are 2^{30} grammars, over a billion – 1,073,741,824; forty binary parameters yield 2^{40} grammars, 1,099,511,628,000, over one trillion. If a child takes eight years to converge on a mature grammar, that number would suggest that children eliminate 261,489 grammars every living minute, regardless of whether they are asleep or awake. Do the math. Trial-and-error learning is not effective for a problem of this magnitude.

One is reminded here of the apocryphal story of the invention of chess, when the inventor, Cessa, invited by the prince to name a reward, asked for two grains of wheat on the first square, double that on the second square, double that on the third square, and so on, in other words 2^{64}. The prince thought that this was too meager and asked him to request something more substantial, without realizing that that much wheat had never been grown.

So if acquisition proceeds by Gibson & Wexler's TLA and there are forty parameters, then there will be over a trillion different data sets to be stored and checked, and each of those data sets will be enormous. If acquisition proceeds by Clark's Fitness Metric and if there are forty parameters, then the metric will be computing and comparing violations (and subset relations and node numbers) for over a trillion grammars, each defined by vast numbers of sentences generated (actual and potential) – in fact infinite numbers, if grammars contain the recursive devices discussed in chapter 3. And, of course, any particular child hears only a miniscule fraction of that potential. Proponents of these systems have never made any suggestions about how memory demands might be handled in a feasible fashion, nor about how comparisons could be managed between so many competing systems.

Recent learnability models are E-language based in this fashion and this is best understood, it seems to me, in the context of the earliest work on generative grammar and ideas about the evaluation of grammars being translated into ideas about language acquisition. That's why I went through that history at the beginning of this section. The models are input-matching in the sense that they seek to have children converge on a grammar if its output matches most closely the set of sentences they experience, even though it is well known that children develop systems that do not match their input.

For example, Thornton (1995) observed three- and four-year-old English-speaking children leaving a copy of a wh- word at the front of the clause where it is understood (5), and she showed that this is systematic.

(5)   a. What do you think what pigs eat?
        b. Who do you think who eats trash?

That kind of thing occurs in dialects of German but not in the experience of English-speaking children evaluating candidate grammars against sets of sentences in the ambient E-language, and there is no input-matching at work in these cases. There are many other cases of children systematically producing sentences that they have not experienced. Another much discussed example is optional infinitives (see section 7.1 and Wexler 1994).

In rendering children as conservative input matchers, these models leave little scope for understanding how children converge on systems that do not match the input data but on new I-languages with different structures.

4.2   An I-language perspective

The problems of E-language-sensitive models seem to be fundamental and suggest that it may be useful to consider alternatives. The models just considered are unhelpful for historical linguists, who are interested in cases of CHANGE. Change may take place where there is massive disruption of a population through an invasion or genocide. However, this is unusual and more often new systems emerge where there is no invasion or similar cataclysmic event, and they nonetheless generate significantly different data sets. In such instances children attain systems that do not generate the structures and sentences generated by earlier grammars, and there may be no close match, as we shall see in the next few chapters.

I have argued in earlier work (Lightfoot 1997, 1999) that children scan their environment for designated structures or "cues," elements of I-language. They are CUE-BASED learners. Elements of E-language play no role in comparing grammars.

A cue is a piece of structure, an element of I-language, which is derived from the input, but it is not a sentence. One example of a cue is the $_{VP}$[V DP] structure for verb–object languages; I will give several other examples in the next section, resulting from the analyses of chapter 3. The full range of cues is provided by UG and children scan the mental representations that result from hearing, understanding, and "parsing" utterances. Hearing and understanding a sentence *He visited Claudia* requires treating *visited Claudia* as a unit headed by the verb, which has Claudia as its complement, hence the $_{VP}$[V DP] cue is identified. As a child understands an utterance, even partially, he/she has some kind of mental representation of the utterance; that involves a syntactic structure, which helps to define a meaning. The learner scans those representations, derived from the input, and finds the necessary elements of structure, cues. A sentence EXPRESSES a cue if the cue is unambiguously required for the analysis of the sentence.[5]

Under this view, the crucial input consists of structures, not sentences, and all triggers are "global" in Gibson & Wexler's sense; in all languages the cue for verb–object order is the $_{VP}$[V DP] structure and not different sentence-types, although there may be different sentence-types expressing the cue in different languages – an important point discussed below.

This comports with Janet Fodor's view; she treats triggers as structures and not sentences, what she called "treelets," where a treelet is "a small piece of tree structure . . . that is made available by UG and is adopted into a learner's grammar if it proves essential for parsing input sentences" (Fodor 1998: 6).

Ironically, the best-worked-out model of parameter setting comes from phonology and the work of Elan Dresher & Jonathon Kaye (1990). The notion of binary parameters has not played an extensive role in the phonological literature, but Dresher & Kaye identified parameters for stress patterns, a rather well-studied area of phonology. Furthermore, they developed a cue-based theory of acquisition (they introduced the term), now clarified, elaborated, and generalized by Dresher (1999). Under their view, UG specifies not only a set of parameters, but also for each parameter a cue. I amend this and say that cues that are realized only in certain grammars are the points of variation between grammars and there is no need for an independent notion of a parameter.

A sentence *I saw the man with a telescope* is structurally ambiguous, as we saw in chapter 3, and therefore does not express the structure of the complement DP. On the other hand, *I saw a man with a brown jacket* is not similarly ambiguous and can only be analyzed with *a man with a brown jacket* as a complex DP; it therefore expresses that structure. Likewise, *I saw a man through binoculars*,

---

[5] Sometimes sentences expressing the cues are referred to as "triggers."

meaning what it means, may only be analyzed with *through binoculars* as an adjunct to the VP *[saw a man]*, since *a man through binoculars* does not refer to any real-world entity, unlike *a man with a brown jacket*. The two unambiguous sentences express structures, each of which can be employed for the ambiguous *I saw a man with a telescope*.

The child scans the linguistic environment for cues only in simple syntactic domains; this is the "degree-0 learnability" of Lightfoot (1991, 1994), to be discussed in chapter 6. Cues are found in simple structures, and children learn nothing new from complex structures with multiple embeddings. A French child can learn that CP and not IP is a bounding node for Rizzi's Subjacency Condition on exposure to a simple sentence like *Combien as-tu vu de personnes?*, as illustrated above (4c). Similarly with other parameters that have appeared to require more complex triggers.

Learners do not rate grammars against sets of sentences; rather, they seek abstract structures derived unambiguously from the input (elements of I-language), looking only at structurally simple domains, and they act on this locally without regard to the final result, building the grammar cue by cue. That is, a child seeks cues and may or may not find them; the output of the grammar is entirely a by-product of the cues that the child finds, and the grammar is in no way evaluated on the basis of sentences that it generates. The child's triggering experience, then, is best viewed as a set of abstract structures manifested in the mental representations that result from parsing utterances.

The essential feature of cue-based models of acquisition is that learners use what they hear as sources of cues. The crucial input is not sets of sentences of the kind that Gibson & Wexler invoked (table 4.1), but rather partially analyzed syntactic structures; these are the mental representations resulting from parsing utterances. Some of those representations may constitute partial parses, which lack some of the information in mature, adult parses (Lightfoot 1999). Cues are intensional elements, grammar fragments, and elements of I-language, Fodor's treelets.

A cue-based learner determines the existence of "prenominal possessive" phrases on the basis of exposure to data which must be analyzed with a possessive DP phrase preceding the head, e.g. $[_{DP}[John]\text{ }'s]\text{ }_N[hat]]$. That determination can only be made, of course, when the child has a partial analysis that treats *John's* and *hat* as separate words, the latter a head noun, connected by the clitic determiner *'s*, etc. The possessive phrase may be much larger than *John*, for example *The woman we met in Chicago*, yielding *The woman we met in Chicago's hat*. Such structures do not occur in the grammars of French speakers and therefore represent a point of parametric variation, but there is no parameter as such, independent of the cue.

The cue-based approach assumes with Lightfoot (1989) that there is a "learning path," an order in which cues are identified. We have seen that a child cannot determine whether possessive phrases precede heads until some analytical vocabulary has been developed. Similarly, the child cannot determine whether a grammar has verb–object structures until he/she has identified phrasal categories. This represents prior stages of acquisition. Representations are elaborated step-by-step in the course of acquisition, and the cues needed become increasingly abstract and grammar-internal. In this model the learning path is part of linguistic theory, a function of the way in which the cues are stated.

The learning path reflects dependencies among cues and follows from their internal architecture. A child determines sounds, morphological elements like past-tense markers, lexical items categorized as nouns, etc., and such levels of analysis are prerequisites for more abstract syntactic representations involving verb phrases (VPs), complement relations, determiner phrases (DPs), etc. Children become sensitive to the particular sounds of their I-language in the first year of life. During the latter part of that year babies lose the ability to discriminate between contrasts N O T found in the ambient E-language (Goldin-Meadow 2003: 4). By nine months, infants begin to recognize words.

UG is involved at all stages and defines the primitives of observation, such as the available sounds and lexical categories – children's experience is analyzed in terms of nouns, verbs, prepositions, and a small number of other categories. Exposure to a phrase *Student of generative linguistics* may trigger an analysis which generates complements to the right of their head noun, but this can happen only when the child already knows that *student* is a noun that assigns a thematic role to the phrasal element *generative linguistics*. We shall see more examples of these dependencies when we consider more specific cues in the next section.

Children are incremental parsers, apparently born to analyze language as best they can. Chomsky (1965: 32) adopted the strong assumption

that the child has an innate theory of potential structural descriptions that is sufficiently rich and fully developed so that he is able to determine, from a real situation in which a signal occurs, which structural descriptions may be appropriate to this signal, and also that he is able to do this in part in advance of any assumption as to the linguistic structure of this signal.

Children scan the environment for elements of I-language. These elements are derived from the input, in the mental representations yielded as children understand and "parse" their input. A cue-based learner acquires a verb–object grammar not by evaluating different grammars against sets of sentences but on exposure to simple $_{VP}$[V DP] structures, utterances which M U S T be analyzed with such structures. This requires identifying verbs and verb phrases and the cue must be represented robustly in the mental representations resulting from parsing the simple structures of PLD.

Different sentences may express the cue in different languages; the $_{VP}$[V DP] cue might be expressed by a subject–verb–object sentence (*He visited Claudia*)

for an English-speaking child or by a subject–auxiliary–verb–object sentence
for a child acquiring a verb-second grammar like Swedish. In Swedish, a simple
subject–verb–object sentence is structurally ambiguous and might be analyzed
with the verb moved out of the VP, hence not expressing the $_{VP}$[V DP] cue.

Some version of this cue-based approach is implicitly assumed in some work
on acquisition – for example, in the work of Nina Hyams (1986, 1996), who
saw Italian and Spanish children acquiring capacities to have null subjects by
identifying expletive structures. In fact, much of the work on acquisition, unlike
models of learnability, views children as converging on particular structures;
Crain & Thornton (1998) provide a comprehensive account of the methods
behind such work.

The cue-based approach also comports well with work on the visual system,
which develops as organisms are exposed to very specific visual stimuli, horizontal lines for example (Hubel 1978, Hubel & Wiesel 1962, Sperry 1968).
Current theories of the immune system are similar; specific antigens amplify
pre-existing antibodies. In fact, this is the kind of thing which is typical of selective learning quite generally (Piattelli-Palmarini 1986). The cue-based approach
has been productive for phonologists concerned with the parameters for stress
systems (Dresher 1999, Fikkert 1994, 1995).

Cue-based acquisition is a radical departure from much current work on
learnability, which portrays children as evaluating grammars against sets of
sentences. It is striking that so much of this work has children dealing with
elements of E-language, often requiring that the system perform elaborate calculations in effect. The model advocated here plays down the centrality of
E-language for a good account of acquisition, and postulates children seeking
elements of I-language in the input and selecting grammars accordingly; the
model makes no reference to elements of E-language or to the output of the
grammar.

Gibson & Wexler's TLA and Clark's genetic algorithms are learning algorithms quite distinct from the grammars assumed. However, the cue-based
approach suggests that there is no relevant learning algorithm beyond the information provided specifically by UG.

In addition, the feasibility issues discussed in the context of error-driven,
grammar-evaluating models do not arise. In that discussion, we pointed to the
difficulties of evaluating grammars against data-sets when billions or trillions
of grammars might be permitted by sets of thirty or forty binary parameters.
In contrast, there might be, say, a thousand different cues without comparable
feasibility problems. If each of those one thousand cues might be present in a
particular I-language or not, then one also allows for a great variety in available
systems, in fact many, many trillions. However, if a child simply has to identify
whether a thousand elements of I-language are present or not, without evaluating different systems against sets of E-language items (effectively, sentences),

then each of those options is comparable to learning an exceptional past-tense verb form. We know that English-speaking children may identify 200 irregular past-tense forms, recognizing *kept, sang, was, chose*, etc. Identifying a structural cue such as $_{VP}[V\ DP]$ might be roughly analogous to identifying particular verb forms and there is no reason to deal with the vast numbers implicated in the E-language-based approaches. So the set of cues found for a particular language organ could be viewed as similar to the lexicon; the child identifies cues in much the way that he/she identifies lexical items. This is a way of accommodating the insight behind the principles-and-parameters model, that children attain their grammar by turning on or off a manageable number of switches.

Cues need to occur with a certain degree of robustness, since there is no reason to believe that children are thrown off course by being exposed to occasional ill-formed expressions, for example an object–verb structure from a native speaker of German with only a partial mastery of English, who said *I think that Gerda tea drank*. There is good reason to believe that children learn only from unambiguous structures, sentences that M U S T be analyzed with the relevant cue, and such unambiguous structures must be sufficiently robust. Some cues may be triggered by just one instance, in the way that children seem able to learn some lexical items on a single exposure; one giraffe may be enough for a four-year-old child to learn the word. But other cues require more robust triggering and one must not characterize children as "trigger happy," responding to everything they hear, including an archaic verb-second sentence from John Milton's *Paradise Lost* (I.1.500), *Then wander forth the sons of Belial, flown with insolence and wine*, and the idiosyncrasies of the German house guest. Nor can we portray children generalizing idiomatic expressions inappropriately, extending *A good time was had by all* to **A piece of cake was had by Kim* or *By and large* to **Through but yellow*.

The required degree of robustness may vary from one cue to another and Goldin-Meadow (2003: 20) distinguishes properties of I-language that are F R A G I L E, properties that might change if the input is slightly different.

4.3   Syntactic cues

Let us now review the claims made in chapter 3, considering how the I-language systems argued for might be acquired and discussing specific cues. If we reject models evaluating grammars against sets of E-language items, we shall want to know what the cues might be. I list the eleven cues in (6). (6a-g) correspond to the computational operations of (28) in chapter 3.

(6)   a. $_C$e
      b. $_{CP}[$wh-
      c. $_V$e
      d. NP+*is*

e. $_{VP}e$

f. $_{VP}[VP \# DP]$

g. $_{DP}[DP _D\text{'s NP}]$

h. $_{IP}[DP_i \ V \ _{DP}[\text{-self}]_i]$

i. $DP_i \ V \ _{DP}[DP\text{'s } _{NP}[NP \ pronoun_i]]$

j. $_N[X\text{-}1 \ N\text{-}2]$

k. $_{XP}[2 \ 1]$

A child identifying these eleven cues will attain the I-language system discussed in chapter 3, given an appropriate contribution from UG, including the three notions discussed in that chapter (the condition on deletion, the Binding Theory, and the bottom-up analysis of intonational structure). Let us go through them one by one, seeing what prerequisites are needed for a child to parse a sentence in such a way that it expresses the cue.

English-speaking children identify empty complementizers (6a) on exposure to expressions like *Peter said Kay left*, comparable to *Peter said that Kay left* with an overt complementizer. The child needs be at the stage of development where he/she understands that *Kay left* is the sentential complement of the verb *said*, thus parsing the sentence with a CP, and such a CP can then only be analyzed as having a null C, an empty complementizer; there is no structural ambiguity here when the child is at the relevant stage of development and has the prerequisites to parse *Kay left* as a CP – at that point *Peter said Kay left* expresses (6a). One can think of this in such a way that identifying the empty complementizer cue yields the operation (28a) of chapter 3: *that* → 0.

Children identify displaced wh- phrases, pronounced at the front of a clause but understood elsewhere (6b). This is done on hearing something like *Who did Jay see?* and understanding it to mean 'Jay saw somebody; who was it?'. This involves parsing what is heard with *who* in a preposed position and with its source deleted. Again there is no structural ambiguity in this regard when the child has the wherewithal to understand *who* as the complement of *see*, and the cue yields the operation Copy wh- ((28b) in chapter 3).

The empty-verb cue $_Ve$ (6c) is expressed by an utterance like *Jay saw Ray and Jim Kim*, understood to mean that Jim saw Kim. That understanding comes from a parse in which *Jim Kim* is a clause, an IP containing a VP with an empty verb understood as 'saw': $_{IP}[Jim \ _{VP}[_Ve \ Kim]]$. Once the sentence is understood in that way, there is no alternative parse in this regard and no structural ambiguity. That parse would yield the operation Gap V, (28c) of chapter 3.

The NP+*is* cue (6d) could be identified on exposure to *Kim's happy*, understood to mean that Kim is happy and pronounced with a reduced *is*. That is tantamount to a parse in which the copula *is* is cliticized to its left (because it is reduced and phonetically assimilated to the last segment of the NP), and that parse would yield the operation *is* → *'s*, (28d) of chapter 3.

Children identify ellipsed VPs on exposure to the cue $_{VP}e$ (6e), which would be expressed in an utterance like *Mary didn't*, understood to mean that Mary didn't do something. That understanding requires an empty VP in the mental representation, which is interpreted in some fashion, and again there is no relevant structural ambiguity. Hence the operation Ellipse VP, (28e) of chapter 3.

A child might hear something like *Jay gave to Ray his favorite racket*, pronounced with an intonational break between *Ray* and *his* and meaning that Jay gave his favorite racket to Ray. Such an understanding would involve a parse containing the structure $_{VP}[VP \# DP]$, the cue (6f), which occurs only with a "heavy" DP, triggering the Copy DP operation. In this particular example from English, there is no structural ambiguity and *his favorite racket* can only be analyzed as adjoined to the VP, but we shall see in chapter 6 that comparable structures in object–verb languages may involve some ambiguity.

As discussed above, children identify prenominal possessive phrases on exposure to *John's hat* or something similar, understood to be a unit with a head noun *hat*, possessed by John, hence a structure $_{DP}[DP _D$'s NP$]$ (6g). A particular instance of the same structure would be *Jay's picture*, understood to mean 'picture of Jay' and an "objective genitive." That understanding would require a parse in which *Jay* is copied to the left and its source deleted, thus triggering an operation Copy DP to leftward Specifier, (28g) of chapter 3. Again, there is no structural ambiguity if that is the understanding of the expression.

This represents a strong and testable claim about how acquisition proceeds. As for a theory of cues, they would constitute the set of available grammatical structures, some occurring in all grammars and others, the ones representing points of variation, occurring only in certain I-language systems. This is reminiscent of the inventory of sounds: children begin with the potential of acquiring any of the distinctions that occur in any language, but by the end of the first year they lose the capacity to acquire distinctions that are not part of their ambient language. Similarly with syntactic structures: if they are not identified, they atrophy and disappear from a child's capacity. We have illustrated some specific cues here in the light of the analyses provided in chapter 3, but it is unlikely that the cues would be stated in this form. More likely, they would be stated more abstractly and more generally, perhaps along the lines of (7), but we will not concern ourselves here with the form of cues beyond these observations. If that is right, then we can reconstitute the notion of a parameter as a metatheoretical relationship between cues: languages are either left-adjunct or right-adjunct.

(7)   a. left/right adjunct
        b. left/right complement
        c. elements may be null if interpretable.

In chapter 3 we also discussed the Binding Theory and indexical relations, positing that children need to learn that reflexive pronouns like *themselves* are anaphors and that forms like *him* and *her* are pronouns subject to Principle B of the Binding Theory. That *themselves* is an anaphor could be learned on exposure to a simple sentence like *They washed themselves*, where the washer and washee are understood to be identical, hence parsed as coindexed. The structure would be $_{IP}[DP_i \ V \ _{DP}[-self]_i]$ (6h), where the subject and object are coindexed, and this is the cue for the anaphor status of *self* forms. Similarly a child could learn that *her* is a pronoun on exposure to *Kim heard Bill's speeches about her*, understood to mean that the speeches were by Bill and about Kim. This would involve a parse containing a structure $DP_i \ V \ _{DP}[DP's \ _{NP}[NP \ her_i]]$, the cue of (6i) that establishes the pronominal nature of *her*. Given the required understanding, the indices follow necessarily, and there is no problem of structural ambiguity. These cues are complex; they presuppose a lot of prior knowledge and therefore could not be identified early in the acquisition process.

We also discussed intonation patterns and argued for a system whereby children learn that noun compounds have a 1–2 pronunciation, while 2–1 is standard in all other structures. A child could learn this on exposure to the word *black-board*, pronounced 1–2 and understood to be a compound noun, a noun with two parts, hence the structure $_N[X-1 \ N-2]$, the cue of (6j). The standard 2–1 pattern could be learned from a host of other units with a 2–1 pronunciation, for example *black board*, meaning a board which is black (unlike a black-board, which is not necessarily black) and pronounced in the usual 2–1 fashion: $_{XP}[2 \ 1]$ (6k).

We are unifying the syntactic analyses of chapter 3, where we were careful to address the apparent poverty-of-stimulus acquisition problems, with a plausible account of how the analyses might be "learned" by children, triggered in some feasible fashion. The child finds the cues of (6) in the sentences he/she hears (all structurally simple) and incorporates the cues into his/her grammar, yielding the computational operations I have specified. Appropriate parsing is the way to an appropriate mature grammar and the child reacts only when forced to do so, not reacting if there is relevant structural ambiguity. That will become clearer when we consider, in the next chapter, cases of structural ambiguity; in the cases discussed here, there is no ambiguity to contend with. The sentences express the cues; that is, they require the cue in order to have any analysis compatible with the perceived meaning and the grammar as it exists so far, prior to exposure to any given cue.

Cue-based learning is "deterministic" in the sense of Berwick (1985), to which we shall return: the learner may not backtrack or undo elements of structure that have already been identified. Once cued, a structure exists in the person's emerging grammar and may not be eliminated. Hence there is no possibility of the learner getting into infinite loops, of the kind discussed by Dresher (1999), flipping from one parameter setting to its opposite. For our cue-based child, forty language-particular structures could be set by forty events. No cue is adopted into the grammar unless it permits analysis of a sentence experienced and indeed is required for that analysis. For the error-driven, grammar-evaluating child, forty binary parameters entail a lot of guesswork among a vast population, over a trillion potential grammars.

4.4   Conclusion

If acquisition is cue-based in this fashion, that has consequences for the nature of what is acquired. For example, it is sometimes said that certain languages have "free word order." Whatever the properties of the language in question, they would need to be acquired through identifying structural cues and it is hard to imagine how there could be a structural cue tantamount to free word order, perhaps best viewed now as a pretheoretical notion. Similarly, Gibson & Wexler's "verb-second" parameter would be seen as a pretheoretical notion, the consequences of a structural cue where a phrasal category occurs in the Specifier of a CP whose head is occupied by a verb: something like $_{CP}$[XP $_C$V ...].

The approach assumes that children are obligated to process speech. There is nothing voluntary here, any more than people decide whether to see. Children are exposed to a visual world and react to horizontal lines, edges, and the other primitives of current work, and come to see in the way that they do. Similarly, children process speech, driven to assign syntactic, morphological, phonological, etc. representations, using context, lexical knowledge, and the structures already existing in their grammar. All input for learning comes through parsing, through the mental representations triggered by utterances. Under the cue-based approach, mere parsing provides the wherewithal for language acquisition, identifying the elements of the I-language with no learning algorithm like Gibson & Wexler's TLA and no evaluation of competing grammars through anything like Clark's Fitness Metric.

The insight behind cue-based learning is that brains make certain structures, cues, available for interpreting what a person experiences. That is the role of the brain in learning, the contribution of the organism to the processing of experience. Sometimes we can see that role particularly clearly when the outside world becomes different. In chapters 5 and 6, we shall see what may happen if the outside world changes a little, and in chapter 7 we shall see what may happen with more dramatic differences in the world outside.

If I-languages have the kinds of properties we discussed in chapter 3 and if acquisition proceeds in the way discussed in this chapter, we are now in a position to ask how I-languages may change from one generation to another, how new languages may emerge.

5   New E-language cuing new I-languages

5.1   Changes in I-languages

We saw in chapter 2 that our nineteenth-century predecessors developed linguistics as a distinct discipline and were concerned exclusively with language change. For them, languages were external objects and changed in systematic ways according to "laws" and general notions of directionality. Languages were related to each other to different degrees, modeled in tree diagrams (*Stammbäume*), and they changed at certain rates that could be discovered. Linguists of the time focused on the products of human behavior rather than on the internal processes that underlie the behavior, although other approaches were put forward towards the end of the century, particularly in the work of Hermann Paul and phoneticians like Eduard Sievers.

From our perspective, they focused on E-languages and sought to explain, for example, how one E-language, Latin, could develop into the new E-languages of French, Spanish, Italian, Sardinian, and the other Romance languages. Those idealizations were useful to a degree, they have been resilient over a long period, and those of us who deny that E-languages have any biological reality and deny that they can be defined in any precise way, nonetheless find it convenient to refer to English, Swedish, and other E-languages for certain purposes. Furthermore, we shall see that E-language, although not systematic, represents a kind of reality that is indispensable for our account of new I-languages.

However, the fact is that dealing only in terms of E-languages and focusing exclusively on change did not bring a scientific, Newtonian-style analysis of language change of the kind that had been hoped for. By the end of the nineteenth century, the data of linguistics consisted of an impressive inventory of sound changes but the changes occurred for no clear reasons and tended in no particular direction, and the idea that there were principles of history to be discovered was largely abandoned in the 1920s.

We shall retain a notion of E-language but I shall argue over the next three chapters that progress can be made if we incorporate, in addition, a different idealization, a notion of I-languages and new grammars.[1] If we attend not only to the products of the language system but also to the system itself, not only to E-language but also to I-languages, we explain new grammars through the nature of the acquisition process. There is more to language change than new grammars and it also involves the changing USE of grammars and social variation, as we shall see. Nonetheless, new grammars, new I-languages, while just one part of language change, are an important, central part and they enable us to reach explanations previously unavailable.

We have seen that grammars are formal characterizations of an individual's linguistic range, conforming to and exploiting the tools provided by a universal initial state (UG), and developing as a person is exposed to his/her childhood linguistic experience. A grammar, in this terminology, is a mental organ, a person's language organ. There is more to a person's language than what is captured by his/her grammar and, indeed, a person may operate with more than one grammar, but grammars, I-languages, are an essential part of the picture, as we have seen in the last two chapters. We will see now how these ideas enable us to approach linguistic change differently.

New grammars may emerge over time: children grew certain grammars in London in the thirteenth century and different ones in the fifteenth century. Nineteenth-century children in Amsterdam grew particular grammars and children in present-day Johannesburg who will become speakers of Afrikaans grow different grammars, despite some continuity with nineteenth-century Dutch. These groups speak differently and use different structures. The only way a different grammar may grow in a different child, under the view that we have developed so far, is when that child is exposed to different experience. Children typically hear the speech of many people and what a child hears may express the cues of UG differently, just because the ambient speech has changed in certain ways. When a new grammar emerges, the linguist wants to find how it emerged and how the relevant childhood experience might have changed just prior to the emergence of the new I-language, in such a way that the new grammar was the only possible outcome. The difference may be slight, perhaps just statistical shifts, but it will be significant if it cues a different grammar.

In this perspective, the study of new grammars, of grammar change, is fused with work on variation, the use of grammars, and the acquisition of grammars. We explain the emergence of the new grammar and the explanation illuminates the nature of the child's triggering experience and the way in which children acquire their linguistic capacities; the study of new grammars has implications for grammatical theory and for theories of language acquisition, and I assume

---

[1] Remember that I-language and E-language are idealizations, competing with idealizations like "English." Matthews (2003) queries the distinction and offers good, succinct, and skeptical discussion but he underestimates the difference between E-language and I-language.

that there is a deterministic relationship between particular experiences and a particular grammar, and the relationship is many-to-one (1); clusters of PLD trigger a single grammar.

(1)   a. $PLD_{x,y,z} \rightarrow grammar_1$
           b. $PLD_{p,q,r} \rightarrow grammar_2$

As noted in chapter 1, grammars differ sharply: a person either has a grammar with a certain property, or not. A person may also have more than one grammar, indeed a family of grammars, but each grammar is discrete and either has a given property or not. People's speech, on the other hand, is in constant flux, and languages, conglomerations of the output of people's grammars, are inherently fluid, unstable, always changing. As a result, no two people have the same initial experiences. While the E-language to which people are exposed is infinitely variable, grammars are not; there is a finite number of grammars, resulting from the identification of a finite number of different cues.

E-language is a group phenomenon. E-language, whatever it may be precisely, reflects the output of the grammars of a community of people, the varying use of those grammars in discourse, and social variation in the set of grammars. E-language change can sometimes be tracked geographically, seeing some new variant attested in different places at different times. And change at the level of languages often seems to take place gradually, spreading through the population socially and geographically.

The linguistic experience of young children (the ambient E-language and their PLD) varies constantly, but sometimes small variations are significant and have bigger, structural consequences, changes in grammars. Grammar change is linked to changes in people's speech; we can only know about it by studying what people say, often through written texts, and it must be studied in conjunction with other kinds of change. However, grammar change, involving new structures, is different from change in E-language; if grammars are abstract, then they change only occasionally and sometimes with dramatic consequences for a wide range of constructions and expressions; grammar change tends to be "bumpy," manifested by clusters of phenomena changing at the same time, as we shall see. New I-languages, new grammars, constitute a distinct type of change, a reaction to contingent factors of language use. To focus on new grammars, on I-language, is to attend to one aspect of language change, one that illuminates the variation and acquisition of grammars by children, but one that is dependent on other kinds of language change. So historians need to distinguish change in E-language from change in I-languages, which is not always easy.

The explanatory model is essentially synchronic and there will be a local cause for the emergence of any new grammar, namely a different set of primary linguistic data. To illustrate this, let us look at the history of certain aspects of

English verbs. These changes have been discussed by many people over the past thirty years and are now well understood.[2]

5.2   English verbs

English modal auxiliaries like *can, could, may, might, will, would, shall, should,* and *must* differ from ordinary verbs in their distribution. A modal auxiliary does not occur with a perfective (2) or present participle (3), unlike a verb; a modal does not occur in the infinitival complement to another verb (4), nor as the complement of another modal (5), unlike a verb like *try*; and no modal may occur with a direct object, whereas some verbs may (6).

(2)   a. *He has could understand chapter 4.
      b. He has understood chapter 4.

(3)   a. *Canning understand chapter 4, . . .
      b. Understanding chapter 4, . . .

(4)   a. *He wanted to can understand.
      b. He wanted to understand.

(5)   a. *He will can understand.
      b. He will try to understand.

(6)   a. *He can music.
      b. He understands music.

The distribution of these modal auxiliaries is peculiar to modern English. For example, the equivalent verbs in French, *pouvoir* 'can,' *devoir* 'must,' etc., behave the same way as a normal verb like *comprendre* 'understand': unlike *can, pouvoir* and *devoir* may occur as a complement to another verb (7), even to another modal verb (8), and may take a clitic direct object (9), and to that extent they behave like ordinary, common-or-garden verbs in French. In French grammars, the words that translate the English modals, *pouvoir, devoir,* etc., have the same distribution as French verbs and are verbs, just like *comprendre*.

(7)   Il a voulu pouvoir comprendre le chapitre.
      'He wanted to be able to understand the chapter.'

(8)   Il doit pouvoir comprendre le chapitre.
      'He must be able to understand the chapter.'

(9)   Il le peut.
      'He can it,'·i.e. understand the chapter.

Furthermore, not only may languages differ in this regard, but also different stages of one language. Sentences along the lines of the non-existent utterances

---

[2] The changes were first discussed in terms of a change in category membership by Lightfoot (1974). Plank (1984) and Warner (1993), among others, added to our understanding, and Lightfoot (1999: ch. 6) gives a fairly full account.

of (2–6a) were well-formed in earlier English. If the differences between Old and Modern English were a function of separate features with no unifying factor (Ross 1969), we would expect these features to come into the language at different times and in different ways. On the other hand, if the differences between Old and Modern English reflect a single property in an abstract system, a categorical distinction, then we would expect the trajectory of the change to be very different. And that's what we find: the new phenomena arise together. If the differences between *can* and *understand* are a function of the single fact that *understand* is a verb while *can* is a member of a different category, then we are not surprised to find that (2–6a) dropped out of people's language in parallel, at the same time. This has encouraged linguists to postulate a single relevant difference between the earlier and later grammars: in the early grammars words like *can*, *must*, etc. were verbs and in later grammars they belonged to a different category. That has become a standard analysis for Modern English grammars. This kind of clustering of phenomena is typical of change in I-languages, a multiplicity of phenomena all reflecting a single difference at the level of I-languages.

In Middle English *Kim can understand the chapter* had the structure (10), where *can* was a verb that may move, like all verbs, copied to a higher Inflection position, I; and in present-day English the structure is (11), where *can* is listed as an Inflection element, entering the structure as I and not as a V, not being copied into a higher Inflection position but originating there. So an expression *Kim can understand the chapter* was analyzed as (10) in early English and then as (11) in later times, being assigned a different structure and being parsed differently. We shall ask why this happened in a moment.

(10)   Middle English   (11) Present-day English

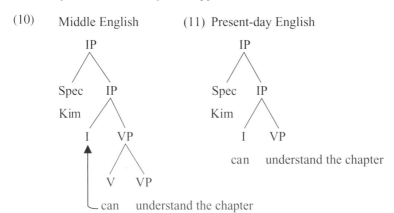

If in present-day English *can* is an I element, then one predicts that it cannot occur to the right of a perfective or progressive marker, as in (2a, 3a) (those aspectual markers *have* and *be* originate within the VP and may co-occur only

with verbs: *Kim has wept, slept, and crept* but not **Kim has could weep*), that
it is mutually exclusive with the infinitival marker *to* (which also occurs in
I) (4a), that there may only be one modal per VP (5), and that a modal may
not be followed by a direct object (6a). Simply postulating the structure of
(11) accounts for the data of (2–6) in present-day English. Earlier English had
structures like (10), where *can* was a verb and behaved like *understand*, moving
to a higher functional position. If one thinks in terms of a certain kind of abstract
system, then there is a single change which accounts for the phenomena of (2–
6) and accounts for why they emerged simultaneously. These are the different
I-languages.

For a simple sentence *Kim understood the chapter*, the structure is (12). In
early English the V-to-I operation moved the verb *understood* to the higher I
position, as in (10), while in Modern English grammars there is no V-to-I operation and the tense marker lowers on to *understood* as a kind of morphological
operation sometimes referred to as Affix Hopping (Chomsky 1957, Lightfoot
1993, Lasnik 1999), here called Inflection lowering.

(12)

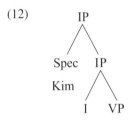

If we attend just to changing phenomena, the historical change consists in the
LOSS of various forms, not in the development of new forms; people ceased to
say some things that had been said in earlier times. Before the change, all of the
utterances in (2–6) might have occurred in a person's speech, but later only
those forms not marked with an asterisk; the (a) sentences disappeared. That
fact alone suggests that there was a change in some abstract system, a change
in I-languages. People might START to use some new expression because of
the social demands of fashion or because of the influence of speakers from
a different community, but people do not CEASE to say things for that sort
of reason. There might be an indirect relationship, of course: people might
introduce new expressions into their speech for external, social reasons, and
those new expressions might entail the loss of old forms; but that is not what
happened here. Changes involving only the loss and obsolescence of forms
need to be explained as a consequence of some change in an abstract, cognitive
system. This methodological point is fundamental.

If one focuses on the final disappearance of the relevant forms, one sees that
they were lost as a set and not individually. The most conservative writer in

this regard was Sir Thomas More, writing in the early sixteenth century. He used all of the starred forms in (2–6a) and had the last attested uses of several constructions. His grammar treated *can*, etc. as verbs in the old fashion (10), and the fact that he used ALL the relevant forms and his heirs none suggests that his grammar differed from theirs in one way and not that the new grammars accumulated unrelated features. Similarly for other writers: either they used all the forms of (2–6a) or none.[3] The uniformity of the change suggests uniformity in the analysis. There was a single change, a change in category membership: *can*, formerly a verb that moved to I in the course of a derivation, came to be analyzed as an I element (11). The fact that there was a single change in grammars accounts for the bumpiness: already we see the advantages of thinking in terms of an abstract system, a grammar. Different verbs may have undergone the shift at different times and different people had the new properties at different times, but several phenomena clustered.

There are two reasons to think of this abstractly, as change in I-languages. First, the key phenomena are the LOSS of forms. Second, the change involves several different phenomena changing simultaneously.

The change in category membership of the English modals explains the catastrophic nature of the change, not in the sense that the change spread through the population rapidly (it did; we will come to that later), but that phenomena changed together. Change in grammars is a way of unifying disparate phenomena, taking them to be various surface manifestations of a single change at the abstract level. Therefore, the theory of categories is part of the explanation of the change: UG provides an inventory of categories, noun, verb, preposition, inflection, determiner, etc., each with a formal definition, and children assign words to these categories as part of the acquisition process.[4] Words are assigned to particular categories on the basis of their morphological properties and their distribution; if they have the same kinds of endings and the same distribution, then they are members of the same category. In addition, Tony Kroch and his associates (see Kroch 1989, for example) have done interesting statistical work on the spread of such changes through populations of speakers, showing that it is grammars that spread. They have shown that the variation observed represents oscillation between two fixed points, two grammars, and not oscillation in which the PHENOMENA vary independently of each other. Also, competing grammars may coexist in individual speakers for periods of time.

We do not appeal to historical forces as explanations under the cognitive view of grammars. If the change in grammars is as I have indicated, then the cause

---

[3] Given the fragmentary nature of historical records, this cannot mean that we have direct evidence for all the forms in all attested authors. For some people, we have only very partial records. Where we have extensive records, we find authors using all the predicted forms, as with Sir Thomas More.

[4] The definitions are formal and not notional. A noun is not the name of a person, place, or thing, as they taught us in school. Rather, a noun co-occurs with a determiner, and a determiner phrase (DP) may act as the subject of a verb phrase or as the complement of a verb or a preposition.

of the grammatical change can only be earlier changes in PLD. So let us ask now W H Y grammars changed in this way. The relevant change in PLD was the dramatic simplification in inflectional morphology. A quick look at a standard grammar of Old English (e.g. Campbell 1959, Quirk & Wrenn 1955) shows nouns and verbs varying in form depending on their function in a sentence. Verbs have different forms depending on their tense, person, and mood, while nouns differ as a function of their case usage, whether they are nominative, accusative, genitive or dative. However, most of these morphological properties were lost over the course of Middle English (eleventh to fifteenth centuries).[5] This had two consequences for the "premodals," the verbs that were to become modal auxiliaries.

First, the modal auxiliaries became distinct morphologically, the sole surviving members of the preterite-present class of verbs. There were many verb classes in early English and the antecedents of the modern modals belonged to the preterite-present class. The preterite-presents (so-called because their present-tense forms had past-tense or "preterite" morphology) were distinct in that they never had any inflection for the third person singular, although they were inflected elsewhere: *þu cannst, we cunnan, we cuðon*. Nonetheless, they were just another class of verbs, one of many, and the forms that were to become modal auxiliaries, the premodals, belonged to this class, along with a number of other verbs that either dropped out of the language altogether or were assimilated to another more regular class of verbs. For example, *unnan* 'grant' was lost from the language and *witan* 'know' simply dropped out of the preterite-present class, coming to be treated like non-preterite-presents. They were not entirely normal verbs and there is evidence that the future modal auxiliaries were already developing some distinct properties in late Old English. Warner (1993) shows that some of these items were not attested with non-finite forms in Old English texts, and Getty (2002) uses metrical evidence from *Beowulf* to argue that the future auxiliaries appear more frequently in weak metrical positions, which sets them off from other, lexical verbs that do not appear there.

After the simplification of verb morphology over the course of Middle English, verb classes collapsed and the O N L Y inflectional property of present-tense verbs to survive was the *-s* ending for the third person singular, a property which the preterite-present verbs had always lacked. The preterite-presents did not change in this regard, but a great mass of inflectional distinctions had disappeared and now the preterite-presents were isolated; they looked different from

---

[5] If one asks why the morphology was simplified, I believe that the reason is to be found in the influence of Scandinavian and the fact that northeast England during the Danelaw had many bilingual, English and Scandinavian, households. For discussion, see Lightfoot (1999: sects. 1.2, 4.5). Old English and Scandinavian were both richly inflected but the inflections differed to a significant degree and the combination did not constitute a single learnable system.

all other verbs in lacking their one morphological feature, that -*s* ending. The surviving preterite-presents were the elements that would be recategorized as Inflectional items.

Second, the morphological distinctiveness of the surviving preterite-presents, the new modals, was complemented by a new opacity in their past-tense forms. The past-tense forms of the preterite-present verbs were phonetically identical in many instances to the subjunctive forms and, when the subjunctive forms were lost, past-tense forms survived with subjunctive meanings rather than indicating past-time reference. While *loved* is related to *love* pretty much exclusively in terms of time reference in present-day English, the relationship between *can* and *could* is sometimes one of time (13a) and sometimes has nothing to do with time (13b). And *might* is never related to *may* in terms of time in present-day English (14a,b); in earlier times, *might* did indicate past time (14c) – but the thought of (14c) would need to be expressed as *might not have intended* in present-day English. So *might, could, should*, etc. came to take on new meanings that had nothing to do with past time, residues of the old subjunctive uses; the past-tense forms became semantically opaque.

(13)   a. Kim could understand the book, until she reached page 56.
        b. Kim could be here tomorrow.
(14)   a. *Kim might read the book yesterday.
        b. Kim may/might read the book tomorrow.
        c. These two respectable writers might not intend the mischief they
           were doing. (1762 Bp Richard Hurd, *Letters on Chivalry and
           Romance* 85)

As a result of these changes, the preterite-present verbs came to look different from all other verbs in the language: they were morphologically distinct and their past-tense forms had become semantically opaque and did not systematically indicate past time. UG provides a small inventory of grammatical categories and elements are assigned to a category on the basis of their morphological and distributional properties. If forms look alike and have the same formal, morphological properties, they are usually assigned to the same category; in addition, if forms have the same distribution and occur in the same contexts, they are assigned to the same category. So, in general, forms may belong to the same category because they look alike or because they behave alike.

Consequently, the morphological simplification entailed new primary linguistic data and they seem to have triggered new category distinctions. In this case, we know that, following the morphological changes, the surviving verbs of the preterite-present class were assigned to a new grammatical category, and that change was complete by the early sixteenth century. The evidence for the new category membership is the simultaneous loss for each verb of the phenomena we discussed in (2–6a).

We have identified a change in E-language, a general loss of morphology, and changes in I-languages in terms of the category membership of the modal auxiliaries, and we have linked the two types of change in such a way that we can understand how the new E-language led children to the new I-language. The E-language change is different from the I-language change but the two are related through the acquisition process. In particular, we have seen how new morphology may trigger a new syntax, a matter that we shall return to in the next section.

This was the first of three I-language changes affecting English verbs (Lightfoot 1999: ch. 6). It was a change in category membership, whereby *can*, etc. ceased to be treated as verbs and came to be taken as manifestations of the Inflection category; this change affected some verbs before others, but it was complete by the sixteenth century. For a sentence like *Kim can sing*, early grammars had structures like (10), where *can* is an ordinary verb that sometimes moves to I, but later grammars had structures like (11), where *can* is a modal, drawn from the lexicon and merged into a structure as an instance of I. As a result, sentences like (2–6a) dropped out of the language and no longer occurred in texts.

Once one child had the new grammar, that would change the ambient E-language for people in that speech community. That child would not produce sentences like (2–6a), which would therefore reduce in frequency, increasing the chances that other children in this community would converge on the new grammar. The new I-language changes the ambient E-language, and hence the spread of the new system. We see new E-language entailing a new I-language, yielding new E-language.

Second, English lost the operation copying verbs into a higher Inflection position (e.g. in (10) and (12)). This change was completed only in the eighteenth century, later than is generally supposed (Warner 1997). At this point, sentences with a finite verb copied to some initial position (15a), or to the left of a negative (15b), or to the left of a VP adverb (15c) became obsolete and were replaced by equivalent forms with the periphrastic *do: Does Kim understand this chapter? Kim does not understand this chapter.* The simultaneous obsolescence of these three constructions is the evidence for the loss of the V-to-I operation. Again, obsolescence suggests a grammatical change and the singularity of the change points to singularity at the level of abstract system, I-language.[6]

(15)   a. *Understands Kim chapter 4?
        b. *Kim understands not chapter 4.
        c. *Kim reads always the newspapers.

---

[6] Corresponding sentences with a modal auxiliary are well-formed, as we would expect if *can* is an Inflectional element and not a verb within a VP: *Can Kim understand chapter 4?*, *Kim cannot understand chapter 4*, and *Kim can always read the newspapers*.

Again French differs: finite forms of both *pouvoir* and *comprendre* occur sentence-initially (16), to the left of a negative (17), and to the left of an adverb (18).

(16)   a. Peut-il $_{VP}$[~~peut~~ comprendre le chapitre]?
            'Can he understand the chapter?'
        b. Comprend-il $_{VP}$[~~comprend~~ le chapitre]?
            'Does he understand the chapter?'
(17)   a. Il ne peut pas $_{VP}$[~~peut~~ comprendre le chapitre].
            'He cannot understand the chapter.'
        b. Il ne comprend pas $_{VP}$[~~comprend~~ le chapitre].
            'He doesn't understand the chapter.'
(18)   a. Il peut souvent $_{VP}$[~~peut~~ boire du vin].
            'He can often drink wine.'
        b. Il boit $_{VP}$[souvent ~~boit~~ du vin].
            'He often drinks wine.'

If verbs do not raise to a higher I position, then they cannot move on to a clause-initial position (15a), they do not occur to the left of a negative (15b), nor to the left of a VP adverb (15c); in French, on the other hand, finite verbs may move out of their VP, as (16b, 17b, 18b) indicate. This change has been discussed extensively and Lightfoot (1999: sect. 6.3) argued that it was caused by prior changes in PLD, most notably the recategorization of the modal verbs just discussed and the rise of periphrastic *do* forms. These two changes had the effect of greatly reducing the availability of the relevant cue, $_I$V, an inflected verb occurring in an Inflection position.

The idea here is the one developed in the last chapter, that children scan their linguistic environment for structural cues, such as $_I$V or $_{VP}$[V DP] (verb–object order), etc. Cues may be E X P R E S S E D in the utterances they hear. An utterance expresses a cue if, given everything that the child knows so far, it can only be analyzed with that cue present. So if a finite verb is separated from its DP direct object (by a negative particle, adverb, or other material), then it must have been copied out of its VP and the only position that a finite verb may move to is the next highest head, necessarily a functional head like I under current assumptions. So (16b) can only be analyzed with the finite verb *comprend* moved to some higher functional position. It therefore expresses the $_I$V cue for a child in a French-speaking milieu. Cues are elements of structure derived from what children hear. They are found in the mental representations that result from hearing, understanding, and "parsing" utterances. As a child understands an utterance, even partially, he/she has some kind of mental representation of the utterance. These are partial parses, which may differ from the full parses that an adult has. That access to partial parses is a key aspect of the cue-based approach, distinguishing it from the approaches that evaluate only complete grammars. The learner scans those representations, derived from the input, and finds certain cues, elements of grammars, I-language.

The two grammatical changes discussed are related in ways that we now understand: first, the Inflection position was appropriated by a subclass of verbs, by the modal auxiliaries, and by *do* (in sentences like *Kim does (not) understand the chapter*, *does* occurs in the same position as *can* in (11)) and the V-to-I operation (10) no longer applied generally to all tensed clauses. It no longer applied to clauses containing a modal auxiliary, because they came to originate in the I position. Somewhat later, the V-to-I movement operation was lost for all other verbs (other than the exceptional *be* and *have*[7]) and I was no longer a position to which verbs might move. The relationship is that the first change dramatically altered the expression of the $_IV$ cue, leading to the loss of that structure.

A cue is expressed robustly if there are many simple utterances that can be analyzed only with the cue present. So, for example, the sentences corresponding to (16b) and (17b) can only be analyzed by the French child (given what he/she has already established in his/her emerging grammar) if the finite verb raises to I, and therefore they express the $_IV$ cue. A simple sentence like *Jeanne lit les journaux*, 'Jeanne reads the newspapers,' on the other hand, is structurally ambiguous and could be analyzed with *lit* raised to I or with the I lowered into the VP in the English style (12); therefore it does not express the $_IV$ cue.

Early English grammars raised verbs to I, as in the grammars of Modern French speakers, but later grammars did not; the operation was lost at some point. Indeed, for a significant period speakers used a V-to-I system that also incorporated periphrastic *do* as an Inflectional item. Here are some examples from Shakespeare's *Othello*, where he alternates freely within the same utterance (19). In (19a) the first verb has periphrastic *do* in the I position and the second verb undergoes V-to-I movement.

(19)   a. Where didst thou see her? – O unhappy girl! – With the Moor, say'st thou? (*Othello* I, i)
         b. I like not that. // What dost thou say? (*Othello* III, iii)
         c. Alas, what does this gentleman conceive? – How do you, madam? (*Othello* IV, ii)

From our perspective, the V-to-I operation eventually ceased to be cued. The $_IV$ cue came to be expressed less in the PLD in the light of at least two developments in early Modern English.

---

[7] Finite forms of *be* and *have* occur in clause-initial position, to the left of a negative, and to the left of a VP adverb and therefore move to I: *Is she happy?*, *She is not happy*, and *She is always happy*.

We have seen that modal auxiliaries, while once instances of verbs that raised to I (10), were recategorized such that they came to be merged into structures as I elements (11); they were no longer verbs, so sentences with a modal auxiliary ceased to include ₁V and ceased to express the cue. Sentences with a modal auxiliary, *Kim could not leave*, are very common in ordinary speech addressed to young children – estimates are typically within the 50 percent range (e.g. Klein 1974) – and the recategorization meant that they no longer expressed the ₁V cue. Sentences of this type existed at all stages of English but they came to be analyzed differently after the change in category membership, first with *could* raising out of the VP, across *not*, to the I position, and later with no movement, as (10, 11) indicate.

Second, as periphrastic *do* came to be used in interrogatives like *Does he understand chapter 4?* (cf. 15a) and negatives like *He does not understand chapter 4* (cf. 15b), so there were still fewer instances of ₁V. Before periphrastic *do* became available, sentences like (15a,b,c) expressed the ₁V cue. Periphrastic *do* began to occur with significant frequency at the beginning of the fifteenth century and steadily increased in frequency until it stabilized into its modern usage by the mid-seventeenth century. For every instance of *do*, there is no verb in I; *Kim does not understand the chapter* is analyzed as (20).

(20)

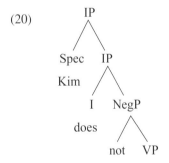

understand the chapter

By quantifying the degree to which a cue is expressed, we can understand why English grammars lost the V-to-I operation, and why they lost it after the modal auxiliaries were analyzed as non-verbs and as the periphrastic *do* became increasingly common. Grammars changed as the available triggering experiences, specifically those expressing the cue, shifted in critical ways. With the reanalysis of the modal auxiliaries and the increasing frequency of the periphrastic *do*, the expression of the ₁V cue in English became less and less robust in the PLD. There was no longer much in children's experience that had to be analyzed as ₁V, i.e. which REQUIRED V-to-I movement, given that the morphological I-lowering operation was always available as a default. In particular, common, simple sentences like *Jill left* could be analyzed with

I-lowering as in Modern English; sentences with modal auxiliaries or periphrastic *do* did not require the $_I$V cue. Meanwhile sentences like *Kim reads always the newspapers* with postverbal adverbs and quantifiers had to be analyzed with a verb in I, but these instances of the cue were not robust enough to trigger the relevant grammatical property, and they disappeared quickly, a by-product of the loss of the V-to-I operation, a domino effect. Sentences like *Understands Kim the chapter?* and *Kim understands not the chapter* also required the $_I$V cue, but they became less and less common as *Does Kim understand the chapter?* and *Kim does not understand the chapter* became more frequent.

So the expression of the cue dropped below its threshold, leading to the elimination of V-to-I movement. The expression of the $_I$V cue reduced because of the changes I have indicated, one a prior change in I-languages (the recategorization of the premodals) and one a result of changes in the use of grammars (the increasing frequency of periphrastic *do*). What is crucial is the point at which the phase transition took place, when the last straw was piled on to the camel's back. Children scan the environment for instances of $_I$V. This presupposes prior analysis, of course. Children may scan for this cue only after they have identified a class of verbs and when their grammars have a distinct Inflection position, I.

This grammatical approach to diachrony explains changes at two levels. First, the cues postulated as part of UG explain the unity of the changes, why superficially unrelated properties cluster in the way they do. Second, the cues permit an appropriately contingent account of why the change took place, why children at a certain point converged on a different grammar: the expression of the cues changed in such a way that a threshold was crossed and cues were identified differently. This relates new E-language to new I-languages and we see how changes in E-language may cue new I-languages and then how new I-languages yield new E-language.

An intriguing paper by Anthony Warner (1995) shows that there is a third stage to the history of English verbs, involving changes taking place quite recently affecting the copula *be*; this turns out to be of current theoretical interest, and is discussed in Lightfoot (1999: ch. 7). The changes only involve the verb *be* but they have the hallmarks of grammatical change, change in I-languages. There are several surface changes, all involving *be*, which can be attributed to one analytical notion concerning the way that elements are stored in the lexicon: forms like *was*, *been*, *being*, etc., once construed as *be*+past, *be*+*en*, etc., came to be stored atomically in the lexicon. The changes reflect quite general properties of the grammar. The structural property that is relevant can be identified and we can tell a plausible and rather elegant story about why and how the grammatical change might have come about.

In brief, the changes have to do with the obsolescence in the nineteenth century of forms like (21). These forms are from Jane Austen's novels and do not occur in present-day English.

(21)   a. I wish our opinions were the same, But in time they will.
        b. You will be to visit me in prison with a basket of provisions.
        c. Two large wax candles were also set on another table, the ladies being going to cards.
        d. I was this morning to buy silk.

That change, which I will not discuss here, is another illustration of the fact that morphology has syntactic effects. The change in the analysis of *be* forms stems from the loss of V-to-I raising and loss of the second singular (familiar) -*st* forms. The loss of V-to-I raising represented new I-languages, as we discussed, but the loss of the familiar usage of the second singulars began as a change in the use of grammars.

The use of those familiar second singular forms was always subtle. They were used for social inferiors, children, animals, and the like, but they also revealed attitudes (Crystal 2004). In the disastrous first scene of *King Lear*, the King uses *thee* and *thine* for his daughters Goneril and Regan but elevates his favorite Cordelia with the plural form: *What can you say to draw / A third more opulent than your sisters?* And then *Mend your speech a little / Lest it may mar your fortunes.* However, when Cordelia continues to resist and he becomes angry, he switches to the condescending second singular: *Let it be so; thy truth then be thy dower!* English democratizing forces eliminated the use of these forms, although they persisted into modern times in the north of England.

In any case, this change is another illustration of the importance of morphology in defining category membership; children assign items to categories on the basis of their morphology.

While morphology clearly influences category membership, one finds a stronger claim in the literature. It is sometimes argued that richly inflected languages differ in a fundamental, global way from poorly inflected languages like English, Swedish, and Chinese. Not many of the world's languages have a richly recorded history, but many that do have undergone morphological simplification, sometimes with category changes. If our historical records included languages with INCREASING morphological complexity, we would be in a stronger position to relate morphological and categorial changes.

In this section I have tracked some changes affecting the English modal auxiliaries, changes that might be labeled "grammaticalization" (see chapter 2). We have shown local causes for each of the two changes in grammars (the new category membership of the modal auxiliaries and the loss of V-to-I movement), taking grammars to be individual, internal systems existing in individual brains.

There was nothing inevitable about these changes: the equivalent words in French and Swedish did not undergo parallel changes, because there were no parallel local causes.

These syntactic changes result to some degree from prior changes in morphology. Let us now consider the relationship between morphology and syntax more generally.

5.3   Syntactic effects of morphological change

The three changes in the syntax of English verbs are each linked to prior morphological change and they suggest that changes in morphology can have syntactic consequences. We have seen that there were structural shifts in grammars after morphological properties were simplified significantly during the course of Middle English. This comports with an intuition shared by many linguists, going back at least to Humboldt (1836/1971), that languages with rich inflectional systems have a different kind of syntax. A language like Chinese, with very few inflectional properties, would be expected to have quite different syntactic properties from a richly inflected language like Latin, Sanskrit, Finnish, or Georgian. If morphological properties determine aspects of a language's syntax, then we have an example of the kind of thing Tinbergen pointed to, mentioned in chapter 1: behavior may be due to properties that appear to be unrelated. His example was of young herring gulls opening their mouths to their mother in response to the red spot under her beak, not because they wanted the food she was carrying. So grammars may have specific syntactic properties as a result of certain morphological properties.

What of this intuition? Can it be made precise? Can we understand which morphological properties might trigger which syntactic properties? One of the premier examples of grammatical parameters is the null subject option, whereby one can say 'rains on Tuesdays' or 'goes to soccer games' for English *It rains on Tuesdays* or *He goes to soccer games*. This option is often supposed to be available to languages with rich inflection like Italian, Spanish, and European Portuguese, but not in less richly inflected languages like French and Modern Brazilian Portuguese. Indeed, Brazilian Portuguese seems to have lost the null subject option as its verb morphology was reduced (Kato & Negrão 2000, Pires 2002, Rodrigues 2002).

Another much-discussed example bears on one of the changes discussed in the last section: it is said that languages with rich verb morphology allow verbs to raise to a higher Inflection position, but languages with poor morphology do not (what Bobaljik 2001 calls the Rich Agreement Hypothesis). Correspondingly, if a language loses many of its verb inflections, it loses the V-to-I movement operation. So English lost its rich verb morphology and then the V-to-I operation, as we just saw. Let us examine this case more carefully.

It is hard to quantify "rich inflection," since verbs may have different numbers of distinctions in different tenses, and somewhat legalistic definitions of rich morphology have been given. For example, Rohrbacher (1999: 116) says that "a language has V-to-I raising if and only if in at least one number of one tense of the regular verb paradigm(s), the person features [1st] and [2nd] are both distinctively marked." Vikner (1997: 207) says that "an SVO-language has V-to-I movement if and only if person morphology is found in all tenses." Koeneman (2000: 72) claims that "the affixes in a paradigm are lexically listed (and hence force V-to-I movement) if the features [1st] and [2nd] and [singular] are each contrasted somewhere in that paradigm."

One troublesome aspect of these definitions is that they are stated in terms of paradigms, not of the morphology of individual verbs. It is not clear how paradigms, organized classes of endings familiar from grammar books (like present tense of a-class verbs or "third declensions"), could function in the kinds of I-languages that generative grammarians work with.

The Scandinavian languages provide an interesting laboratory, because they vary in richness of inflection and in whether they have verb movement. Icelandic (21a,b) and the Swedish dialect of Älvdalsmålet, spoken in Dalecarlia in eastern, central Sweden, (21c) are richly inflected by Rohrbacher, Vikner, and Koeneman's standards, because they distinguish both number and person, and have V-to-I raising: finite verbs in embedded clauses (but not non-finite verbs) occur only to the left of negative particles, having moved over them, now separated from their complement direct object.[8] On the other hand, the Norwegian dialect of Hallingdalen, spoken in central, southern Norway, distinguishes singular and plural forms of the present-tense verb but not person, and does not have V-to-I raising (21d). In Hallingdalen the verb 'throw' is *kasta* in all forms of the singular and *kastæ* in all forms of the plural in the present tense and there is only one past-tense form. In Älvdalsmålet, on the other hand, the plural is *kastum* in the first person, *kaster* in the second person and *kasta* in the third person, varying not only for tense but also for person.

(21)   a.   . . . að   hann keypti ekki bókina.
               . . . that he   bought not the-book
         a'. . . . að hann ₁keyptiᵢ ekki ᵥₚ[keyptiᵢ bókina]
         b.   . . . að   Jón hafa   ekki komið.
               . . . that John has   not come
         c.   . . . ba fo dye   at   uir uildum int fy   om.
               . . . just because that we would not follow him

d. . . . at me ikkje kjøpæ bokje.
* . . . at   me kjøpæ ikkje bokje
. . . that we buy   not   the-book

In addition, finite verbs in Danish (22a,b) and Swedish (22c,d), both poorly inflected, only occur to the right of negative markers in embedded clauses, suggesting that the verbs have not moved and that their grammars lack the V-to-I operation.

(22)   a. . . . at   hen   ikke   købte bogen.
        . . . that he   not   bought the-book
    a'. . . . at hen $_I$[] ikke $_{VP}$[købte bogen]
    b. *. . . at hen købte ikke bogen.
    c. . . . om Johan inte   köpte boken.
        . . . if   John   not   bought the-book
    d. *. . . om Johan köpte inte   boken.
        . . . if   John bought not   the-book

One should bear in mind that the position of the negative is not definitive evidence for lack of movement to I, since the negative element may occur to the left of IP as in Italian.[9] Indeed, there is some evidence that the negative in Swedish occurs to the left of IP. In (20) the VP has been fronted and there is a dummy finite verb, *gör*, more or less equivalent to the periphrastic *do* of English. If *gör* is in the I position, then (23) indicates that the Swedish negative occurs to the left of I, just as Italian *non* is to the left of I in a sentence like *Non lo prendo* 'I am not taking it' (Lightfoot 1991).

(23)   [läser boken]   kanske Allan inte gör
        reads the book maybe Allan not does
        'Read the book maybe Allan doesn't.'

However, the position of the finite verb with respect to VP adverbs gives a clearer indication that finite verbs do not move but remain adjacent to their complement direct objects, as in English: *Mary smokes often cigars.* (24a,b) shows the verb staying to the right of the adverb 'often' in a Danish complement clause, and (24c,d) in a relative clause. See Vikner (1994) for discussion. Swedish and Norwegian work similarly.

(24)   a. Peter tvivler på at Maria ofte køber islandske aviser.
        b. *Peter tvivler på at Maria køber ofte islandske aviser.
        'Peter doubts that Maria {often buys/buys often} Icelandic newspapers.'
        c. Den kiosk hvor Maria ofte køber islandske aviser ligger på gågaden.

---

[9] Belletti (1994) analyzes Italian Negative Phrases as occurring higher than IP, yielding the order *Non prendo il libro* 'I am not taking the book.'

     d. *Den kiosk hvor Maria køber ofte islandske aviser ligger på
        gågaden.
        'The kiosk where Maria {often buys/buys often} Icelandic
        newspapers lies in the pedestrian street.'

English also reveals a significant correlation between syntax and morphology. One of the few verbs with rich morphology in standard dialects is *be*, which varies between *am*, *are*, and *is* in its present tense. And it moves to a higher position, to the left of the negative and to a clause-initial position in interrogatives (25).

(25)   a. Kim is not happy.
       b. Is Kim happy?
       c. What is Kim?

Furthermore, certain forms of English show uninflected forms of *be* (26a). Black English Vernacular shows (26b) and some forms of child English show (26c). Strikingly, the syntax does not yield (26d), which is what one would expect if the uninflected *be* behaved like its inflected counterpart (25). Rather we find the forms of (26b,c), which do not manifest movement to a higher position.

(26)   a. Bill be angry.
       b. Bill don't be angry.
          Do Bill be angry?
          What do Bill be?
       c. I don't be angry?
          Do clowns be boys or girls?
          Did it be funny?
       d. *Bill ben't angry.
          *Be Bill angry?
          *What be Bill?

All of this strongly suggests a one-way implication: rich morphology entails V-to-I movement. If a language does not have rich inflection, its verbs may or may not move to higher positions. They do not move in English and the standard dialects of Danish, Norwegian, and, according to most analyses, Swedish. But they do move in Japanese, Chinese, and Korean (Otani & Whitman 1991), and Swedish verbs might move, depending on how sentences like (23) are analyzed. Also the Kronoby dialect of Finland Swedish (27a) and the Tromsø dialect of Norwegian (27b) have poor morphology but do nonetheless have V-to-I movement, with embedded finite verbs occurring to the left of negative markers.

(27)   a. He va   bra   et   an tsöfft   int bootsen.
          it was good that he bought not the-book
          'It was good that he didn't buy the book.'

b. Han kom så seint at   dørvakta vilde ikkje slæppe han inn.
   he came so late that the-guard would not   let   him in
   'He came so late that the guard wouldn't let him in.'

So there is a one-way implication: richly inflected verbs raise to a higher functional position, while uninflected verbs may or may not raise (Lightfoot 1993: 207–208, Thráinsson 2003). This follows from what is known as "checking theory": inflectional features are located in functional categories and verbs must raise to "check" those features and we need no notion of paradigms. If there are no inflectional features, the morphology gives no reason for verbs to raise. This means that the cue $_1$V is EXPRESSED both by inflected verbs and by uninflected verbs that are displaced. That is, an inflected verb and a manifestly displaced verb must be analyzed in the Inflection position. An inflected verb must (by checking theory) be analyzed as occupying a higher functional position; an uninflected verb may be analyzed there or in its base-generated position within the VP. It will be analyzed in a higher functional position if and only if there is syntactic, distributional evidence for that position. There will be syntactic evidence if the verb occurs to the left of a negative marker or to the left of a VP adverb or is copied to the front of a clause.

We can now understand why loss of V-to-I lags behind the loss of morphology. English verb morphology was simplified during the Middle English period (1066 to 1500) but verbs continued to occur to the left of negative markers and adverbs and in clause-initial position through the seventeenth century. Similarly for Scandinavian: Platzack (1988) and Thráinsson (2003) claim that person markers on verbs were lost by the beginning of the sixteenth century but verb raising in embedded clauses continued to be found through the second half of the seventeenth century. Platzack (1988) counts verbs occurring to the left of VP adverbs: 80% in authors born 1480–1530, 36% in authors born 1570–1600, and 24% in authors born 1620–1665. So verb-raising order continued to be used in embedded clauses in written Swedish for some 200 years after the loss of rich verbal morphology, but diminishingly so.

All of this indicates that rich verb morphology means that finite verbs must be analyzed in a higher functional position, raised out of the VP. If a grammar lacks rich morphology, then verbs may be analyzed in such a position if only syntactic evidence demands it. It is striking, however, that both English and Scandinavian lost V-to-I raising a few hundred years after losing the morphology. That suggests that morphological markers demand V-to-I movement, whereas mere distributional factors are a more fragile trigger for the operation.

We see a connection now between verbal morphology and syntax: richly inflected verbs occur in Inflection positions. What about nouns inflected for case? Some languages show distinct forms for nouns occurring in different cases. For example, Old English showed the case distinctions of table 5.1. These endings were lost over the course of Middle English. The inherent cases

Table 5.1 *Old English case distinctions*

	'that	stone'	'that	ship'	'that	tale'	'that	name'
singular								
nom.	sē	stān	þæt	scip	sēo	talu	sē	nama
acc.	þone	stān	þæt	scip	þā	tale	þone	naman
gen.	þæs	stānes	þæs	scipes	þǣre	tale	þæs	naman
dat.	þǣm	stāne	þǣm	scipe	þǣre	tale	þǣm	naman
plural								
nom.	þā	stānas	þā	scipu	þā	tala	þā	naman
acc.	þā	stānas	þā	scipu	þā	tala	þā	naman
gen.	þāra	stāna	þāra	scipa	þāra	tala	þāra	namena
dat.	þǣm	stānum	þǣm	scipum	þǣm	talum	þǣm	namum

were lost early; by 1200 nouns were no longer marked for case and dative merged with accusative. Noun phrases continued to be marked for accusative case on the definite article into the thirteenth century. The change spread from north to south, with the conservative southern dialects preserving case through the fourteenth century.

Roberts (1997) analyzed inflected nouns in a similar fashion to the way we have treated inflected verbs. He argued that in a sentence like (28), the inflected noun phrase has been copied to a higher position (Specifier of AgrO[10]), yielding object–verb order. If the case marker is in the Spec of AgrO position, then the inflected DP must move there to check the inflection. With the loss of case marking, noun phrases do not move to Spec of AgrO to check the ending, hence no more object–verb word order and English changes to verb–object. In this way Roberts links the change in word order, from object–verb to verb–object, to change in nominal morphology.

(28)   Þæt   hi   mihton $_{\text{AgrOP}}$[$_{\text{DP}}$heora fynd$_i$]
        So-that they might   their foes
        AgrO $_{\text{VP}}$[oferwinnan ~~heora fyndi~~]]
                     overcome
        'So that they could overcome their foes.' (Bede 44.14)

Pintzuk (2002) argues against this analysis by showing that distinctions in case marking have no effect on position. The frequency of postverbal DPs does not vary if the case-marked DP is ambiguous or not, nor if an unambiguously marked DP shows structural (accusative) case or inherent (genitive, dative) (table 5.2). Furthermore, there is a steady loss of object–verb order in Old

---

[10] The assumption here is that there are many functional projections above VP, including distinct positions for subject agreement (AgrS) and object agreement (AgrO). Each of these heads projects to a phrasal category, giving AgrS phrases and AgrO phrases. See Haegeman (1994: ch. 11) for introductory discussion and Cinque (1999) for the most elaborated structures.

Table 5.2 *Case marking and word order in Old English*
(Pintzuk 2002)

Case marking	Preverbal	Postverbal	Total	%postverbal
Unambiguous				
accusative	113	57	170	33.5%
genitive	35	21	56	37.5%
dative	76	47	123	38.2%
Total unambiguous	224	125	349	35.8%
Ambiguous	336	216	582	37.1%
Total	590	341	931	36.6%

Table 5.3 *Word order before and after 950*
(Pintzuk 2002)

Date	Preverbal	Postverbal	Total	%postverbal
before 950	380	144	524	27.5%
after 950	210	197	407	48.4%
Total	590	341	931	36.6%

English and the change is well under way by 950, even though the case system is intact until Middle English. If Roberts' correlation were right, one would expect word order to shift dramatically in early Middle English when the morphology changes, but that is not the case (table 5.3).

There is also comparative evidence against Roberts' analysis. Icelandic has richer case morphology than German and much richer than Dutch, but has verb–object order, while German and Dutch are object–verb, suggesting that object–verb order cannot be a simple function of rich case morphology.

So noun morphology does not seem to express the syntactic position of the noun analogously to verb morphology and inflected DPs do not move to positions in order to check their inflections. Bejar (2002) argues correspondingly that the movement of DPs to other DP positions ("A-movement") in English is triggered not by morphological properties but by distributional, syntactic cues. She examined the loss of dative experiencers in the history of English, sentences like *I gave the book John*, where *John* had dative case, and argues that the LOSS of morphology correlates with the EMERGENCE of movement in such instances (yielding *I gave John the book*). In that event, movement clearly is not induced by inflectional properties. In fact, she argues that the relation between overt morphology and movement in such constructions is closer to being disjunctive than conjunctive: as morphology was lost, so movement became necessary and forms like *I gave the book John* were lost.

Similarly, Sundquist (2002) shows that Danish, Norwegian, and Swedish have undergone significant simplification in nominal and verbal inflection, but at different rates, quite different from the far more conservative Icelandic. He finds no relevant syntactic changes in the distribution of DPs from Middle Norwegian onwards despite the loss of case endings on nouns, which he tracked in a large corpus of diplomatic letters.

So the movement of DPs is not triggered by morphological properties in the way that inflected verbs are always copied to a higher functional position. However, there may be larger effects and it may be that languages fall into two basic classes. DPs are associated with particular thematic roles, being agent, recipient, patient, etc. – this is an essential part of the interpretation or meaning of sentences – and certain grammars may link DPs with their thematic role by virtue of their inherent case properties. In such grammars a verb like 'give' or 'tell' might be listed in the mental lexicon along the lines of (29), whereby it is specified that a verb meaning 'give' occurs with three DPs with the inherent cases and corresponding thematic roles indicated (structural cases are not linked with particular thematic roles).

(29)   DP with a particular case has a particular thematic role
         {V DP   DP   DP}
            nom   dat   acc
            agent recip patient

Alternatively another kind of grammar might have the verb listed as in (30), linking thematic roles to position and not to inherent case properties. The subject DP preceding the verb is the agent, the complement DP following the verb is the recipient, and the third DP is the patient, as in *I gave John the book.*

(30)   Positional syntax *give, tell,* etc.
         DP ____ DP   DP
         agent   recip patient

Such grammars with a positional syntax would be subject to the kind of principle that we examined in chapter 3. In these grammars DPs can be copied only from certain positions, perhaps motivated by the parsing considerations mentioned there: listeners need to assign copied DPs to the position in which they are understood in order to establish their thematic role. In grammars with rich case marking, on the other hand, thematic roles might be established as a function of the inherent case marking, as in (29). So in languages like Latin and Sanskrit and others with rich case morphology, word order is much less restricted than in grammars with positional syntax and one does not find the kinds of distinctions noted in chapter 3. That would give us a way of understanding why languages with rich case morphology tend to have freer word order than languages without rich morphology and are immune to the effects discussed in section 3.3.

Under this view, one child might grow a grammar with lexical entries like those of (30) and have a positional syntax, subject to principles like that of chapter 3, and with comparatively restricted word order. Another child in a different speech community and hearing different E-language, might grow a grammar with lexical entries like that of (29), identifying thematic roles through inherent case markings. The difference lies in the richness of case morphology: positional syntax if little case morphology and non-positional syntax if rich case morphology. If movement of DPs is construed as copying and deletion (chapter 3), then one way of thinking of this is that copied DPs may be deleted if they are (in) the complement of an adjacent, overt head (condition 10 of chapter 3) or if they are inherently case-marked. There are some indications that something like this might be plausible, although still speculative. Again, the general idea is old: Humboldt (1836/1971) viewed word order and inflectional morphology as alternative means of realizing grammatical relations.

Kiparsky (1997) took up Humboldt's view and distinguished a class of positional languages, where particular principles of UG are activated. He was concerned with several changes that he depicted as emerging simultaneously in the late fourteenth century and linked them all, directly or indirectly, to the loss of case morphology on nouns. His analysis differed from the one given here but his concern was the same, to flesh out the old intuitions about the relationship between morphology and syntax in some principled way, and to characterize "inflectional morphology and positional constraints [as] functionally equivalent elements of grammatical structure" (Kiparsky 1997: 461).[11]

5.4   Results

The emergence of a grammar in a child is sensitive to the initial conditions of the primary linguistic data. Those data might shift a little, because people came to use their grammars differently in discourse, using certain constructions more frequently, or because the distribution of grammars had shifted within the speech community, or because there was a prior change in I-languages. In that case, there may be significant consequences for the abstract system. A new system may be triggered, which generates a very different set of sentences and structures. Contingent changes in the distribution of the data (more accurately,

---

[11] Kiparsky's analysis is, in a sense, the opposite of what I have argued, at least for inflected verbs. He posits a one-way implication that "lack of inflectional morphology implies fixed order of direct nominal arguments" (Kiparsky 1997: 461).

There are interesting analyses featuring correlations between morphological and syntactic properties. For example, Haeberli (2002) offers an intriguing analysis for the loss of verb-second effects in English. He distinguishes two positions for subjects, arguing that DPs may stay in the lower position (yielding certain verb-second effects), if there is an empty expletive in the higher position. The loss of verb-second in English results from the loss of empty expletives, which, in turn, results from the weakening of verbal morphology.

changes in the expression of the cues) may trigger a grammar that generates significantly different sentences and structures, and that may have some domino effects.

Changes often take place in clusters: apparently unrelated superficial changes occur simultaneously or in rapid sequence. Such clusters may manifest a single theoretical choice that has been taken differently. If so, the singularity of the change can be explained by the appropriately defined theoretical choice. So the principles of UG and the definition of the cues constitute the laws that guide change in grammars, defining the available terrain. Any change is explained if we show, first, that the linguistic environment has changed and, second, that the new phenomenon (*may, must,* etc. being categorized as I elements, for example) must be the way that it is because of some principle of the theory and the new PLD.

Sometimes we can explain domino effects. Loss of inflectional markings had consequences for category membership and changes in category membership had consequences for computational operations moving finite verbs to an I position. In that event, one establishes a link between a change in morphological patterns and changes in the positions of finite verbs.

Historical change is a kind of finite-state Markov process, where each state is influenced only by the immediately preceding state: new grammars have only local causes and, if there is no local cause, there is no new grammar, regardless of the state of the grammar or the language some time previously. In that way, the emergence of a grammar in an individual child is sensitive to the initial conditions, to the details of the child's experience. The historian's explanations are based on available acquisition theories, and in some cases our explanations are quite tight and satisfying. Structural changes are interesting precisely because they have local causes. Identifying structural changes and the conditions under which they took place informs us about the conditions of language acquisition; we have indeed learned things about properties of UG and about the nature of acquisition by the careful examination of diachronic changes. So it is if we focus on changes in grammars, viewed as biological entities, and we gain a very different approach to language change than the ones that focus exclusively on E-language phenomena, on the group products of cognitive systems rather than on the systems themselves.

Linking language change to the acquisition of grammars in this fashion has enabled us to understand certain grammars better and has refined UG definitions. It has also been the source of two fairly fundamental notions: the idea of coexisting grammars and internal diglossia, whereby apparent optionality can be viewed as the effects of speakers using more than one grammar (Kroch 1989); and the idea that the PLD consist of structures, indeed only simple structures, instead of sets of sentences (Lightfoot 1999).

6 The use and variation of grammars

6.1 The use of grammars

Children hear E-language, language out there, and E-language may change; it may change in such a way that it triggers new I-languages, as we saw in the last chapter. New E-language may result from prior changes in I-languages or because people come to use their grammars differently or because there are new social mixes of grammars. There is more to a person's speech than his/her I-language.

Grammars are used and some elements of their use result from general properties of the human cognitive system, others are more idiosyncratic, and that distinction is fundamental. In fact, we need two distinctions: grammars need to be distinguished from the way in which they are used (Newmeyer 2003), and general use functions need to be distinguished from specific, learned strategies. Let us consider some examples.

(1a) is ambiguous between a deontic and epistemic reading. It might mean that John is under an obligation to study or it must be the case that John is a student (for example, because he drinks cheap wine). (1b) is ambiguous in precisely the same way. That would lead us to expect that (1c) would be four-ways ambiguous: deontic–deontic, epistemic–epistemic, deontic–epistemic, or epistemic–deontic. This turns out to be false: (1c) is only two-ways ambiguous and each conjunct must have either the epistemic reading or the deontic, but no mixing is possible. Either it means that it must be the case that John is a student and Susan a teacher or it means that John and Susan are under obligations to be a student and a teacher respectively.

(1) a. John must be a student.
   b. Susan must be a teacher.
   c. John must be a student and Susan must be a teacher.

So much for the facts. There is good reason to believe that such facts should not be treated as part of a person's grammar. First, it is unclear how to state the facts in terms of grammatical structures and it would complicate the grammar enormously. Second, there is no reason to try to complicate the grammar because there is an alternative and preferable non-grammatical account possible. Third, one would be missing generalizations if one pursued a clumsy, grammatical analysis.

The alternative strategy is to invoke a general cognitive property that treats two adjacent ambiguous objects in parallel. One sees this property at work in vision. A Necker cube is ambiguous in terms of which side is closest to the observer. However, two juxtaposed cubes present two possible interpretations and not four: for each cube, the same side is closest to the observer (figure 6.1).

Figure 6.1

This is a general property of the visual system that can also account for the two-way ambiguity of our linguistic examples. This looks like a general property of cognition, not a property of people's grammars. The grammar can remain simple, overgenerating four interpretations for (1c), but only two interpretations can actually be perceived by humans under normal conditions because of the way that grammars are used, embedded alongside other cognitive properties. Furthermore, the phenomenon seems to be quite general in all languages and not a property of particular grammars.

Another example: English allows (2a,b), where the clause *that the moon is round* is the subject of *is obvious* (2a) or *bothers me* (2b). But not the more complex (2c), where the clause of (2a) is the subject of *bothers me*.

(2)   a. [That the moon is round] is obvious.
         b. [That the moon is round] bothers me.
         c. [That [that the moon is round] is obvious] bothers me.

Building into the grammar a statement that VPs may have sentential subjects (2a,b) but not if they are complex (2c) would be very difficult. There is another cognitive strategy that might account for this phenomenon, namely that human systems do not do well with multiple center-embedding, as discussed in Chomsky (1965) – the lowest clause is embedded in the middle of the higher clause. Grammars may generate (2c) but people do not use such structures.

These are examples of general use functions, plausibly common to the species. Distinguishing grammars from their use enables us to keep the grammars simple and we have a two-track approach to the language capacity, involving structural grammars and their use functions. In addition, there are use functions that are not common to the species and are learned in the course of a person's lifetime. People learn to use their grammars in particular ways and this has been the subject-matter of discourse analysts.

It has been argued that women use tag questions, *It is raining, isn't it?*, more frequently than men (Lakoff 1975). There is no reason to believe that the sexes have different grammars, because all English speakers have the capacity to use tag structures. Rather, some people use their grammars differently and employ such structures more frequently, for reasons that are learned. Such use functions may be very specific and we find different use functions associated with specific genres of speech, for example in sports commentaries, sermons, political speeches, jokes, and a host of other modes.

It is worth noting how central these considerations are to broader linguistic inquiries. Investigations of language change have appealed to properties of language acquisition by children. For such accounts to work, one needs to be able to assume that children have different linguistic experiences. That can happen if there is a population shift whereby people are exposed to new linguistic forms through invasions or other such political dramas or are exposed to different experiences because segments of the population have been using their grammars differently, using certain kinds of constructions more frequently, perhaps for social or even self-conscious reasons. Such varying use functions are the engines of linguistic change. If some people use their grammars differently, that sometimes has the effect that children have different experiences to some threshold level, where a new grammar is triggered, as happens when a language acquires new split genitive constructions, undergoes an object–verb to verb–object shift, or loss of verb-second properties.

Three such innovations are the subject-matter of this chapter and the study of the variable use of grammars is central to questions of language acquisition and change. First, we will continue to explore the ramifications of the loss of case endings in Middle English.

6.2   Split genitives and more syntactic effects of the loss of case

We will begin with a different angle on the relationship between inflectional morphology and syntax.[1] Nouns and determiner phrases (DPs) are pronounced only in certain positions in English: as the subject of a finite clause (*The students left*), as a Specifier of a larger DP (*The students' books*), or as a complement to a verb or a preposition (*Read the books*, *From the teacher*). These are positions

---

[1] The change in split genitives was discussed more fully in Lightfoot (1999: sect. 5.2) and an abbreviated version also appeared as section 8.4 of Anderson & Lightfoot (2002). Here I offer a different analysis.

that typically receive nominative, genitive, and accusative cases in languages with morphological case and English pronouns show the various case forms: *They left*, *Their books*, *Read them*, *From them*. In fact, one approach to this is to specify that DPs must have some sort of case, even if it is not overt, a kind of abstract case, and these are the positions to which abstract case is assigned.

If a DP is merged first into another, non-case-marked position, then it must somehow acquire case. Such positions are the complement to a participle, adjective, or noun or as the subject of an infinitival verb. So initial $_{IP}$[was $_{VP}$[arrested Kim]] or $_{NP}$[portrait Kim] or $_{IP}$[seems $_{VP}$[Kim to be happy]], where Kim follows a passive participle or a noun or occurs as subject of an infinitive, surface as *Kim was arrested*, *Kim's portrait*, and *Kim seems to be happy*, where Kim has moved to a position where it receives nominative or genitive case. Initial $_{AP}$[proud Kim] surfaces as *proud of Kim*, where a meaningless, dummy preposition *of* has been inserted simply in order to assign case; similarly $_{NP}$[portrait Kim] may surface as *portrait of Kim* with the dummy preposition. This is a hallmark of languages with what we called "positional syntax" in the last chapter. In languages with rich morphological case (and non-positional syntax), on the other hand, nouns may be pronounced in all those positions and have their own overt case markers, e.g. Latin (3); no movement or dummy prepositions are required.

(3)   a. Creditur Marco.
          It-is-believed to-Marcus.
          'Marcus is believed'
       b. Historia Romae
          'History of Rome'
       c. Carus Marco
          'Dear to Marcus'

So morphological case and abstract case work somewhat differently. In this section I shall examine some curious syntactic effects resulting from the disappearance of the morphological case system of early English; the effects, we shall see, were triggered in part by the ways that grammars were used in the formulation of names.

If heads assign case to the left or to the right in particular languages in accordance with the order of heads, one is not surprised to find Old English nouns assigning case to the left (4a) AND to the right (4b). One finds genitive–head order alternating with head–genitive, with the genitive suffix, singular *-es* and plural *-a*. There is good reason to believe that the order of heads was shifting in late Old English: one finds verbs preceding and following their complement, object–verb order alternating with verb–object, as we shall see in the next section.

(4)   a. Godes lof
           'Praise of God'
           Cristes læwa
           'Betrayer of Christ'
        b. Lufu godes and manna
           'Love of God and of men' (Ælfric, *Catholic Homilies* ii. 602.12)
           Ormæte stream wæteres
           'Huge stream of water' (Ælfric, *Catholic Homilies* ii. 196.5)

If Old English nouns assigned case to the left and to the right, and if in both positions it was realized as a morphological genitive, then one is not surprised to find that Old English also manifested "split genitives." They were split in that a single genitive phrase occurred on both sides of the head noun. In (5) we see examples where the split element occurring to the right of the noun was a conjunct. Jespersen (1909: 300) notes that with conjuncts, splitting represents the usual word order in Old English.

(5)   a. Inwæres broþur ond Healfdenes
           Inwær's brother and Healfden's
           'Inwær's and Healfden's brother' (*Anglo-Saxon Chronicle* 878)
        b. Sodoma lande 7 gomorra
           'The Sodomites' and the Gomorreans' land'
                                     (*West Saxon Gospels* (Ms A), Matt 10.15)

In addition, appositional elements, where two DPs are in parallel, were usually split: the two elements occurred on either side of the head noun (6a–c), although (6d) was also possible, where *Ælfredes cyninges* is not split. Notice that (6a) comes from the Peterborough version of the *Anglo-Saxon Chronicle*, a copy dating from 1122. The Parker [A] version, copied more than 200 years earlier, shows no splitting of the genitive phrase (6d), indicating that there was dialectal or diachronic variation.

(6)   a. Ælfredes godsune cyninges
           'King Alfred's godson'
                (*Anglo-Saxon Chronicle* 890 (Laud (Peterborough) [E] 1122))
        b. Þæs cyninges dagum herodes
           'In the days of Herod the king'
                                     (*West Saxon Gospels* (Ms A), Matt 2.1)
        c. Iohannes dagum fulwihteres
           'From the days of John the Baptist'
                                    (*West Saxon Gospels* (Ms A), Matt 11.12)
        d. Ælfredes cyninges godsunu
                            (*Anglo-Saxon Chronicle* 890 (Parker c900))

    e. *The book's cover about Rio (= 'The book about Rio's cover')

    f. *Þæs cyninges godsune Frances

       The king's godson of-France (= 'The king of France's godson')

Splitting within DPs was restricted to conjuncts (5) and to appositional elements (6a–c). In particular, Old English did not show split constructions with a preposition phrase, along the lines of (6e). Nor does one find anything like the non-appositional (6f), where *Frances* has no thematic relation to *godsune*; *Frances* is neither a conjunct nor appositional and is thematically related to 'king' (Nunnally 1985: 148, Cynthia Allen, Willem Koopman, personal communication).

Split genitives in Old English had a structure along the lines of (7). *Ælfredes* was in the specifier of DP; *godsune* assigned case to the left and to the right (Allen 2002 argues that *cyninges* is an adjunct to *godsune*, not a complement).

(7)   _DP_[_Spec_[Ælfredes] D _NP_[_N_godsune [cyninges]]]

These grammars had an overt genitive case on the right or on the left of the head noun; and they had split genitives. So much for splitting in Old English grammars.

Now for the changes, the new languages. Middle and early Modern English also manifested split genitives but they included forms that are very different from the split genitives of Old English (8), and the Old English forms were lost.

(8)   a. The clerkes tale *of Oxenford* (Chaucer, *Clerk's Tale*, Prologue)

        b. The Wive's Tale *of Bath* (Chaucer, *Wife of Bath's Tale*, Prologue)

        c. Kyng Priamus sone *of Troy* (Chaucer, *Troilus & Cressida* I, 2)

        d. This kynges sone *of Troie* (Chaucer, *Troilus & Cressida* III,1715)

        e. The Archbishop's Grace *of York*

                         (Shakespeare, *1 Henry IV* III.ii.119)

The meaning is 'The clerk of Oxford's tale,' 'King Priam of Troy's son,' etc., and the genitive is split: the rightmost part of the genitive phrase (italicized) occurs to the right of the head noun that the genitive phrase modifies. Mustanoja (1960: 78) notes that "the split genitive is common all through ME" and is more common than the modern "group genitive," *The clerk of Oxford's tale*. Jespersen (1909: 293), exaggerating a little, calls this splitting "the universal practice up to the end of the fifteenth century." However, these Middle English split forms are different from those of Old English grammars, because the rightmost element is neither a conjunct nor appositional, and it has no thematic relation with the head noun, *tale*, *son*, *Grace*.

  We can understand the development of the new Middle English split genitives in the light of the loss of the overt morphological case system. Old English had four cases (nominative, accusative, genitive, and dative) and a vestigial instrumental, but they disappeared in the period of the tenth to thirteenth centuries, the loss spreading through the population from the north to the south – probably under the influence of the Scandinavian settlements, as noted in the last chapter (O'Neil 1978). In early Middle English, grammars emerged that lacked the morphological case properties of the earlier systems, in particular lacking a morphological genitive, as we saw in the last chapter.

Put yourself now in the position of a child with this new, caseless grammar; your I-language has developed without morphological case. You are living in the thirteenth century; you would hear forms such as (6a) *Ælfredes godsune cyninges*, but the case endings do not register – that's what it means not to have morphological case in one's grammar. You are not an infant and you are old enough to have a partial analysis, which identifies three words. *Ælfredes* was construed as a "possessive" noun in the Specifier of DP.

The modern "possessive" is not simply a reflex of the old genitive case. Morphological case generally is a property of individual nouns. On the other hand, "possessive" in Modern English is a property not of nouns but of the DP: in *My uncle from Cornwall's cat* (9a) the possessor is the whole DP *My uncle from Cornwall*. Allen (1997) shows that the *'s* is a clitic attached to the preceding element and that the group genitive, where the clitic is attached to a full DP, is a late Middle English innovation. As the case system was lost, the genitive ending *-es* was reanalyzed as something else, a Case-marking clitic. If *'s* comes to be a clitic in Middle English, which Case marks whole DPs, this would explain why "group genitives" begin to appear only at that time, as Allen argued.

(9)   a. DP[My uncle from Cornwall]'s cat
       b. Poines his brother (Shakespeare, *2 Henry IV* II.iv.308)
          For Jesus Christ his sake (1662 *Book of Common Prayer*)
       c. Mrs. Sands his maid (1607 Sir John Harington, *Nugae Antiquae* II.238, ed. T. Park, 1804)
       d. Job's patience, Moses his meekness, and Abraham's faith
                              (1568 Richard Franck, *Northern Memoirs* 31)

It is likely that there was another parallel reanalysis of the genitive *-es* ending, yielding the *his*-genitives that were attested in the sixteenth and seventeenth centuries (9b) for 'Poines' brother,' 'Jesus Christ's sake,' etc. The genitive ending in *-s* was sometimes spelled *his*, and this form occurs even with females (9c) and occurs alongside possessive clitics (9d).

UG, we have noted, dictates that every phonetic DP has case, either morphological or abstract, with abstract case assigned in a more restricted fashion. The new children without morphological case reanalyzed the old morphological genitive suffix *-es* as a clitic, which was recruited as a case marker occurring in the D position (9a). The clitic *'s* case marks the element in the Specifier of the containing DP. So *Ælfred* has case and the case is realized through the *'s* marker (usually analyzed as the head D, as in (10a′)). In short, the *Ælfredes* of the parents is reanalyzed as *Ælfred's* (10a), although orthographic forms like *Ælfredes* occur in texts when mental grammars surely yielded *Ælfred's*. Orthographic *'s* is a recent innovation.

So now what about *cyninges* in (6a)? The evidence suggests that the phrase became (10a) *Ælfred's godsune king*. One finds phrases of just this form in (10b,c), where the postnominal noun is not case marked, and Jespersen (1909: 283–284) notes that these forms are common in Middle English. However, they did not persist, dying out before long.

(10) a. Ælfred's godsune king
      a′. DP[DP[Ælfred] D's NP[Ngodsune [king]]]
      b. The kynges metynge Pharao
         'Pharaoh the king's dream' (Chaucer, *Book of the Duchess*, 282)
      c. The Grekes hors Synoun
         'Sinon the Greek's horse' (Chaucer, *Squire's Tale*, 209)

The forms of (10), where the rightmost element is appositional, are direct reflexes of Old English split genitives like (6), corresponding exactly, except that the split element, *king*, *Pharao*, *Synoun*, has no overt case. They died out because there was no longer any morphological genitive case and there was no other case marker, hence neither morphological nor abstract case.

There was another option for assigning case to the rightmost element: the preposition *of* came to be used as a case marker, as in (8), and it assigned its own thematic role, Location (unlike in *proud of Kim* or *portrait of Kim*, where *of* is a dummy element, only assigning case and not assigning an independent thematic role). This explains why we do not find **Ælfred's godsune of king*, because if *of* case marked the DP, it would assign a Location role and that would not be consistent with the meaning of the phrase, where *king* is in apposition with *Ælfred*. So *of* shows up in different sentences: the sentences of (6) are not like those of (8) and have different meanings. In (8b), for example, *Wive* and *Bath* are not appositional and *of* assigns a Location role.

With the introduction of the *of* case marker in these contexts, the split genitive construction is extended to new expressions (8). In Old English, the postnominal genitive always had a thematic relation with the head noun. In Middle English, on the other hand, one finds postnominal, split DPs where there is no thematic relation with the head noun, and the postnominal items are case marked by *of*. So, in (8a) *Oxenford* is construed with *clerkes* and not with *tale*, and it is case marked by *of*. The Middle English split expressions only involve *of* phrases: one does not find *The book's cover about Rio* for 'The book about Rio's cover,' mirroring the situation in Old English and showing that there is no general operation "extraposing" PPs in Middle English, any more than there was in Old English. In fact, the postnominal noun in (8) always has a thematic role of Location/Source. I know of no claim to this effect in the literature but it has been confirmed for me by Cynthia Allen, Olga Fischer, and Willem Koopman in independent personal communications. So, for example, one does not find forms like (11), where the postnominal noun is a Theme (11a) or a Possessor (11b).

(11)   a. The portrait's painter of Saskia (= the portrait of Saskia's painter)
         b. The wife's tale of Jim (= the wife of Jim's tale)

The properties of the new grammar must have emerged in the way that they did, (a) if children heard expressions like *Ælfredes godsune cyninges* (6a), (b) if their I-languages did not have the morphological case system of their parents, and (c) if they knew that *of* assigns a Locative thematic role – we come to this point in a moment. That provides a tight explanation for the new properties of Middle English grammars. In particular, we explain the distinction between (6), (8), and (10), and we explain the non-occurrence of (9) and (11).

We see that change is bumpy; if one element of a grammar changes, there may be many new phenomena (8). Children do not just match what they hear and they may produce innovative forms. UG defines the terrain, the hypothesis space, and a change in initial conditions (loss of morphological case) may have syntactic effects, as children develop new I-languages.

This is an explanation for the form of the split genitives of (8) in Middle English. They were around for four centuries and then dropped out of the language. This was probably a function of the newly available clitic *'s* that made possible group genitives like *The clerk of Oxford's tale*; these became possible only when *'s* was construed as a clitic, which case marked DPs, and that in turn was a function of the loss of morphological cases, including the genitive in -*es*. As *'s* was recruited as a case marker for NP/DPs, the split constructions disappeared.[2]

The central idea is that children scan their linguistic environment for morphological cases and, if they find them, the children have a non-positional syntax. If children do not find morphological cases, different cues are identified and the syntax is positional. In that event, a P or V may case mark an adjacent NP/DP. The little study of this section shows what happens when everything else remains constant. There came a point in the history of English when children ceased to find morphological cases. Those children were exposed to pretty much the same kind of linguistic experience as their parents but the transparency of overt case endings had dropped below a threshold such that they were no longer attained. Given a highly restrictive theory of UG, then other things had to change; that is how change is often bumpy.

---

[2] *'s* marks case on a noun (*Kim's book*) or a DP (*My uncle from Cornwall's cat*).

However, our account so far leaves open the question of WHY these extended split genitives (8) should have arisen, and this is where we see how the changing USE of grammars may play a role.

An explanation may be found in one special type of Old English split genitive, those involving double names (henceforth, "split names"). Ekwall (1943: 15) finds "a really remarkable profusion" of these forms in his examination of the English Patent Rolls for the thirteenth and early fourteenth centuries (12). He notes that the documents originated in indictments drawn up by local lawyers and that "we may assume that the split genitives represent local usage and everyday speech. Many of the descriptions, especially those which contain a pet form of a personal name, have a very homely and colloquial ring" (Ekwall 1943: 17). These forms are comparable to the appositional types of (6a–c): *Thomas* and *Doreward* have the same relationship to *prest* in (12a) just as *Ælfredes* and *cyninges* have the same relationship to *godsune* in (6a). These surnames often describe social functions: *Doreward* was 'ward of the door,' *Ward* was 'guard.'

(12)   a. Thomasprest Doreward (= priest of Thomas Doreward)
                        (1318 *Patent Rolls* (Elmstead, Ess.))
        b. Simundeschamberleyn Ward (= chamberlain of Simon Ward)
                        (1318 *Patent Rolls* (Hornington, YW))
        c. Thomasservantcornyssh (= servant of Thomas Cornish)
                        (1450 *Patent Rolls* (Great Waltham, Ess.))

Ekwall also finds split names where the second part of the name begins with the French preposition *de* and where the following noun indicates the place of origin (13). This is a common form of name in Middle English and "the preposition begins to be dropped already in the first half of the fourteenth century and is sometimes replaced by *of*" (1943: 48).

(13)   a. Nicholesknave de Moeles (= servant of Nicholas de Moeles)
                        (1314 *Patent Rolls* (Compton Pauncefoot, So.))
        b. Williamesprest de Reigny (= priest of William de Reigny)
                        (1318 *Patent Rolls* (East Lydford, So.))
        c. Alicesbailiff de Watevill (= bailiff of Alice de Watevill)
                        (1323 *Patent Rolls* (Panfield, Ess.))

Comparable split names where the second part begins with English *of* are (14).

(14)   a. Thomasefelagh of Barneby (= fellow of Thomas of Barneby)
                        (1311 *Patent Rolls* (Lockington, YE))
        b. Rogereswarenner of Beauchamp (= warrener of Roger of
            Beauchamp) (1316 *Patent Rolls* (Bennington, Hrt.))
        c. Julianesservant of Weston (= servant of Julian of Weston)
                        (1348 *Patent Rolls* (Tetbury, Gl.))

Forms like (14), being colloquial and therefore readily available to child language learners, might have been a trigger for the new split genitives of Middle English (8), a model for *of* serving as a marker of Locative role. In these names (14) children heard forms introduced by *of* in a kind of appositional structure. In (14a) *Thomas* and *of Barneby* are on a par, just like (12a) where *Thomas* and *Doreward* are similarly on a par, both names of the same person, and initially *of Barneby* was perhaps treated as a unit with no internal structure, a literal translation of the *de* forms like those in (13); if this is correct, then the structure of (14a) is parallel to that of (12a), and the rightmost element is a complex noun with no internal structure (15).

(15)   DP[Spec[Thomas] D NP[Nfelagh N[of-Barneby]]]

However, as *of* became established as a preposition in Middle English, *of Barneby* came to be construed with an internal preposition–noun structure, which would explain why it later gets dropped from names, which then become Thomas Barneby, Roger Beauchamp, Julian Weston, etc. We would expect *of* to drop out as it is recognized as a case-marking preposition assigning a Locative thematic role: if Barneby, Beauchamp, and Weston have the same thematic roles, respectively, as Thomas, Roger, and Julian, a prepositional *of* would be an embarrassment, inviting the interpretation of the following noun as having a distinctive thematic role. But my point here is more limited: forms such as (14) might have been a trigger for the extended split genitives like (8). If *of* assigns case and a Locative/Source role in these names, all of which indicate the place from which Thomas, Roger et al. originate, then forms like (14) provide a model for the split genitives of (8). The new, caseless children heard forms like *Ælfred's godsune king* (10a) and knew from split names like (14) that *of* could case mark a noun and assign Locative role, hence (8).

This is an explanation for the rise of the split genitives of (8) in Middle English and it is a function of the use of grammars. Grammars were used in such a way that people produced split name constructions with *of* assigning a Location role, because of their French origins. It was a way of talking that caught on and provided a trigger for the new split genitives of (8). If we had more data, modern discourse analysis might reveal the social value of these forms and who used them under what circumstances. The grammar that emerged under those conditions was shaped by contingent factors, notably by the form of names.

In this section and in chapter 5 we have seen that changes in morphology, the great simplification in inflectional endings that took place in Middle English, had significant effects on the syntax of the language. This is reminiscent of Tinbergen's famous demonstration that young herring gulls, waiting in the nest, open their mouths when their mothers fly in with food, not because they observe and want to eat the food, but rather in response to a red spot under her beak. Similarly, syntactic properties may be due to apparently unrelated phenomena.

If children attain grammars without the inflectional endings of their parents, then their syntax may also differ as a result, if syntax and morphology are linked in the ways I have suggested here.

6.3   Object–verb to verb–object

Languages differ in their word order, particularly with regard to the order of verbs and their complements. It is clear that these are often differences at the level of the internal system, differences between I-languages. English speakers typically say things like (16a), where the verb of the embedded clause, *visiting*, precedes its direct object, *Amsterdam*, while Dutch and German speakers say (16b,c), showing the reverse order in the embedded clause. We need to illustrate the orders in embedded clauses because several of the languages we will discuss have finite verbs in second position in matrix clauses, which disguises the order of verbs and complements.

(16)   a. Kim thinks $_{CP}$[that Tim is visiting Amsterdam].
         b. Kim denkt $_{CP}$dat Tim Amsterdam bezoekt].
            Kim thinks   that Tim Amsterdam visits.
         c. Kim denkt, $_{CP}$[dass Tim Amsterdam besucht].

English and Dutch differ systematically in this regard and neither is unusual. Object–verb languages, along with Dutch and German, include Basque, Turkish, Latin, Hindi, Kannada, the Dravidian languages, Japanese, Korean, Quechua, Zapotec, and several Amerindian languages, among others; verb–object languages, on the other hand, include English, the Scandinavian languages, Icelandic, the Romance languages, Greek, Serbian, Finnish, Thai, Swahili, and several other African languages. A number of the European verb–object languages were formerly object–verb systems, all with fairly strong verb-second tendencies in matrix clauses, and underwent a change: English, Icelandic, Danish, Norwegian, and Swedish. In addition, the Romance languages all descended from Latin, an object–verb language, and have subsequently become verb–object; similarly the Western Finno-Ugric languages, including Finnish (Kiparsky 1996: 172).

The first question to ask is what the structural difference is between the I-languages of English and Dutch speakers, and there are very different approaches. One approach stems from Greenberg's (1966) analysis of harmonic properties and notes that object–verb languages all have verbs following preposition phrases (PP) and adverbial phrases (AP), they tend strongly also to have V-auxiliary order and, somewhat less strongly, to have all heads (nouns, adjectives, prepositions) following their complement, while verb–object languages are the mirror image, having auxiliary–verb and head–complement order. Hawkins (1979) offers a fairly full listing of these properties in a large number of languages, not all analyzed with the same degree of rigor. This would suggest that there is a single mega-parameter that yields not only verb–object order but also auxiliary–verb and head–complement quite generally.[3]

A very different approach says that "verb–object" is too big a category and that verb–object order may result from several more primitive operations, each of which could differ from one system to another. Hróarsdóttir (2000a,b) is an instance of this approach. She postulates a universal initial verb–object order and several functional categories. The details are not important – the point is that she multiplies the points of possible variation. Verbs merge to the left of their complement to form a VP and then three quite abstract transformations apply to yield object–verb order and grammars may vary in terms of whether they have any one of these transformations (and perhaps in terms of the formulation of the operations). First, the verb–object VP raises to the left of a finite verb, to PredP$_{fin}$; second, the direct object moves out of the moved VP to a still higher position in AgrOP; and third, the finite VP moves to a yet higher functional position, to the Specifier of FP, to yield [V$_{fin}$ – object – V$_{main}$] order (17) (Hróarsdóttir 2000a: 283–285). Hróarsdóttir does not consider how any of these operations might be learned by a child, what PLD would trigger each of the operations, which makes the proposal hard to evaluate.[4]

(17) $_{FP}$[VP$_{fin}$] $_{AgrO}$[DP $_{PredPfin}$[$_{VPmain}$[Vmain ~~DP~~] [$_{VPfin}$[~~Vfin VPmain~~]

When the first of these three operations was lost, the language began to show verb–object order, and the loss of that operation raising the verb–object VP constituted the change in I-grammars when verb–object order was first introduced.

Needless to say, formulating the correct I-grammar analysis of verb/complement order is crucial. Different analyses entail very different kinds of local causes for the change. If Hróarsdóttir is correct, then we would seek an explanation for why the VP-raising operation was no longer triggered in children's grammars (she is not able to offer one – Hróarsdóttir 2000b: 319). If a larger-scale analysis is right, where the change in verb/complement order is part of a larger shift, for example the idea of Vennemann (1975) that Operators and Operands are serialized in a uniform order, then we could look for very different causes. Vennemann's Natural Serialization Principle was that verbs, nouns,

---

[3] Where the correlations are absolute, that may indicate that grammars with property x must also have property y. It is harder to evaluate correspondences that hold partially, grammars with property x having property y, say, 80 percent of the time. One cannot require the theory of grammar to have property x entailing property y, because that would exclude the other 20 percent of systems. The fact that property x entails property y most of the time might be an accident or due to non-systematic factors.

[4] The analysis also has its own internal problems and she notes three (Hróarsdóttir 2000b: 314–315).

and adjectives are ordered uniformly with respect to complements, preposition phrases, and complement, relative, and adverbial clauses.

As observed in note 3, there are too many exceptions to the mega-harmony approach for it to be plausible to seek a single parameter that determines verb/complement, auxiliary/verb, and head/complement order. Watkins (1976) called this approach "Cyclopean," a well-chosen adjective. It may be the case that there are different types of object–verb and verb–object languages, such that we need to think in terms of more primitive notions, perhaps along the lines of Hróarsdóttir. If Hróarsdóttir were right, then there would not be just two relevant grammars, object–verb and verb–object, but eight grammars, depending on whether they have each of the three transformations or not. However, for our present purpose I will assume that there is a single point of variation, verb–XP or XP–verb (where "XP" refers to any phrasal category: DP, PP, AP, VP), in principle one structural difference between two such languages: verbs may precede or follow their direct object or a preposition phrase, an adverbial phrase, or another VP. Those properties seem to cluster reliably: if a language has verb–DP order, then PPs, APs, and VPs also follow the verb. Under that view, children must identify either a $_{VP}$[XP V] cue or $_{VP}$[V XP].

The languages that we know underwent an XP–V to V–XP shift all had fairly strong verb-second properties in main clauses or, in the case of Latin, relatively free word order in main clauses. They differ in this regard from languages that have remained with stable XP–V order, such as Japanese and Korean. This is a big fact; it shapes the account to be given here, and brings us to the idea that children seek cues only in structurally simple domains.

This idea, sometimes referred to as "degree-0 learnability," holds that children learn only from data in unembedded domains. That means simple clauses and the topmost elements of an embedded clause (complementizers and the subjects of infinitival clauses).[5] We can illustrate this by looking at Dutch, an XP–V language with strict verb-second properties in main clauses. That means that Dutch has VPs with XP–V order and finite verbs moving to a high functional position in main clauses. Embedded clauses show XP–V order uniformly (16b), but main causes often have verbs preceding their direct objects, because they have moved to a higher C position. So a simple expression *Maria drinkt vodka* 'Maria is drinking vodka' is analyzed as (18a). The subject *Maria* is copied to the Specifier of the CP and the finite verb *drinkt* is copied to C. Similarly *In Utrecht drinkt Maria vodka* 'Maria is drinking vodka in Utrecht' is analyzed as (18b) and we see how verb-second effects are treated: a phrasal category, the subject DP in (18a) and a PP in (18b), is copied to the Specifier of CP and finite verbs are copied in C.

---

[5] Lightfoot (1991, 1994) states this in terms of unembedded binding Domains.

(18)   a. CP[Maria drinkt IP[~~Maria~~ VP[vodka ~~drinkt~~]]].
        b. CP[in Utrecht drinkt IP[Maria VP[~~in Utrecht~~ vodka ~~drinkt~~]]].

When these clauses are embedded under a main clause *Ik denk dat* 'I think that,'
then there are no verb-second effects and the finite verb appears in its VP-final
position (19).

(19)   a. Ik denk CP[dat Maria VP[vodka drinkt]].
        b. Ik denk CP[dat Maria VP[in Utrecht vodka drinkt]].

This analysis has been well established for many years and we ask now how
it might be attained by children. Children would know that finite verbs are displaced, moving away from their complement phrases and occurring standardly
in second position. Since verbs are first merged with their complement phrase
alongside and may occur separated from that phrase, they must be displaced;
since they generally occur in second position, it seems not hard for children to
learn that they are copied and where they are copied TO.

However, the question now arises of how the child knows where the verb is
copied FROM. If grammars of Dutch speakers have verbs in VP-final position,
we want to know how a child can learn this, if she does not learn from the VPs
of embedded clauses and if main-clause finite verbs are typically displaced. It
turns out there is a good deal of main-clause evidence for the VP-final position
of the verb. It consists of the expressions of (20), which can only be analyzed
with a verb in the VP-final position, i.e. VP[XP V].

(20)   a. Jan belt IP[~~Jan~~ VP[de hoogleraar op~~belt~~]].
           'John calls the professor up.'
        b. Jan   moet IP[~~Jan~~ VP[de hoogleraar opbellen]].
           John must   the professor   up call
        c. En ik maar VP[fietsen repareren].
           'I ended up repairing bicycles.'
        d. VP[Hand   uitsteken].
           Hand   outstretch
           'Signal.'
        e. Jantje VP[koekje hebben].
           'Jantje has a cookie.'
        f. Ik VP[de vuilnisbak   buiten zetten]? Nooit.
           I   the garbage-can   outside set?   Never
           'Me put the garbage out? Never.'

(20a) involves the complex verb *opbellen* 'call up,' a verb consisting of a separable prefix *op* and a stem *bellen*; in Dutch (and German: *Hans ruft den Professor
an*) separable particles occur uniformly at the end of main clauses and are
not moved (unlike English, which allows the order to vary: *call the professor*

up and *call up the professor*) – they mark the VP-final position of the verb. The "clause-union" structure (20b) has a modal verb in the C position and the non-finite verb is in its original VP-final position. (20c) is a productive kind of "historical infinitive," occurring with the particles *en . . . maar*. (20d) represents a colloquial alternative to the usual form of the imperative with the verb fronted; this may be an elliptical form with *je moet* 'you must' missing. (20e) is the kind of thing found in speech addressed to young children, representing a kind of baby-talk in which functional categories are missing. (20f) is an exclamatory question.

So there are several types of primary linguistic data (PLD), all drawn from simple clauses, which must be analyzed with a verb in VP-final position, hence expressing the $_{VP}$[XP V] cue. If this is correct, then children do not need access to embedded domains to determine that Dutch verbs are VP-final.[6]

Not only is this possible and consistent with a degree-0 account, but acquisitional data strongly suggest that something along these lines is correct, that children find the $_{VP}$[XP V] cue in unembedded domains. In work from twenty years ago, Clahsen & Smolka (1986) identified four stages in the acquisition of German (21).

(21)   a. Stage 1 (25–29 months): no fixed order between sentence constituents; all verbal elements occur in first/second and final position with a preference for final position.

b. Stage 2 (31–33 months): verbal elements with particles occur regularly in final position; other finite verbs occur in both first/second and final position.

c. Stage 3 (36–39 months): all and only finite verbs occur in first/second position; verbal complexes with finite and non-finite parts appear in discontinuous positions.

d. Stage 4 (41–42 months): as soon as embedded sentences are produced, their finite verbs are in final position.

This account requires revision in the light of work on optional infinitives (Wexler 1994). However, strikingly, from the earliest relevant stage children identify sentence-final position as one of the possible positions for verbs, including finite verbs, despite the fact that they are not commonly heard in this position in German main clauses, and finite verbs never. At stage 3 there is a dramatic increase in the frequency of verb-second structures: in stages 1 and 2 they are used in only 20–40 percent of the utterances, but at stage 3 they are used in 90 percent; Clahsen & Smolka (1986: 149) report that this increase takes place explosively, within a month for all the children studied. Children at this stage seem to have the $_{VP}$[XP V] order and an operation displacing the finite verb

---

[6] For more details, see Lightfoot (1991: 51–56).

obligatorily, copying it to a fronted position; to this extent the adult system is in place. Importantly, when they begin to use embedded structures (stage 4), finite verbs are invariably in VP-final position and there seems to be no "experimentation" or learning based on embedded-clause data. This is exactly what one would expect if children are degree-0 learners, and not at all what would be expected if children scan embedded domains for cues.

With this approach to acquisition, whereby children scan for structural cues in unembedded domains, let us turn to early English. Like Dutch and German, Old English showed verb-second order in main clauses and verb-final in embedded clauses. However, Old English differs from Dutch and German in that, first, it was not strictly verb-second in main clauses and, second, coordinate sentences often show in the second conjunct the XP–V order typical of embedded clauses (22).

(22)   a. ... & his eagen astungon
              '. . . and they stuck his eyes out'
                         (*Anglo-Saxon Chronicle* (Parker 797))
          b. ... & þone æþeling ofslogon & þa men
              '. . . and (they) killed the prince and the men'
                         (*Anglo-Saxon Chronicle* (Parker 755))

Third, literary Dutch and German almost never show finite verbs still within their VP in main clauses, but this order occurs in Old English texts.[7] Bean (1983) examined 593 main clauses in the first four sections of the *Anglo-Saxon Chronicle* and found 65 cases (i.e. 11 percent of all main clauses) where the verb could not plausibly be analyzed as copied out of its VP. Fourth, Old English shows more variation than Dutch or German texts in the position of its verbs. This may reflect the fact that our information is based on somewhat fragmentary texts of different genres, which have been filtered through a complex web of editorial and scribal practices and which predate the standardization of the literary language, one of the consequences of the Norman Conquest. It may also reflect the fact that changes were taking place affecting the position of the verb.

Another factor obscuring the initial position of the verb in early English was the availability of operations putting non-finite verbs to the right of a finite auxiliary, so called "verb raising" (23a) and "verb projection raising" (23b). Without these operations, one would expect the orders *þæt he Saul ne ofslean dorste* and *þæt he his feorh generian mehte*.

(23)   a. ... þæt he Saul ne   [dorste ofslean]
              ... that he Saul not   dared murder
              '. . . that he didn't dare to murder Saul.' (*Cura Pastoralis* 199, 2)

---

[7] For details, see Lightfoot (1991: 57–72).

b. ... þæt he mehte [his feorh   generian].
    ... that he could   his property save
    '... that he could save his property.' (*Orosius* 48, 18)

These confounding orders from embedded clauses would not be relevant for
degree-0 learners, scanning only unembedded domains, but they would be com-
plicating factors for non-degree-0 learners.

Despite the four differences between Old English and Dutch and German,
it seems clear that grammars had underlying XP–V order with the option of
moving a finite verb to a high functional position, C. Assuming this to be so
and bearing in mind the variation manifested by the texts, we can proceed to
ask how Old English children found the relevant cue, $_{VP}$[XP V].

Children of the Old English period, like their modern Dutch and German
counterparts, had plenty of evidence that finite verbs could move to C, expressions where the verb is to the left of its complement and not adjacent to it
(24).

(24)   a. Þa gegaderode Ælfred cyning his fier.
             then gathered Alfred king his army
             'Then King Alfred gathered his army.'
                                          (*Anglo-Saxon Chronicle* (Parker 894.6))
          b. Þær hæfdon Romane sige.
             there had Romans victory
             'There the Romans were victorious.' (*Orosius* 232.11)
          c. ... & feng Ælfric Wiltunscire bisceop to þam arcebisceoprice.
             ... and succeeded Ælfric, Wiltshire's bishop, to the archbishopric
             '... and Ælfric, bishop of Wiltshire, succeeded to the archbishop-
             ship.' (*Anglo-Saxon Chronicle* (Parker 994.1))

But how did children find the position from which verbs were copied? What
were the unembedded indicators for the position from which the verb was
displaced? First, Old English verbs had prefixes that could occur in a separate
position. The most usual order in main clauses was ... V ... particle (25).
The particle sometimes moved with the verb to its fronted position (26), and
occasionally one finds the particle between the subject and object (27).

(25)   a. Þa *sticode* him mon   þa eagon *ut*.
             then stuck   him someone the eyes   out
             'Then someone stuck his eyes out.' (*Orosius* 168.4)
          b. Þa *geat*   mon   þæt attor *ut* on þære sæ.
             then poured somebody the poison out into the   sea
             'Then somebody poured poison out into the sea.'
                                                            (*Orosius* 258.16)

    c. Ond þa *ahof* Drihten hie *up.*
       and then raised God   them up
       'Then God raised them up.' (*Blickling Homilies* 157.22)
    d. Þa *astah* se Hælend *up* on anre dune.
       'Then went the Savior up on to a hill.'
                           (*Homilies of the Anglo-Saxon Church* I, 182)

(26)   a. He þa *ut awearp* þa sceomolas þara cypemanna.
        he then out threw   the benches   of the   dealers
        'He then threw out the benches of the dealers.'
                          (*Blickling Homilies* 71.17)
    b. Stephanus *up-astah* þurh his blod gewuldorbeagod.
       'Stephen rose-up, through his blood crowned.'
                 (*Homilies of the Anglo-Saxon Church* I, 56)

(27)   a. Þa *ahof* Paulus *up* his heafod.
        then lifted Paul   up his head
        'Then Paul lifted up his head.' (*Blickling Homilies* 187.35)
    b. *Nime* he *upp* his mæg.
        take   he   up   his   kinsmen
        'Let him take up his kinsmen.'
    c. Þær *bær* Godwine eorl *up* his mal.
        then set   Godwin   earl forth his case
        'Then set forth Earl Godwin his case.'
                     (*Anglo-Saxon Chronicle* an.1052)

The prevalence of the order in (25) may have sufficed to express the $_{VP}$[XP V] cue, with the separated particle marking the position of the copied verb. However, the availability of the alternative orders would have made this a less reliable trigger than in modern Dutch and German.

    Second, Old English, like modern Dutch and German, also had clause-union structures like (28), where a modal verb was in C and the main verb remained in its VP-final position.

(28)   Swa sceal geong guma $_{VP}$[gode gewyrcean].
       'Thus shall a young man good things perform.' (*Beowulf* 20)

    Third, unlike Dutch and German, Old English had verb-final main clauses, where the finite verb remained in its VP (29).

(29)   a. . . .   Cuþan   mon   ofslog.
        . . . and Cutha-acc somebody slew
        '. . . and somebody slew Cutha.'
        (*Anglo-Saxon Chronicle* (Parker 584.2))

b. Þa   him Hroþgar   gewat.
   then him Hrothgar   recognized
   'Then Hrothgar recognized him.' (*Beowulf* 662)

c. He Gode   þancode.
   He God   thanked
   'He thanked God.' (*Beowulf* 625)

d. He hine an   bigsell ahsode.
   He him   about parable asked
   'He asked him about the parable.' (*OE Gospels*, Mark 7.17)

Another possible trigger for the $_{VP}$[XP V] cue is sentences with object pro-nouns, which occurred overwhelmingly in object–V order even in simple, main clauses: *He hine seah* 'He saw him.' However, it is not clear how children would have analyzed such forms, whether the pronoun was treated as a clitic, attached to the verb and not reflecting the order of merger. Van Kemenade (1987) shows that pronouns occur in positions barred to full DPs. So one must remain agnos-tic on the point: object pronouns may or may not have been critical. Similarly, nothing is known about colloquial data equivalent to Dutch (20c–f), providing unembedded triggers for the $_{VP}$[XP V] cue.

These seem to be the possible triggers for the $_{VP}$[XP V] cue. If that is right, then there must have been some change in the availability of these triggers, because XP–V order was lost during the Middle English period. We saw in chapter 5 that this cannot be accounted for as a function of the loss of morpho-logical case endings. So what might the changes have been such that by the end of the Middle English period children were not finding the $_{VP}$[XP V] cue and, instead, were finding the $_{VP}$[V XP] cue and manifesting verb–object order consistently?

There was a steady decline of XP–verb order in matrix clauses (29) through the Old English period. For example, Bean (1983) examined nine sections of the *Anglo-Saxon Chronicle*, taking them as representative of different stages of Old and Middle English. She counted four constructions that needed to be analyzed with the verb remaining in its VP. She found 50% of such verbs in the section until 755, 37% in the period 755–860, 25% in 865–884, 23% in 885–891, 13% in 892–900, 12% in 958–1001, 18% in 1048–1066, 17% in 1122–1124, 22% in 1132–1140. Correspondingly, there was an increase in the expressions where the verb needed to be analyzed as displaced to some higher functional position. She offered similar data from other prose texts, King Alfred's *Letter on Learning* and *Ohthere*, Wulfstan, and Ælfric's preface to Genesis.

This change, affecting main-clause verbs, was slow and gradual and proba-bly involved no change in grammars. That is, Old English grammars permitted options of moving the verb to a higher functional position or leaving it in its

VP-final position. The option of moving the verb to a higher position was exercised increasingly over a period of several hundred years. This no more reflects a difference in grammars than if some speaker were shown to use a greater number of passive or imperative sentences. Rather, grammars were being used differently and the difference reflects the kind of accidental variation that is familiar from studies in population genetics. Nonetheless, changes in primary linguistic data, changes in E-language, representing changes in the use of grammars, if they show a slight cumulative effect, might have the consequence of changing the robustness of the expression of cues, leading to new grammars. That seems to be what happened during Middle English.

There are two striking facts that now become comprehensible. First, while main clauses were showing a slowly diminishing number of XP-V orders, embedded clauses remained consistently XP–V. Gorrell's (1895) massive study of Old English embedded clauses showed verbs in final position 80–90 percent of the time in all prose texts examined and there seems to be no change at work in this regard.

Second, when the new verb order began to affect embedded clauses, it did so rapidly and catastrophically, unlike the gradual changes affecting main clauses. One way of measuring this is to determine the rise of V . . . particle order in embedded clauses with verbs like *call up*, formerly consisting of prefix+verb. Since embedded verbs could generally not move to a higher functional position and since they occurred to the right of their prefix, they could not precede their particles until the grammar was reanalyzed as having V–XP order. Consequently, a verb preceding its particle reflects a change in grammars. Figure 6.2 shows that the development of V . . . particle order in embedded clauses took place significantly more quickly than in main clauses. Hiltunen (1983) did the relevant study and he comments that the loss of prefixes and the emergence of verbs separated from their particles happened in early Middle English: "Right from the first pages of [*The Ancrene Riwle*], for instance, one cannot avoid the impression of the prefixes having been swept away almost overnight. The suddenness of the change is remarkable in view of the longish and stable OE period" (1983 : 92).

Correspondingly, main clauses showed steadily declining object–verb order, as noted, but embedded clauses show a very different pattern. In figures provided by Bean (1983), we see a big change in embedded XP–V order between the seventh and eighth sections of the *Anglo-Saxon Chronicle*. In 1048–1066 she finds object–verb order in 65% of relative clauses and 49% of complement clauses, but in 1122–1124 she finds only 27% of object–verb relative clauses and 7% of complement clauses. If one aggregates her relative, subordinate, and conjunct clauses, one finds 66% showing object–verb order from the beginning of the Chronicle until 1066, and then 11% in the last two sections, a rapid drop. Canale (1978) has similar figures based in part on different texts.

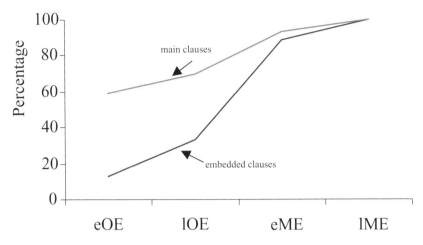

Figure 6.2 Increase in verb . . . particle order (Lightfoot 1991, adapted from Hiltunen 1983)

The historical record, then, shows that matrix clauses underwent some grad- ual statistical shifts through the Old English period: particles were increasingly separated from their associated verbs and appeared to their right, and instances of object–verb order diminished. The net result was that by the eleventh century there were fewer unembedded indicators of object–verb order and more data pointing to verb–object.

The historical record also shows that by the twelfth century there is a fairly consistent V–XP order, becoming quite uniform by the end of the Middle English period. Grammars during this period must have changed to having VPs with V–XP order. Under our view of acquisition, whereby children are sensitive to data from structurally simple domains, the new grammar manifested itself primarily in new patterns in embedded clauses, which emerged much faster than in main clauses. The speed of the change is not a new observation; it has been made by many traditional grammarians who have examined aspects of the transition. Kellner (1892: 290) noted a "sudden stop" in embedded object– verb order, and Kohonen (1978: 101, 125) a "dramatic" change in embedded clauses; Stockwell & Minkova (1991) write of "an abrupt halt" in embedded "verb-lateness."

Certain properties of Old and Middle English grammars remain obscure or ambiguous, and the difference may need to be formulated differently from the way I have characterized it here, in terms of different orders within an initial VP. However, the contrast between the way the changes emerged in main and embedded clauses is a big and robust fact, which we can understand through our cue-based, degree-0 approach to language acquisition. Until the twelfth century,

embedded clauses were robustly XP–V, providing plenty of data expressing the
$_{VP}$[XP V] cue, if children scan for cues in embedded clauses. In contrast, it is
easy to see how degree-0 children attained V–XP order, given the changes in
unembedded domains.[8]

There are two approaches to the intermediate situation when one finds both
XP–V and V–XP order. One is to say that XP–V grammars came to have
"extraposition" operations, in which elements were copied to the right to yield
V–XP order, much more so than in the modern XP–V languages like Dutch
and German. So a sentence like (30a) had an analysis along the lines of (30b),
and (30c) as (30d).

(30)   a. . . . þæt ænig mon atellan mæge ealne þone demm.
          . . . that any   man relate can   all the misery
          '. . . that any man can relate all misery.' (*Orosius* 52. 6–7)
       b. Þæt ænig mon $_{VP}$[$_{DP}$[ealne þone demm] atellan] mæge $_{DP}$[ealne
          þone demm].
       c. . . . þæt micel manncwealm becom ofer þære Romaniscan leode.
          (*AHTh* II, 122,15)
          '. . . that great pestilence came over the Roman people.'
       d. Þæt micel manncwealm $_{VP}$[$_{PP}$[ofer þære Romaniscan lede]
          becom] $_{PP}$[ofer þære Romaniscan leode].

The alternative is to say that there were coexisting grammars, one with XP–V
order and the other with V–XP order, and that people could alternate between
each system (Kroch & Taylor 2000, Pintzuk 1999). There is much to be said
about these two hypotheses, but each of them has in common a notion that
grammars may be used differentially. A grammar with an extraposition operation may be used with that operation applying more or less frequently; if
there are distinct grammars, then people may tend to use one grammar more
or less frequently under various conditions. Under either scenario, it is the USE
of grammars that varies and entails different E-language for children to attend
to. Grammars, either singly or in combination, offered a range of possibilities
that were exercised differently over time, entailing new E-language. Children
came to hear different things, a different distribution of data, which eventually
entailed new I-languages with V–XP order. We know that I-languages had
changed within the population at large when XP–V order ceased to be attested
in embedded clauses; at that point there were new I-languages and the old

[8] There were no significant changes in embedded clauses that might have helped to trigger the
new I-grammar. Furthermore, the consistency of XP–V order in embedded clauses would have
militated against a shift to a V–XP grammar. Lisa Pearl (2004) has produced an interesting
computational model which shows that children who are not degree-0 learners and have access
to embedded clauses would therefore not have attained a V–XP system, given the conservative
pull of embedded clauses.

XP–V I-languages had disappeared. This affected some people before others and reflected gradually changing linguistic experiences.

The experiences may have changed gradually, but the change in I-languages was sharper, more catastrophic. People either had an XP–V I-language or V–XP. If they had two systems coexisting, that typically does not last long; it is an interim stage before the new system comes to be uniform across the population. Indeed, even the change across the population was rapid. Up until 1122, the syntax of the Peterborough version of the *Anglo-Saxon Chronicle*, the manuscript that extends furthest into the twelfth century, is overwhelmingly XP–V, with the option of verb-second main clauses, representing the earlier system. Then in the first quarter of the thirteenth century, several West Midlands prose texts appear, the *Ancrene Riwle* and the Katherine group of saints' lives, and they are overwhelmingly V–XP (Kroch & Taylor 2000: 132). The new V–XP order first shows up in Old English texts but the demise of the old system was rapid. When the old system had disappeared, the new grammar was in place for all speakers.

The pattern of change seems similar to what happened later in Icelandic. Records from the fourteenth century show alternations between XP–V and V–XP order. The distribution, due either to changing applicability of operations within grammars or to changing use of one grammar as opposed to another coexisting grammar, changed over time. Hróarsdóttir (2000b) shows roughly 60% XP–V order in the fourteenth century dropping steadily until the nineteenth century, when the drop becomes more precipitous. Through the eighteenth century, XP–V order is well represented but then disappears rapidly in the first half of the nineteenth century. Within the nineteenth century, she distinguishes people born 1730–1750, who used XP–V order 26% of the time, and those born 1850–1870, who used XP–V order 6% of the time, noting that the disappearance of XP–V order is rapid. Unfortunately she does not distinguish main and subordinate clauses.

In fact, the similarities in the changes in the two languages are more extensive. XP–V order was most resilient in both languages with negative or quantified objects, which survived belatedly in English into the fifteenth century (31a,b); similarly in relative (31c) and coordinate clauses (31d). Van der Wurff (1999) demonstrates the parallelism between the two languages.

(31)   a. Þei schuld no meyhir haue.
            'They could have no mayor.' (Capgrave *Chronicles* 62.23)
       b. He haþ on vs mercy, for he may al þynge do.
            'He has mercy on us, for he can do everything.' (*Barlam* 2740)
       c. And þou dispisist hym þat such þynge suffred for us.
            'And you despise him that suffered such things for us.'
                                                        (*Barlam* 197)

d. Oþer he shal hate þat one and þat oþer loue, or þat one he shal
susteyne and þat oþer dispice.
'Either he will hate the one and love the other, or he will support
the one and despise the other.' (*Barlam* 1800)

It is difficult to see how such distinctions could be made if speakers had
coexisting XP–V and V–XP grammars. If both grammars are available, why
should speakers only use the XP–V grammar in these four contexts. Rather, it
seems more likely that people had a V–XP grammar that yielded XP–V order in
those contexts; van der Wurff offers one possible analysis of the displacement
operations but more work is needed.

6.4   Verb-second and variation in grammars

It is clear that the change from XP–V order to V–XP was not a function of
contact with an external system with the new order – it was not due to the
influence of French. French itself had XP–V order at the time of the English
change and, indeed more generally, French speakers had a major influence on
literary and learned vocabulary but very little influence on syntactic structures.
Rather, the new word order was due to variation stemming from changing use
of pre-existing, indigenous systems, as we have shown – there is no reason and
no opportunity to appeal to external influences in this case.

One case where it now seems clear that there were competing, coexisting
grammars concerns the development of a Scandinavian-style verb-second system in northeast England during the Middle English period. Kroch & Taylor
(1997) discovered that there were two systems determining the position of finite
verbs in Middle English. They argue that Old English was an "IP–V2" language,
meaning that the position to which finite verbs moved was the head of IP, I,
as in Yiddish and Icelandic, where there is verb-second word order in a broad
range of subordinate clauses. This system persisted into Middle English in the
southern part of the country. However, during the Middle English period, the
northeast part of the country, the area invaded by the Danes and Norwegians,
developed a "CP–V2" system, with the finite verb moving to the head of CP in
matrix clauses, as in modern Dutch, German, and Scandinavian, as we saw in
the last section.

The differences are fairly subtle and we will not detail them here, but Kroch &
Taylor show convincingly that they are systematic. A key idea is that pronouns
occur at the CP–IP boundary and then cliticize to the left. In the indigenous
system where the verb moves only to I, the verb is not at the CP–IP boundary
and does not host clitic pronouns, which therefore attach to anything in the
Specifier of CP, and we find the verb occurring in third position (32). On the
other hand, if the verb is copied to C, as in the Scandinavian-influenced system,
pronouns cliticize on to the verb (33).

(32)   a. Ælc yfel he mæg don.
            'Each evil he can do.' (*WHom* 4.62)
         b. Scortlice ic hæbbe nu gesæd ymb þa þrie dælas . . .
            'Briefly I have now spoken about the three parts.' (*Orosius* 9.18)
         c. Æfter his gebede he ahof þæt cild up . . .
            'After his prayer he lifted the child up.' (*ÆChom.* 2.28)

(33)   a. Hwi   sceole we   oþres   mannes niman.
            why   should we   another   man's   take (*ÆLS* 24.188)
         b. Þa   gemette he   sceaðan.
            then   met   he   robbers (*ÆLS* 31.151.)
         c. Ne   mihton hi   nænigne fultum æt   him begitan.
            not could   they   not-any help   from him get
                                                  (Bede 48.9–10)

Distinguishing two coexisting grammars along these lines was an important
piece of progress. Earlier researchers had assumed there was a system with
a kind of optionality that one does not otherwise find in natural languages.
Postulating two parallel systems along these lines was theoretically more parsimonious and congenial, because it was no longer necessary to weaken the
theory to permit a wider range of grammars than was truly necessary.

Kroch & Taylor's explanation for this development in northeast England is
that it stems from language contact and specifically from the imperfect second-
language learning of English by the Danish and Norwegian invaders of the
ninth to eleventh centuries. They claim that these speakers replaced the Old
English inflections in -þ, which did not occur word-finally in Norse, with -s.
This reduced the number of distinct inflectional endings and therefore, they
suppose, eliminated the motivation for finite verbs to move to I, which moved
to C instead. Parts of this analysis are questionable but it seems clear that
there were two systems, one developing due to Scandinavian influences and
lacking the inflectional distinctions of the southern dialect, due, in Kroch &
Taylor's view, to imperfect learning in a language-contact situation (but see
Westergaard 2005 for an interesting new approach in terms of varying use of a
single grammar).[9]

The Scandinavian influence was due to the large numbers of Danes and Norwegians who settled in England during the three centuries before the Norman
Conquest. The Viking seafarers stayed permanently, soldiers married English

---

[9] One problem, for example, is that the order illustrated in (i), whereby the finite verb of the relative
     clause *vnderstandis* occurs to the left of the negative marker *noht*, indicates that the verb has, in
     fact, moved to I.

(i)   Þe   barnis   þat   ere yunge þat vnderstandis noht what paine   fallis til cursing
           the children   that are young that understand   not what punishment falls to cursing
                                                                                     (*Benet* 23.101)

women, and then many Scandinavians, including women, came later as immigrants after areas of Norse control were established. Sometimes, particularly in the northwest, the settler-invaders came from already established Norse settlements in Ireland. Furthermore, the Anglo-Saxon settlement of these northern parts was not dense and the Scandinavians formed majorities in many places.

Kroch & Taylor (1997: 299) note that "the linguistic effect of this combination of population movement and population mixture was extensive, comparable in some ways to the pidginization/creolization phenomena of more recent centuries." Several Scandinavian vocabulary items found their way into English. Unlike French borrowings, they included closed-class items, like the pronoun *they*, the anaphoric noun *same*, the preposition *till*, and the complementizer *at*. "Second-language learners with an imperfect command of English [inflections] were a sufficiently large fraction of the population in the North to pass on their mixed language to succeeding generations, what is traditionally known as the substratum effect" (1997: 318).

Kroch & Taylor contrast a text of the Kentish dialect, the "Ayenbite of Inwit," and the first surviving prose document in the northern dialect, the *Rule of St. Benet*, which shows the invariant verb-second properties of modern Dutch and German, while the southern text has much more variable order and virtually no verb movement over pronominal subjects.

6.5   Summary

In this chapter we have seen that the way people use their grammars may entail new E-language for future generations, to the point that eventually new I-languages are triggered. In section 6.3 we saw an instance of two systems coexisting within one speech community. In that context, the mix may change for children, to the point where new I-languages are triggered. Chapter 5 showed new E-language emerging largely because of new I-languages and this chapter has shown new E-language emerging for different kinds of reasons, for reasons of how speakers used their grammars and how coexisting grammars may mix differently in a social context.

We have seen how ideas about language acquisition enable us to understand otherwise perplexing facts about the way in which word-order changes proceeded, and how, therefore, facts of language change lend credence to ideas about language acquisition. Let us now turn our attention to new language emerging explosively and we shall learn more about acquisition.

7   The eruption of new grammars

7.1   Creoles

Sometimes new grammatical properties emerge in rapid succession and well-defined, new languages erupt as if from the craters of Mount Vesuvius. This might happen in response to an especially heterogeneous triggering experience consisting of expressions from a variety of languages, including perhaps a PIDGIN.[1]

Some owners of coffee, cotton, sugar, and tobacco plantations deliberately mixed slaves and workers from different language backgrounds. For example, when demand for Hawaiian sugar boomed just over a hundred years ago, workers were shipped in from China, Japan, Korea, the Philippines, Puerto Rico, and Portugal. Because of the nature of life on plantations and the practice of splitting up workers with a common language, no one of the languages could be fully acquired by everybody and serve as a lingua franca. When speakers of different languages, the SUBSTRATE languages of the labor force, had to communicate in working contexts, they often developed makeshift jargons. These were pidgins and consisted of strings of words borrowed from the languages of the plantation owners, with little complexity and not much structure. The languages of the plantation owners, the European capital owners, and other socially dominant groups, were the SUPERSTRATE languages.

Pidgins are created typically by adults with their own native tongues, using the evolving pidgin for limited purposes, specifically for interethnic communication; nobody uses a pidgin as a native language acquired under the normal conditions of childhood. Sometimes a pidgin becomes a common currency, a lingua franca, and gradually develops some complexity and stabilization over a period of years; under those circumstances a pidgin can develop rapidly into a full, complex language, which we call a CREOLE, and that happened when children were isolated from their parents and encountered the pidgin as a significant part of the E-language to which they were exposed.

Creoles, unlike pidgins, are acquired as native languages in the first few years of children's lives. Children introduce complexity and their language becomes

---

[1] Material for this chapter is drawn in part from Lightfoot (1991: sect. 7.3, 1999: sect. 6.4).

not just longer strings of words but a real, full-fledged, natural language, functionally unrestricted and used for all the usual purposes, including talking to
oneself, formulating internal propositions, and speaking with intimate partners,
with a normal word order, grammatical markers, and the operations found in
other grammars. All the evidence suggests that creoles have the structural properties of well-established languages, reflecting mature I-languages. Those are
the differences between a pidgin and a creole, and this much represents a broad
consensus among linguists of very different persuasions.

Once we move beyond that consensus, we find a wide range of views within
a particular subfield of "creolistics." Linguists who see themselves working
within this subfield often view creole languages as exceptional, emerging in
special ways and having special properties of one kind or another. DeGraff
(2001) is scathing about the tendency to view creoles as exceptional, different in
kind from other languages, and attributes it in part to missionary and colonialist
preconceptions. Recently, the journal *Language* staged a fiery debate on this
point: Bickerton (2004) and DeGraff (2004).

There are two kinds of exceptionalists: substratists and superstratists. Substratists see creoles as reflecting the syntactic and semantic properties of the
most influential substrate languages, despite the fact that the phonology and
lexicon are derived from the lexifier language, the language that provided most
of the vocabulary. So Haitian Creole is said to draw the sound and other properties of its words from French and its syntactic structures from one of its West
African substrates, Fongbe. So essentially Fongbe is "relexified" with French
words (Lumsden 1998).

Superstratists, on the other hand, see creoles emerging from non-standard
varieties of the superstrate language. French-based creoles, for example, emerge
from layers of approximations of approximations of colloquial dialects of
French spoken in the colonies, where there are no standardizing pressures.
Successive restructurings took place as waves of adults tried to learn a range
of French dialects, with only limited effects from the substrate languages (Hall
1966, Chaudenson 1992).

There is a wide range of views on how creoles come into existence but
both substratists and superstratists view creoles and other languages in now-
familiar E-language terms, entities existing out there and subject to linguistic principles of various kinds. They are particularly concerned with how to
treat creoles in the context of principles of language change, for example the
nineteenth-century *Stammbaumtheorie* discussed in chapter 2, which has new
languages (like Spanish and French) emerging from a single parent language
(like Latin), splitting at particular points. Some have sought to force creoles
into genetic affiliations with their superstrates (Hall 1966), and others have
distinguished normal, genetic transmission of languages from the imperfect,
non-genetic transmission of abrupt creoles (Thomason & Kaufman 1988). The

most common view is that creoles are special, exceptional, and subject to special principles.

Another approach, the one adopted here, views creoles in less exceptional terms, integrating their study with what we know independently of language acquisition and language change. Creoles are acquired, at least in their early stages, under unusual conditions. For the first generation of children, the E-language to which they are exposed, some kind of pidgin alongside a variety of other languages, differs quite dramatically from the capacity they manifest as they grow up and show much richer, novel speech in a new language, the emerging creole. If we can discover some properties of the grammars that emerge in these children, and if we know something of the childhood experience that triggered those properties, we may be able to learn something about triggers in general and about the limiting cases. The particularly dramatic contrast between the ambient polyglot E-language and the mature capacity of the first creole speakers might make it easier to identify which elements of their experience acted as triggers for the emerging grammars, if we can take advantage of the experiment that nature has permitted.

Under usual circumstances, the triggering experience is a small subset of a child's total linguistic experience; I argued in earlier chapters that it consists only of data from unembedded domains that express cues. In that case, the total experience involves considerable redundancy in the "information" normally available to children. Much of what a child hears has no effect on the emerging grammar. From this perspective, the restrictedness of the experience of the first creole-speaking children is not as dramatic as when one is concerned with children's total experience.

The question now arises: to what extent does the creole child lack RELEVANT input for finding the cues provided by the linguistic genotype? The answer to this question might be: not at all, or not very much. This would explain how children with apparently impoverished and heterogeneous experiences nonetheless attain a mature capacity, as rich structurally as that of children with more extensive and more uniform experiences. It would simply mean that children with these kinds of unusual experiences are not exposed to as much redundant information.

Answering the question, of course, requires fairly detailed knowledge of the ambient E-language for the first creole speakers. This kind of information is sometimes available, and this is one reason why Sankoff's work on Tok Pisin is so important (see Sankoff & Laberge 1973). These days there are studies of hybrid languages, for example the Camfranglais found in Cameroon, a flexible mode of local identification, a language that "speaks through" pidgin forms of English and French with localized vocabulary from many sources. Usually, however, the triggering experience of the original creole speakers is covered by layers of historical mist, and written records of early stages of creole languages are meager. This is not to say that no information is available. Derek Bickerton has done interesting detective work on the early context of Saramaccan. Singler (1988) discusses relevant demographic material for other creole languages, which indicates roughly which languages were available as potential triggers and to what degree. Hilda Koopman (1986) derived some interesting results by considering properties of various West African languages that might have made up part of the trigger for the early stages of Haitian.

Under a research program seeking to find how children acquire their mature linguistic capacity, creole languages can be studied profitably in the context of unusual triggering experiences, and one can expect that the sharp contrast between the initial experiences and the eventual mature capacity, at least in the early stages of creole languages, will provide a useful probe into the nature of triggering experiences in general. However, one finds claims in the literature that go far beyond this, another kind of exceptionalism. It is sometimes claimed that creolization is the key to understanding language change in general. Bickerton (1984a) argued that all creoles had the same structures, differing only in vocabulary. This would be surprising, because creoles evolve out of different pidgins. However, Bickerton expected the study of plantation creoles to yield "special evidence" about the nature of genetic principles, particularly about the value of the unmarked settings of parameters of Universal Grammar.

The particular form of Bickerton's claim has changed somewhat. In his articles published around 1984, he argued that the grammars of creoles were genetically given; this was his Language Bioprogram Hypothesis. He drew an analogy with Herodotus' story about the king who isolated a child and waited to hear the first word the child produced; the child allegedly produced a Phrygian word, *bekos* 'bread,' which convinced the king that this was the oldest language. Bickerton's idea was that children who had no real triggering experience would have to rely almost entirely on their bioprogram, which would thus be manifested directly in creole grammars.

This position was soon abandoned in favor of a weaker position: every option-point of UG has an UNMARKED setting, and the unmarked setting is adopted unless experience instructs the child differently; creoles emerge as children select the unmarked setting for every option-point, or sometimes the setting of the superstrate language (Bickerton 1984b).

Markedness values, like most other aspects of Universal Grammar, have been postulated on the basis of arguments from the poverty of the stimulus. We return to an example that we have appealed to previously (section 4.1, where we were discussing subset relations). Some languages restrict wh- displacement, so that a wh- phrase may be copied as in (1a) within a simple clause (analyzed as (1a′)), but not in (1b), where the wh- phrase is copied from within an embedded clause (analyzed as (1b′)). Rizzi (1982) argued that a locality condition limited movement/copying to cross at most one bounding node, and that bounding nodes vary from language to language. In all languages DPs are bounding nodes and in this first class of languages, both CP and IP are bounding nodes in addition; a wh- phrase cannot be extracted from an embedded clause without crossing both IP and CP (1b′).

(1)   a. What did she read?
        a′. what did $_{IP}$[she ~~did~~ read ~~what~~]
        b. What did she say he read?
        b′. what did $_{IP}$[she ~~did~~ say $_{CP}$[~~what~~ $_{IP}$[he read ~~what~~]
        c. How many did she read books?
        c′. how many did $_{IP}$[she ~~did~~ read $_{DP}$[~~how many~~ books]]

In languages where only IP is a bounding node, i.e. most forms of English, that movement is possible and one hears sentences like (1b) – only one bounding node is crossed, the IP indicated. (1c), on the other hand, does not occur in English-type languages, because the movement would cross two bounding nodes, DP and IP.

In other languages, such as French and Italian, IP is not a bounding node but CP is; in such languages one hears things like (1c), *How many did she read books?*, where only one bounding node is crossed (DP).

Anything you can say in the first class of languages, you can say in English, plus sentences like (1b), and anything you can say in English, you can say in French and Italian, plus sentences like (1c) (French *Combien a-t-elle lu de livres?* 'How many books has she read?' or Italian *Ne ho visti molti corrergli incontro* 'Of them I saw many run toward him' and the long *Tuo fratello, a cui mi domando che storie abbiano raccontato, era molto preoccupato*, 'your brother, to whom I wonder which stories they told, was very troubled'). So the languages are in a superset relation. Languages with DP, IP, and CP as bounding nodes represent the "smallest" languages, English the next, and French and Italian the largest.

This means that there are markedness relations, where children begin with the least marked setting and learn to adopt more marked settings.[2] If the starting point, the least marked setting, is where both IP and CP are bounding nodes, then the English-speaking child can "learn" to go to the next level of markedness, where only IP is a bounding node, and this is learned by experiencing sentences like (1b). Italian and French children can go the next level of markedness, "learning" that IP is not a bounding node as a result of hearing sentences of a kind that occur in Italian and French (1c). The most restricted languages, which do not allow wh- items to be extracted from a subordinate clause, represent the least marked case, and then we can account for the learning on the part

---

[2] The notion of markedness originated in the work of the Prague school, particularly in the writings of Nikolai Trubetzkoy and Roman Jakobson. They thought of markedness in what we would call E-language terms: unmarked values are attested in most languages and acquired first. Here we adapt the notion in I-language terms, reflecting properties of UG.

of children who come to speak some form of English, Italian, and French. We can point to primary data that trigger each value. If, on the other hand, there were no ranking among these values, we would not be able to point to primary data that trigger each grammar. There would be no basis for determining that both IP and CP were bounding nodes unless a child knew that sentences like (1b,c) did not occur; but evidence that sentences do not occur, negative data, are not part of the primary linguistic data that trigger the development of grammars, as we discussed; children learn only from positive data, from things they hear.

Given this ranking among grammatical properties, we can see that Bickerton's prime example of a "radical creole," Saramaccan, has a marked setting for at least one option-point. Saramaccan is like English in that wh- items can be extracted from subordinate clauses.

Supposing that we had no evidence along these lines from Saramaccan, I would see no reason to expect only unmarked settings in "radical" creoles. Such an expectation presupposes that marked settings require access to more extensive experience, and perhaps to fairly exotic data, and that this is not available to the first speakers of a creole. This presupposition seems to me to be unwarranted. One can easily imagine a marked setting being triggered by readily available data, even in the first forms of a creole. For example, suppose that Bickerton is right and that every option-point has an unmarked setting. One option is that a DP consists of a D and NP, with the order to be fixed depending on the language to which the child is exposed. Suppose, with Bickerton, that one of those orders is marked. The marked cue (say, NP–D) would be established on the basis of data which would be available every minute – expressions such as *horse that* and *trees two*.

However, that raises the question of why one would want to say that either of the cues, D–NP or NP–D, should represent a marked value. The same point could be made for the cues that put a complement in front of its verb or behind it, object–verb or verb–object; why should one of these cues be marked? Why are they not equipotential? It is hard to see that specifying that one value is marked would contribute to solving any poverty-of-stimulus problem, which is the rationale for all properties of the linguistic genotype, including the markedness properties of Rizzi's locality condition.

Roberts (1998a) also argues that generally creoles have unmarked values. Specifically he claims that they lack the V-to-I movement we discussed in section 5.2, because the movement represents a marked value (a strong feature, in his terms), and this despite movement in the lexifier language. It is not surprising, of course, that English-based creoles lack V-to-I, since English lacks it. Also, it is not surprising that French-based creoles may lack it, because the most robust evidence for V-to-I in French, namely V-in-C, is limited to contexts where the subject is a pronoun: *Lisez-vous ces journaux?* 'Do you read these newspapers?' but not **Lisent les ouvriers ces journaux?* 'Do the workers read these newspapers?' If V-to-I is less common in creoles than one expects, that might be a function of problems in recognizing the cue, $_I[V]$, in the kind of restricted input that early speakers have.

It is known that children have some difficulty in recognizing these structures even in languages where they seem to be somewhat transparent. That difficulty is manifested in children's use of optional infinitives in many languages, forms that adult speakers do not use and for which children have no models (Wexler 1994). Examples from Dutch are (2). Children hear adult forms like *Pappa wasst schoenen* 'Daddy washes shoes,' *Pappa doet weg kranten* 'Daddy throws newspapers away,' where the verb is finite and in second position, but produce (2a,b) respectively, where the verb is not raised as in the language they hear but is in non-finite form and in its original position.

(2)   a. Pappa   schoenen   wassen.
          Daddy   shoes   wash
       b. Pappa   kranten   weg   doen.
          Daddy   newspapers   away   does

On the matter of UG biases and creole evidence for them, consider Berbice Dutch, a better-worked-out example where the debate can be sharpened. A striking property of this Guyanese creole is that it has subject–verb–object order while its source languages, Dutch and the Kwa language Eastern Ijo, are both underlyingly object–verb and verb-second. Roberts (1998a) takes this to illustrate the fact that subject–verb–object order represents an unmarked option and that creoles generally adopt unmarked values. A cue-based, degree-0 approach to acquisition would tackle things differently.

Dutch is the lexifier language for this creole, the language providing most of the vocabulary, but Ijo provides a high proportion of the basic vocabulary, some morphological material (including the verbal ending *-te* 'past' and the nominal ending *-apu* 'plural'), and some syntactic patterns (e.g. locative postpositions such as *war ben*, house in, 'in the house'). Dutch and Ijo have underlying object–verb order but verb–object order often occurs in matrix clauses because of the verb-movement operation that moves the verb to I and then to an initial C position, yielding verb-second order in the way we discussed in chapter 6. Our theory of constituent structure demands that verbs be generated adjacent to their complements, either right-adjacent or left-adjacent. A degree-0 learner resolves the verb-order option on the basis of unembedded data that reveal the position of the verb, as argued in Lightfoot (1991) and in chapter 6 here. In Dutch these data are the position of separable particles (3a), negation elements (3b), certain adverbs (3c), and clause-union structures (3d), each of which mark the underlying position of the verb to the right of its complement.[3]

---

[3] When we discussed this in chapter 6, we did not discuss the position of negative markers (3b) and adverbs (3c).

(3)   a. Jan belt de hoogleraar op.
           'John calls the professor up.'
        b. Jan   bezoekt de   hoogleraar niet.
           John   visits   the professor   not
        c. Jan belt de hoogleraar soms/morgen op.
           'John calls the professor up sometimes/tomorrow.'
        d. Jan moet de hoogleraar opbellen.
           'John must call up the professor.'

Furthermore, there are non-finite constructions in colloquial Dutch, which manifest object–verb order directly in unembedded contexts (4).

(4)   a. En ik maar fietsen repareren.
           'I ended up repairing bicycles.'
        b. Hand uitsteken.
           hand outstretch 'signal'
        c. Jantje koekje hebben?
           'Johnnie has a cookie?'
        d. Ik de vuilnisbak buiten zetten? Nooit.
           'Me put the garbage out? Never.'

Ijo has similar properties, often showing verb–object order in matrix clauses, despite having original object–verb order (Kouwenberg 1992). In each language children identify the verb-order cue on the basis of indirect evidence in unembedded domains. If that indirect evidence is obscured in some way, children may not be able to identify the old $_{VP}$[XP V] cue and may, instead, find the $_{VP}$[V XP] cue expressed more robustly. That is what happened toward the end of the Old English period, as we saw in section 6.2.

We can understand this in terms of cue-based acquisition: the cue for XP–V order is $_{VP}$[XP V], where the V may be deleted after copying. In each language, children set the verb-order parameter on the basis of evidence in unembedded domains; the evidence may be indirect and show that the original, displaced verb was to the right of the direct object. This is necessarily the case for a degree-0 learner confronting a consistently verb-second language, because in simple, unembedded domains verbs are consistently moved to C and are pronounced in that position. Hence the role of indirect evidence. So (3a) contains the structure *Jan belt $_{VP}$[de hoogleraar op~~belt~~]*; the child knows that this is the structure by virtue of knowing that *opbellen* is a phrasal verb and that *belt* must therefore have originated in a position to the right of *op* and been copied from there. Similarly the negative *niet* occurs to the right of the direct object and marks the position from which the verb has moved (3b). In this way, the child finds instances of the $_{VP}$[XP V] cue in unembedded domains in Dutch. If the evidence for the position of the deleted verb is obscured in some way, the PLD would fail to some extent to express the cue for object–verb order.

In the case of Berbice Dutch, if the first speakers did not have robust evidence about the distribution of separable particles, or if negative elements were no longer retained in their original postverbal position (marking the original position of the verb), or if clause union was not triggered in the same way as in Dutch, then there would arise a situation comparable to that of late Old English: there would no longer be adequate data to require the $_{VP}$[XP V] cue.

In that event, we would understand the emergence of Berbice Dutch analogously to the emergence of verb–object order in Middle English. Negation, for example, works differently in Ijo and Dutch. In Dutch the negative element occurs to the right of an object DP, marking the position from which the verb is displaced, but in Ijo the negative particle "is adjoined directly to the verb in its proposition-negating role" (Smith, Robertson, & Williamson 1987) and moves with it, as in Old English (5).

(5)   Á nimi-γá.
        I know not

Ijo provided the negative for the creole, *kane*, which is a clitic attached to the verb, and because Ijo provided the basis for negation patterns, one of the Dutch indicators of the position of the deleted verb was obscured.

We lack good records for the early stages of Berbice Dutch, and therefore it is hard to be more precise and to show exactly how the primary data failed to express sufficiently the $_{VP}$[XP V] cue. Lack of good records is a general problem for work on the early stages of these kinds of historical creoles. However, the negation example is suggestive and shows that one indicator of underlying object–verb order may be nullified if the other language is dominant in the relevant aspect. Conversely, Dutch may have been dominant in an area of grammar that expressed the cue for the position of the deleted verb in Ijo. Of course, if children are not degree-0 learners, then the $_{VP}$[XP V] cue would be expressed, because this is the standard order for embedded domains in both Dutch and Ijo. In fact, we know that early learners of Berbice Dutch acquired verb–object order and therefore were unaffected by this embedded-clause evidence, as expected if they were degree-0 learners, searching for cues only in simple structures.

Indeed, if children learn only from simple domains, the creole's verb–object order is less mysterious: cue seekers who are degree-0 learners are insensitive to embedded domains, where there would otherwise be much evidence for object–verb order in each of the languages to which they were exposed. Instead, they rely on indirect evidence from unembedded domains, and minor shifts in those patterns must have entailed a different setting for the verb-order cues. Consequently, one can understand how a creole might emerge with quite different properties from both the languages on which it is based, if one assumes that the relevant data for language acquisition are structurally limited and that some of the simple data might be analyzed differently by children as a result of the contact situation.

It is not difficult to see how a degree-0, cue-based learner might acquire a verb–object grammar when the source grammars are object–verb and verb-second, and we do not need to say that there is a UG bias in favor of verb–object order or that creoles always manifest unmarked cues. Verb-second grammars generate simple clauses that may begin with a subject DP, an object DP, a PP or an adjectival or adverbial phrase, but in practice subject–verb is by far the most common order. Statistical studies on a variety of European verb-second languages consistently show about 70 percent subject–verb order in informal conversation (Lightfoot 1993). If it is the subject that is most often displaced to initial position, there would be frequent verb–object order in the E-language, as in the Dutch *Jan bezoekt de hoogleraar* 'John visits the professor' (6).

(6)   Jan bezoekt $_{IP}$[~~Jan~~ $_{VP}$[de hoogleraar ~~bezoekt~~]].

Creole children, like all other children, scan their environment for cues. They interpret what they hear, heterogeneous or impoverished though it may be, as expressing cues and they converge on grammars accordingly. They are not subject to any bias built into UG of the type that Bickerton and Roberts have suggested. So new languages may emerge rapidly and fully formed despite unusual, polyglot experiences, and this view receives striking support from recent work on signed languages, as we shall see in the next section.

There are other approaches that treat creoles as a special type of language. One treats them as directly reflecting universal semantic structures; another treats them as the crystalization of some stage in the development of second-language learning, because the first creole speakers do not have sufficient access to a model and thus arrive at an approximative system; another regards them as reflecting a simplified baby-talk provided by speakers of European languages; another derives the similarity among different creole languages from the common communicative requirements imposed by the plantations on the slaves, who did not have a common language of their own. These and other approaches were surveyed in Muysken (1988).

Muysken pointed to some general properties of creole languages: preverbal particles, a simple morphology, and subject–verb–object order, as in (7).

(7)   a. Wanpela man i   bin   skulim mi long Tok Pisim. (Tok Pisin)
           one   man PR ANT teach me in   Tok Pisin
           'A man was teaching me in Tok Pisin.'
        b. Sō   mō   ka   ta   toka   pálmu. (Senegal Kriol)
           one   hand NEG   HAB   touch   palm
           'One hand can't touch its palm.'
        c. M te   pu   bay   lazā. (Haitian)
           I   ANT   MD   give   money
           'I had to give the money.'

The prevalence of preverbal particles in creole languages played an important role in shaping Bickerton's Language Bioprogram Hypothesis. Where these particles do not exist in the source languages but represent innovations in the creole, they may be supposed to reflect some sort of ill-understood tendency on the part of children to analyze primary data in terms of preverbal particles. Where the particles reflect properties of one of the source languages, one may ask why these items are attainable but elements of inflectional morphology are not. Put differently: why do elements of inflectional morphology require a more robust triggering experience than is generally available to the first speakers of a creole language? We may learn something about this by considering the way in which inflectional systems may be lost in non-creole languages when children are exposed to multiple systems. We indicated in the last chapter that English inflections were radically simplified, many endings being lost, when children were exposed to both the indigenous morphology and the somewhat different Scandinavian inflections; something like that may be a factor in the simple inflections of creole languages.

However, if we do not understand in detail why inflectional morphology is so impoverished in creole languages, we do understand some of the consequences. In earlier chapters it was noted that morphological properties help to identify various cues with widespread syntactic consequences. As Muysken discusses, the absence of inflectional morphology entails that creoles based on Spanish and Portuguese show no null-subject option and no subject–verb inversion, which are dependent on a rich morphology. Consider (8).

(8)   a. E   ta   kome. (Papiamentu)
           he   ASP   eat
           'He is eating.' (cf. Spanish *él está comiendo*)
        b. *Ta   kome.
           ASP eat (cf. Spanish *está comiendo*)
        c. *Ta   kome Maria.
           ASP eat   Maria (cf. Spanish *está comiendo Maria*)

The uniformity of verb–object order is interesting, particularly when it does not reflect properties of the source languages. It is not surprising that English and French creoles have verb–object order, since that order occurs in the superstrate languages. However, some explanation is required for creoles based on Spanish and Portuguese, which show frequent verb–subject–object order, and for those based on Dutch, which has underlying object–verb order. The explanation might be found in the substrate languages, if they show verb–object order. But Hilda Koopman (1984) has argued that many of the relevant languages of the West African peoples from which the slaves were drawn had object–verb order, like Dutch, along with a verb-fronting operation. If they also had verb-second operations in matrix clauses like Dutch and Ijo, then our notion that primary data that trigger grammars are drawn only from unembedded domains may help us understand why children acquired verb–object systems in certain contexts, as we have just discussed.

Although we know little of the primary data to which early creole speakers had access, there is no reason to believe that there is a qualitative difference in the acquisition of the first stages of a creole and the acquisition of Dutch and Ijo under usual circumstances. For example, Koopman (1986) considered various aspects of Haitian and showed that they reflected properties either of French or of a cluster of West African Kru and Kwa languages. She thereby argued against the notion that creoles are not influenced by the structural properties of substrate languages; by focusing on general West African properties she avoided the danger of postulating substrate influence by arbitrarily invoking one particular language, like Yoruba, when one could not show that its speakers were dominant among the slave communities as the creole emerged.

Koopman argued that although the phonetic shapes of Haitian verbs are clearly derived from French, many of their selectional properties differ from those of French and are strikingly similar to those observed in West African languages. For example, one finds double-object constructions (*Give Kim the book*) in Haitian and the West African languages but not in French; Haitian and the West African languages lack subject-raising verbs, which occur in French (e.g. *sembler: Jean semble aimer le soleil* 'John seems to like the sun'); Haitian and the West African languages lack infinitival indirect questions and infinitival relatives, in contrast with French (*Je ne sais pas que faire* 'I don't know what to do,' *Il a quelque chose à boire* 'He has something to drink,' *Elle n'a rien avec quoi réparer sa voiture* 'She has nothing with which to fix her car'); French modal verbs (*pouvoir, devoir*, etc.) are followed by an infinitive, whereas the corresponding verbs in Haitian and some West African languages may select either an infinitive or a tensed complement (the Kru languages have ONLY tensed complements to modal verbs). Koopman also points out that some Haitian verbs, for which there are no equivalents in the West African languages, have the same properties as French verbs. Also, the order of heads and their complements coincides with that of French and not with those of West African languages, which often have mixed or head-final properties. Haitian numerals occur prenominally, as in French, whereas West African numerals uniformly occur postnominally. Koopman found only one way in which Haitian resembled neither French nor the West African languages: besides the pleonastic pronoun *li*, Haitian has a zero pleonastic pronoun for certain contexts, in contrast with French and the West African languages (*Semble pleuvoir* 'It seems to be raining').

The earliest form of Haitian was a pidgin, a contact language, which made up some of the triggering experience, the ambient E-language, for children as they scanned for their cues and acquired their I-language. This pidgin was spoken by African slaves, by fugitives, and by some of the free population, as a second language, alongside their native African languages. Koopman notes that a well-known strategy in second-language learning and in language-contact situations is relexification: the transfer of lexical properties from the native language to the target language. So if the primary data that made up the triggering experience for subsequent forms of Haitian contained West African properties, via relexification, one can understand the correspondences between Haitian and the West African languages that Koopman observed.

This scenario, accounting for lexical parallelisms, does not explain the absence of infinitival relatives and indirect questions (above). One must claim that devices generating such forms were not triggered by the contact language. It is likely that the primary data that triggered the formation of Haitian lacked such infinitival forms or lacked them with sufficient robustness: these constructions do not occur in the West African languages and are not very frequent in French, and furthermore they occur only in restructured (clause-union) embedded clauses. Consequently, it seems plausible to claim that they would not have been robust enough in children's experience to have any long-term effect.

If one views the genesis of creole languages in this way, focusing on familiar properties of Universal Grammar and trying to tease out likely properties of the simple structures in the ambient E-language, there is no need to invoke any special procedures or devices. In particular, there is no reason to believe with Bickerton and Roberts that the cues in creole languages are generally unmarked or determined by the superstrate language. Creole languages may have failed to incorporate oddities like historical relic forms or infrequent constructions, which require a lot of exposure for learning, but that is a very different claim. The properties of Haitian suggest that there was a fairly well-developed contact language, influenced on a continuing basis by the substrate languages. This conforms to the findings of Sankoff & Laberge (1973), who pointed to an increasing complexity in the pidgin Tok Pisin before it was acquired by native speakers (i.e. before it triggered child I-languages). Also, Koopman notes that "because of high mortality, low birthrate, mass suicides, and mass desertions on the labor intensive sugar plantations, massive importation of slaves took place. New speakers of African languages were thus arriving all the time . . . These circumstances leave plenty of space and time for African languages to be spoken and learned" (1986: 253–254).

The early stages of creole languages are particularly interesting in that sharp contrasts between the triggering experience and children's mature capacities show how normal, rich systems of knowledge may arise on exposure to polyglot, impoverished input. This is surprising for somebody who believes that children need access to rich and complex structures for a normal grammar to emerge, but less so for somebody arguing that the emergence of grammars depends on access only to simple structures expressed robustly in the ambient E-language.

From this perspective, there is no reason to invoke special learning strategies for creole languages, or to argue that creoles have a special status, reflecting Universal Grammar in a direct or privileged fashion.

7.2   Signed languages

Work on creoles is limited by the sketchiness of the data available for the earliest stages, but the view that new languages emerge rapidly and fully formed despite impoverished input receives striking support from work on signed languages. The big fact here is that only about 10 percent of deaf children are born to deaf parents who can provide early exposure to a natural sign language like ASL (American Sign Language).

Much of the work on signed language has focused on ASL, used in North America, but work has also been carried out on British Sign Language, Japanese Sign Language, and many others. There are hundreds of distinctive sign languages around the world and, in developing countries, deaf people may use the sign language of educators from other countries. For example, some deaf people in Madagascar use Norwegian sign language.

The work has shown that, where there are communities of interacting deaf people, there are rich, grammatically complex signed languages that are quite different from the spoken languages of the area and different from and mutually incomprehensible with the signed languages of other areas. To this extent, natural signed languages are the same as natural spoken languages acquired in the same way. This is striking, because even if signed languages are acquired in the usual way by children in the first few years of life, they are often acquired under very different circumstances if only a small minority are born into signing homes.

Few deaf children are born to deaf parents using a native signed language, and the vast majority of deaf children are either kept away from other signers by educators in the "oralist" tradition, who want them to master lipreading and speech, or they are exposed initially to fragmentary signed systems that have not been internalized well by their primary models.

Oralist methods dominated US deaf education until the 1960s, offering intense training in sound sensitivity, lipreading, and speech production. These programs actively discouraged the use of signed language, on the grounds that learning a sign language interferes with learning a spoken language. It is very rare for children with severe to profound hearing loss to achieve the kind of proficiency in a spoken language that hearing children achieve routinely. These methods were undermined by the pioneering work of William Stokoe, who published the first analyses of ASL, showing it to have the richness of natural spoken languages (Stokoe 1960).

The fragmentary signs encountered by deaf children born to hearing parents are often drawn from some form of Manually Coded English (MCE), which maps English into a visual/gestural modality and is very different from ASL (which is not English-based and does not resemble British Sign Language). Goldin-Meadow & Mylander (1990) show that these are not natural systems and they offer a useful review of work on how deaf children go beyond their models in such circumstances and NATURALIZE the system, altering the code and inventing new forms that are more consistent with what one finds in natural languages. Goldin-Meadow & Mylander show that children exposed to models who use morphological markers irregularly and spasmodically, nonetheless regularize the markers, using them consistently and "in a system of contrasts . . . akin to the system that characterizes the productive lexicon in ASL" (1990: 341).

Elissa Newport (1998, Singleton & Newport 2004) extends these ideas by reporting work on a single child, Simon, showing how he comes to use morphology consistently and "deterministically," where his models used it inconsistently and "probabilistically." She notes that Simon does not create "an entirely new language from his own innate specifications," as the Language Bioprogram Hypothesis of Bickerton (1984a) would suggest. "Rather, he appears to be following the predominant tendencies of his input, but sharpens them, extends them, and forces them to be internally consistent." Inconsistent input, then, presents no problem for young children, who simply generalize across-the-board. However, adult learners, on the other hand, are seriously impeded by inconsistent input, she reports, and they often perform even more inconsistently than their models.

Simon's primary models, when he was young, were his parents, also deaf; they had acquired ASL only in their late teens, and consequently acquired it inaccurately, attaining a kind of pidgin. He attended a school where none of the teachers or other students knew ASL. Remarkably, although Simon's access to ASL was initially only via his parents' very defective version of it, his own language was much closer to ASL than theirs; he seems not to have been misled by his parents' grammatical "noise," and seems to have pursued his own private creolization.

ASL verbs are morphologically complex, with seven to fifteen morphemes along the lines that linguists have found in American Indian and indigenous Australian languages. A verb of motion might have a morpheme indicating the path (straight, arc, or circular), the manner (bouncing, rolling, etc.), the semantic category of the subject (human, vehicle), and others. Simon's parents used many of these morphemes but often not in the ASL fashion. Simon reorganized what he heard and had a cleaner, more organized system, producing his own version of ASL, with a structure more like that of other natural languages.

Work by Supalla (1990) on MCE casts more light on this. MCE systems were invented by educators to teach English to deaf children. They rely on a lexicon borrowed heavily from ASL. However, while ASL morphology is generally NON-LINEAR, with simultaneous spatial devices serving as morphological markers, MCE morphology generally is LINEAR and uses invented signs that reproduce the morphological structure of English; those signs precede or follow the root word. The English *take/took* alternation is an example of non-linear morphology and *walk/walked* is an instance of a linear alternation, where the verb stem precedes the tense marker. Supalla studied Signed Exact English (SEE2), the dominant version of MCE, where all bound morphemes are invented and based on English. For example, the SEE2 suffix -ING involves the single handshape "I"; the suffix -s (for singular present tense or plural) is a static upright "S" handshape in the neutral signing space; the -MENT, -TION, -NESS, and -AGE suffixes are all syllabic, /M/, /S/, /N/, and /G/ respectively. Of the 49 English affixes that have an equivalent in SEE2, 44 consist of at least one distinct syllable. They are strictly linear and, importantly, phonologically independent of the root.

Supalla cites several studies showing that SEE2 morphology fails to be attained well by children, who do not use many of the markers that they are exposed to and use other markers quite inconsistently and differently from their models. He focuses particularly on deaf children who are exposed only to SEE2 with no access to ASL, and he found that they restructure SEE2 morphology into a new system. The SEE2 "bound morphemes were rejected and replaced with devised forms. Moreover, in the devised forms, the affixation type was predominantly non-linear in nature . . . not exactly like that of ASL, [but] formationally within the constraints of affixation in ASL" (1990: 46). Unlike in Newport's study, children did not simply generalize markers that were used inconsistently in the input. Rather, there were particular problems with inflectional morphemes and children invented a new system.

Supalla's approach to this was to postulate a Modality-Constraints Model, which limits signed languages to non-linear morphology, while spoken languages tend to have linear morphology. However, this approach seems suspect. First, the correlation does not hold reliably: spoken languages often have non-linear morphology (e.g. the *take/took* alternation of English above), and non-linear morphology is comprehensive in Semitic and other languages; and Supalla (1990: 20) points out that ASL has some linear morphology, e.g. agentive (analogous to the English -er suffix) and reduplicative markings. Second, the model fails to account for the fact that SEE2-type morphology does not exist even in spoken languages. What is striking about the inflectional morphemes of SEE2 is that they "are produced in terms of timing and formation as separate signs" (1990: 52). Supalla shows that they are not subject to assimilation;

they are phonologically independent, articulated distinctly, even emphasized. In general, this kind of phonological independence is characteristic of free morphemes but not of inflectional, bound morphemes (linear or not), and the system seems not to be learned by children.

Clearly this cannot be modeled by any learning device rating the generative capacity of grammars against the set of expressions experienced, because, quite simply, the input is not matched. Not even close. Furthermore, it is not enough to say that SEE2 morphology just violates UG constraints, because that would not account for the way in which children devise new forms. Nor is it enough to appeal to a UG characterization of functional categories. More is needed from UG. The unlearnability of the SEE2 morphology suggests that children are cue-based learners, programmed to scan for clitic-like, unstressed, highly assimilable inflectional markers. That is what they find standardly in spoken languages and in natural signed languages like ASL. If experience fails to provide such markers, then markers are invented. Children seize appropriate kinds of elements that can be interpreted as inflectional markers. In signed languages there seems to be at least a strong statistical tendency to reinterpret linear elements in this fashion.[4] It would be interesting to see work examining how this reinterpretation takes place and how new morphology is devised when children are exposed to unlearnable systems like SEE2. This would flesh out the general perspective of Goldin-Meadow & Mylander (1990) and Newport (1998).

Goldin-Meadow, for example, differentiates mothers' gestures from those of their children, showing that "neither the way that parents respond to the children's gestures, nor the gestures that the parents produce when talking to the children can explain the structure found in the deaf children's gestures" (2003: 160–161). She distinguishes RESILIENT linguistic properties from FRAGILE (2003: ch. 16). Resilient properties appear in a child's communication whether or not the child is exposed to a natural language model, for example consistent word order and consistent inflections. Fragile properties, however, need more specific and particular environmental triggering.

Deaf children are often exposed to artificial input and we know a good deal about that input and about how it is reanalyzed by language learners. Therefore, the acquisition of signed languages under these circumstances offers a

---

[4] Supalla (1990: 50–51) hints at an intriguing explanation for this tendency to non-linear morphology. He points to studies showing that individual ASL signs take about 50 percent longer to produce than English words, but comparable propositions take about the same amount of time. This is achieved by having signs with more morphemes per sign and non-linear morphological structure. This could be explained if there is a natural rhythm to natural language, if language processing takes place naturally at a certain speed, and if a language with ASL-type signs and a linear, affixal morphology would just be too slow.

wonderful opportunity to understand more about abrupt language change, cre-olization, cue-based acquisition, and how new languages can erupt out of craters of heterogeneity.

One particularly dramatic case is the emergence of Nicaraguan Sign Language, as described by Kegl, Senghas, & Coppola (1998). Linguists have effectively been able to document the birth of a new human language. Until a generation ago, government policy under the Somoza dictatorship (1934–1979) treated the deaf as subhuman and kept deaf people isolated from each other. Older people, brought up under that regime, have only primitive homesigns and are known as *no-sabes* 'know nothings.' However, when the Sandinista govern-ment took over in 1979, they provided schools for the deaf and therefore places where they could come together and form a community. The largest of these schools, in Managua, drew over 500 deaf children within a few years. There are now about 800 deaf signers in Nicaragua, ranging from infants to fifty years old. The schools pursued oralist goals, training children to lipread and to speak, with the usual dismal results. Meanwhile the children were inventing their own sign system, pooling the gestures used with their families at home. This settled into a kind of pidgin, called Lenguaje de Señas Nicaragüense (LSN) and used these days by deaf adults, who were born before 1970 and developed LSN when they were ten or older. Everybody uses it differently and with varying degrees of fluency.

However, children born after 1970, who learned to sign in their first few years of life, are very different and use a full-blown system so different from LSN that it goes by a different name, Idioma de Señas Nicaragüense (ISN). This seems to be a signed creole with the usual properties of natural languages, used fluently and consistently, and created rapidly when the younger children were exposed to the pidgin signing of the older children. It looks very different from the pidgin LSN: it uses less space and signs are restricted almost entirely to the limbs, head, and upper torso. The use of the two hands is more asymmetric. Signs are made simultaneously. The communication has a distinct rhythm and flow. Children use ISN for the usual purposes, expressing anger, jokes, stories, poems, lies, and life histories; and linguists who became aware of these developments in the 1980s have been able to watch and study the eruption of a well-defined, new language.

Senghas, Kita, & Özyürek (2004) studied cohorts of ISN signers according to the year that they were first exposed to the language and found that they differed in expressions that describe complex motion events, such as rolling down a hill or climbing up a wall. They considered the kind of phenomena that Newport investigated with Simon (above). Motion events may incorporate the manner of the movement (rolling) and the path (downwards). When speakers describe such events, they often gesture to represent the movement iconically, the gestures indicating manner and path simultaneously.

Languages, in contrast, typically encode manner and path in separate elements, combined according to the rules of the particular language. For example, English produces one word to express manner (rolling) and another to express path (down), and assembles them into the sequence "rolling down." Signing that dissects motion events into separate manner and path elements, and assembles them into a sequence, would exhibit the segmentation and linearization typical of developed languages, and unlike the experience of motion itself. (Senghas, Kita, & Özyürek 2004: 1780)

So this is a difference between ordinary gesturing and linguistic signing. Essentially, they found that the oldest signers tended to use the simultaneous representations typical of gestures, a single hand movement, while the younger signers, the ones who developed their language at younger ages, used sequential manner-only and path-only segments typical of natural language. They show ISN changing so that it acquired the discrete, combinatorial nature that is a hallmark of natural language.

Senghas, Kita, & Özyürek observe that "elements and sequencing provide the building blocks for linguistic constructions (such as phrases and sentences) whose structure assigns meaning beyond the simple sum of the individual words" (2004: 1781), as we observed in our discussion of the ambiguity of *I saw old men and women* and *I saw a man with a telescope* in section 3.1; there we saw the two meanings each associated with a distinct structure. The difference between the older and younger signers indicates what young children can do and adolescents cannot. "Such an age effect is consistent with, and would partially explain, the preadolescent sensitive period for language acquisition" (2004: 1781), the so-called "critical period" that we will discuss in section 8.1. ISN is a young language, recently created by children, and its development reveals children's learning mechanisms. Senghas, Kita, & Özyürek conclude that "even where discreteness and hierarchical combination are absent from the language environment, human learning abilities are capable of creating them anew" (2004: 1782).

What is striking about the Nicaraguan case is that there were no substrate languages, no preexisting signed systems with any communal standing nor any spoken language that was relevant. Therefore, since no ambient languages had any influence, similarities between ISN and other languages must be due to other forces, to what is called variously the Language Bioprogram or Universal Grammar. Kegl, Senghas, & Coppola conclude that "the source of language is within us but that the conditions for its emergence depend crucially on community" (1998: 223).[5]

---

[5] Another new sign language has emerged *ex nihilo* over the last seventy years. Al Sayyid Bedouin Sign Language is used in a village of 3,500 people in the Negev Desert of Israel; it is not related to Israeli or Jordanian sign language, and it has a word order quite different from the surrounding spoken languages. The villagers are descendants of one founder, who arrived 200 years ago from Egypt and married a local woman. Two of the couple's five children were deaf, as are about 150 members of the village today (Sandler, Meir, Padden, & Aronoff 2005).

The work in Nicaragua shows that the community is important; it was only when there was a community that ISN began to develop, reflecting natural I-languages, triggered in childhood in the usual fashion. The shaping effects of community were identified by Humboldt (1836/1971: 36) and Goldin-Meadow (2003: 222) points to work on chaffinches. If young chaffinches are taken from the nest after five days and reared by hand in isolation from other chaffinches, each develops its own song but idiosyncratically and unlike normal chaffinch songs. However, if the young chaffinches are raised as a group, isolated from adult birds, they develop a communal song, unlike anything recorded in the wild but one that sounds somewhat like typical chaffinch song, divided into similar phrases (Thorpe 1957). So developing song without an adult model but in a community of other young chaffinches leads to something that has more structure than the songs of birds raised in isolation.

7.3   Conclusion

I submit that work on abrupt creolization, the acquisition of signed languages, and on catastrophic historical change shows us that children do not necessarily converge on grammars that match input. This work invites us to think of children as cue-based learners: they do not rate the generative capacity of grammars against the sets of expressions they encounter but rather they scan the environment for necessary elements of I-language in unembedded domains, and build their grammars cue by cue. The cues are not in the input directly, but they are derived from the input, in the mental representations yielded as children understand and "parse" the E-language to which they are exposed. So a cue-based child acquires a verb–object grammar not by evaluating grammars against sets of sentences but on exposure to structures that must contain $_{VP}[V\ XP]$. This requires analyzing the XP as in the VP, i.e. knowing that it is preceded by a verb. $_{VP}[V\ XP]$ is a cue and the cue must be represented robustly in the mental representations resulting from parsing the PLD.

Under this view, one would expect there to be grammatical changes that are abrupt, and one would expect languages to differ from each other in bumpy ways. We may seek to quantify the degree to which cues are expressed by the PLD, showing that abrupt, catastrophic change takes place when those cues are expressed below some threshold of robustness and are eliminated.

We can produce productive models for historical change along these lines, relating changes in simple cues to large-scale grammatical shifts, and therefore our results have consequences for the way in which we study language acquisition.

Alongside creolization contexts, there are other unusual triggering experiences that shed light on the way in which cues are identified. In extreme cases there is no triggering experience, as with "wolf children" raised by animals or raised by humans who have deprived them of the usual physical, social, and linguistic experiences. Examples are the Californian woman, Genie, deprived of normal human interactions through adolescence (Curtiss 1977), or the wild boy of Aveyron portrayed in François Truffaut's movie *L'enfant sauvage*, or deaf children raised in non-signing homes. Sometimes the triggering experience is more diverse and heterogeneous than usual, as when children are raised in multilingual homes. Or there may be an exceptional amount of degenerate input, as in the case of children raised monolingually by immigrant parents who do not fully command the language in which the children are being raised. We will understand more of these unusual conditions as we understand better the less unusual, more regular conditions. That is more likely to be productive than treating each of these kinds of cases as exceptional, subject to special principles of creolization, or special principles of signed language acquisition, and so on.

Since a child's triggering experience is a subset of the total linguistic experience, the research program followed here will gain little from costly experiments in which tape recorders are strapped to the backs of children for long periods, recording what kinds of expressions are uttered around them. The earliest studies of language acquisition had researcher-parents making diaries of their own children's speech, recording the new utterances produced. Diary studies were later amplified by audio and video samples of groups of children. This work is labor-intensive but it has yielded descriptions of what children know at different stages. It is harder to know HOW children come to develop new knowledge. Much experimental work argues that children have adult capacities at the earliest stage they can be tested (Crain & Thornton 1998). That means that we are unlikely to learn from that kind of experimental work what aspects of the input, the ambient E-language, are shaping the emerging system.

On the other hand, I have argued that much can be learned from studying the way in which languages change historically by considering how expressions cease to trigger grammatical elements under certain conditions, becoming obsolete, and how changes arise which appear only to affect embedded clauses. Properly construed, this material can illuminate the way in which grammatical properties emerge and under what conditions new properties emerge. We can never know the details of an individual's relevant experience, but examining historical changes enables us to work at a macro-level, identifying, where we have good records, the gross changes in E-language that may have facilitated the emergence of new systems.

There is much more to be said about the chaotic elements of the environment, about catastrophes that follow from new I-languages, about creolization, and about the development of grammars in general, but studying the way in which new properties emerge suggests that the primary data that serve to trigger grammars are drawn entirely from unembedded binding domains and consist of grammatical cues, pieces of grammatical structure identified one at a time. That provides us with a way of thinking about the emergence of new languages under normal and unusual conditions, a better way than viewing children as evaluating the generative capacity of grammars against inventories of the sentences they experience.

8 A new historical linguistics

8.1 Language change, contingency, and new systems

So languages change, both I-languages and E-language. There is a deep inter-relationship and new languages are always emerging, of both kinds. Adults and children both play roles. The perspective we have developed, particularly the distinction between external E-language and individual I-languages, recasts matters of the role of children and adults, the gradualness of change, directionality, the spread of changes through populations, explanation, and other issues that have been central for traditional historical linguistics; see Janda & Joseph (2003) for a recent survey.

E-language, a group phenomenon, language out there, is amorphous and in constant flux. No two people are exposed to the same E-language and everybody hears different things. E-language is in flux because people say different things and use their grammars differently, both differently from other people and differently themselves over time. Some people use certain constructions provided by their I-language more or less frequently than others, and more or less frequently than themselves at other times or in different contexts. There may be whims and fashions, whereby people take on the speech forms of public figures, popular singers, politicians, or comedians, and certain expressions take on new forces or come to be used more or less frequently. Furthermore, people's speech may change through their lifetime, as one can see by looking at one's own letters written over a period of years. E-language incorporates the output of many I-languages and their varying use, but there is little systematic or predictable about E-language as a whole beyond the general properties of I-languages and their use.

There are many forces at work influencing how people use their grammars, reflecting both conscious and subconscious choices. Several European languages have retained two second-person pronoun forms, one for children, intimates, and social inferiors: *tu* versus *vous* in French, *du* and *Sie* in German, *je* and *U* in Dutch, and *tu* and *Usted* in Spanish. Usage varies and changes over time, and English eliminated a similar distinction between *thou* and *you* and the accompanying verbal forms in *-(e)st* (*Thou shalt*, *Thou shouldest*) in the eighteenth century as a deliberate function of social and political changes taking place at the time. German usage seems to be changing with respect to prenominal modifiers: expressions like *Die im Herbst abgeschlossene Übernahme des Konzerns dient der Firmenexpansion* 'The in fall completed take-over of the business serves the expansion of the company' are giving way increasingly to the "unpacked" *Die Übernahme des Konzerns, die im Herbst abgeschlossen wurde, dient der Firmenexpansion* 'The take-over of the business that was completed in the fall serves the expansion of the company.' One or other form may be favored in particular contexts or in particular editorial practices. Indeed, people's speech may be affected by stylistic modes adopted, for example, for professional purposes. People adopt particular styles for writing obituaries, for presenting legal briefs in court, for speaking to patients in hospitals, for writing letters to shareholders, for composing rap poems, for writing a novel set in medieval times, and those styles may spill over and affect their everyday speech.

None of this results from new I-languages, but it reflects different use of one's internal system, one's I-language. As a result, E-language, the kinds of things that people say, is always in flux; sociolinguists try to track such variations and sometimes they can identify changes in progress by showing differences in usage between generations of speakers (for a classic, Labov 1963 studied generations of speakers on Martha's Vineyard). In this way, people change the ambient E-language through their lifetime, including in adulthood, short of adopting new I-languages.

Indeed, I-languages are quite different and there is good reason to believe that they are formed within a critical period, the first few years of a person's life. This is the period in which elements of sound structure and basic phrase-structure properties are determined, whether the system is object–verb or verb–object, whether the negative particle precedes or follows the head of the inflection phrase, whether a DP may be licensed in a Specifier position and, if so, how; and similarly the computational operations, whether wh- words move, whether verbs move to a higher Inflectional position and, if so, whether they may move on to a higher C position, as early English *Understands Kim chapter 4?* and in "verb-second" languages (section 5.2). Such properties are determined and fixed within the critical period, essentially before the age of puberty, for neurophysiological reasons, and they do not change later.

The critical period was argued for by Lenneberg (1967) and the idea has stood the test of time. It is well known that, with a few rare exceptions, adults cannot acquire a second language with anything like the speed and proficiency of children. We also know from studies of children deprived of normal human interactions that their capacity to acquire the elementary structures of a first language deteriorates dramatically beyond this critical period (Curtiss 1977), while certain aspects of learning are unaffected, such as the acquisition of certain kinds of words, which continues through a person's lifespan. Something similar has been shown in studies of the new Nicaraguan Sign Language (section 7.2). Newport, Bavelier, & Neville (2002) have argued that there is more than one critical period and that different linguistic properties are subject to different internal time constraints. Sociolinguistic studies such as Kerswill (1996) and work on dialect acquisition (Chambers 1992) support the age-sensitivity theories; they show that adult acquisition of new varieties of language does not involve a new grammar or I-language, but a modification of the native system through use. This makes it likely that adults introduce words and idioms into their I-language, but not new structures.

So adults modify their speech through changes in the use of their natively acquired system and that changes the ambient E-language. Slight changes in E-language may have crucial effects on how the next generation of I-languages develops in the brains of young children within the critical period. The usual flux of E-language most commonly does not affect the way in which children acquire their I-language – for long periods structural shifts may not happen – but from time to time E-language may change in a way that triggers the growth of a new grammar. In chapter 4, we developed a model whereby children scan their environment for speech that expresses grammatical cues and they develop their individual I-language accordingly. If E-language crosses some threshold such that cues are expressed differently and a different I-language is triggered, we have a different kind of change, a new I-language.

New I-languages tend to spread through populations quickly, for reasons that are not hard to understand: one child acquires a new I-language, because the ambient E-language is on the cusp of triggering a new system and does just that for this child. Once the first child has grown the first new I-language, that changes the ambient E-language some more, because the new I-grammars generate different kinds of structures and sentences. That makes it more likely that a second and third child within the speech community may acquire the same new I-grammar, with cumulative effects.

There is a gradualness to change and a suddenness. E-language most often changes gradually and chaotically, sometimes word by word, often without being noticed (Humboldt 1836/1971: 43), and primarily through the subconscious choices of adults in the use of their internal systems. I-languages change more quickly and systematically through the acquisition of new systems by children under normal conditions. So new I-languages are introduced quickly across speech communities, bringing a kind of bumpiness into the general gradualness of E-language change, whereby E-language then changes abruptly through the new I-languages being acquired. The changes from object–verb to verb–object (section 6.3) and from verb-raising to Inflection-lowering (section 5.2) took place quickly within speech communities and then across geographical and other communities through wider populations.

New E-language may cue new I-languages, which, in turn, entail new E-language. We have new languages at different levels, children and adults are involved in different ways, and we find never-ending cycles of change, driven ultimately by the fact that people use their grammars creatively, expressively, and idiosyncratically, so that speech is highly individual within the bounds of shared I-language . . . and, of course, shared UG; I-language is shared within a speech community and UG is shared by all humans, across the species.

This means that there are coexisting grammars within speech communities and even within the brains of some individuals, who have multiple competencies. That, in turn, entails oscillation between certain fixed points, particular I-languages, and not random variation. Recent computational work has modeled this in different ways. Colleagues have developed partially parsed computer corpora for various stages of English. Texts are analyzed in terms of their principal syntactic constituents and stored in computers. This permits researchers to test hypotheses against large banks of data, to conduct large-scale statistical studies in short periods, and to model variation between fixed points, showing which authors have which systems at which times. For short, transitional periods, some speakers may have coexisting grammars and that idea has enabled us to understand some variation more productively. I have not focused much on these statistical studies here and the field awaits a good introductory treatment, but Pintzuk (1999) is a good study that exploits the new techniques, which we discussed in chapter 6, and Kroch (1994) discusses some of the key ideas.

Many elaborate statistical studies of varying grammatical patterns were conducted in the nineteenth and twentieth centuries, but the work was painstaking, slow, not always reliable, and it was hard to compare hypotheses with much richness of internal structure, identifying differences in texts from individual speakers. The availability of computerized corpora has had dramatic consequences on the sophistication of diachronic studies and in the quality of results achieved. This has been conspicuous in the biennial Diachronic Generative Syntax (DIGS) meetings, initiated in 1990.

In addition, we can also build computer simulations of the spread of grammars through populations under different hypothetical conditions (Briscoe 2000, Niyogi & Berwick 1997, Pearl 2004, Yang 2002). This enables us to compare different models of language acquisition and change, and to see what kinds of contrasting predictions they make.

Under this view, structural change in I-languages is contingent, resulting from changes in the grammars or in the use of grammars of earlier generations that have the effect of changing the availability of grammatical cues. There is no particular direction to these cycles and the never-ending efforts of historical linguists to find such directions have not been successful; we discussed nineteenth-century quests for universal directions in chapter 2. More recently it has been shown that languages sometimes "grammaticalize" and show distinct words coming to manifest what were formerly purely grammatical functions, prepositions coming to serve as case endings, or verbs like *may* and *must* coming to be Inflectional elements. Conversely, they sometimes undergo "anti-grammaticalization" and employ former prepositions as verbs, as we discussed in sections 2.6, 5.2, and 6.2.

Change is not random, but there is no overall direction to it. Historically related languages show considerable variation in their syntactic properties, and new languages often emerge through divergence, taking different directions. We are dealing with contingent systems, not predictions. Linguists can offer satisfying retrospective explanations of change in some instances, but there is no reason to expect to find a predictive theory of change, offering long-term, linear predictions about what will happen to English in 200 years.

In this way, linguists are like biologists and offer historical-narrative explanations, unlike the predictions of physicists. Ernst Mayr (2004) noted that variability and the genetic program combine to impart a fundamental difference between the organic and inorganic world. The planets move with exquisite predictability, an electron remains an electron, but of the six billion humans, no two are identical.

The emergence of a grammar in a child is sensitive to the initial conditions of the primary linguistic data. If those data shift a little, changing the distribution of cues, there may be significant consequences for internal systems. A new system may be triggered, which generates a very different set of sentences and structures. Even twins, it has been shown, raised in the same households, may converge on different grammars. There is nothing principled to be said about why the set of sentences a child is exposed to should shift slightly; those shifts represent chance, contingent factors.

Changes in languages often take place in clusters and that often indicates a single change at the level of I-language: apparently unrelated superficial changes occur simultaneously or in rapid sequence. We now have a substantial number of well-researched case studies. Such clusters manifest a single theoretical choice that has been taken differently. The singularity of the change is explained by the appropriately defined theoretical choice at the level of I-languages. So the principles of UG and the definition of the cues constitute the laws that delimit change in grammars, defining the available terrain. Any phenomenal change is explained if we show, first, that the linguistic environment has changed in a way that affects the expression of a cue (like $_IV$), and, second, that the new phenomenon (e.g. the obsolescence of *Kim understands not the answer*) must be the way that it is because of some principle(s) of the theory and the lack of $_IV$ structures. In other words, grammatical change is contingent, due to local causes, new triggering experiences, but takes place within the limits of UG.

What we cannot explain, in general, is why the linguistic environment should have changed in the first place (as emphasized by Lass 1997 and by others).

Why should the use of periphrastic *do* (*Kim does not understand the answer*) have spread from the southwest of England as verbal inflections were being lost (section 5.2)? Environmental changes are often due to what I have called chance factors, effects of borrowing, changes in the frequency of forms, stylistic innovations, which spread through a community and, where we are lucky, are documented by variation studies. Changes of this type need not reflect changes in grammars. But with a theory of language acquisition that defines the range of theoretical choices available to the child (the cues) and specifies how the child may take those choices, one can predict that a child will converge on a certain grammar when exposed to certain environmental elements. This is where prediction is possible, in principle.

We take a synchronic approach to history. We observed in section 5.4 that historical change is a kind of finite-state Markov process: changes have only local causes and, if there is no local cause, there is no change, regardless of the state of the grammar or of the language some time previously. In that way, the emergence of a grammar in an individual child is sensitive to the initial conditions, to the details of the child's experience. So language change is chaotic, in the same way that weather patterns are chaotic. We have as little chance to predict the future course of English as the weather on 17 October next year in Hamburg from what they observe in today's measurements. The historian's explanations are based on the acquisition theory that our synchronic colleagues have devised, and in some cases our explanations are quite tight and satisfying. There are no principles of history and, in this sense, history is an epiphenomenon, a function of many interacting factors.

This constitutes a different take on a number of matters that have been central for historical linguists. Traditional historical linguistics did not achieve the ambitious levels of explanation that its nineteenth-century proponents sought. In order to understand language change more fully, we need to distinguish I-languages from E-language and to work with grammatical theory, principles of language acquisition, language use, social variation, computer models, and with philological sensitivity. The new historical linguistics harmonizes this range of work. If we are generalists in this way, then linguists can attain a level of explanation quite unlike what one finds in historical studies in other domains, such as the history of biological species or political systems.[1]

One of the primary activities of traditional historical linguists has been the reconstruction of proto-languages, hypothetical, unrecorded languages that are supposed to have been the antecedents of attested daughter languages, and we turn now to that work.

---

[1] "We develop theories in historical linguistics of a sophistication quite unheard of in most other fields of history" (Matthews 2003:7).

8.2   Reconstruction

If there are no principles of history and no basis for predicting the long-term future of languages, there would seem to be little basis for working backwards and reconstructing proto-languages, except where there is stasis and the most archaic languages show the same properties. Reconstruction of prehistoric systems has been a major preoccupation of historical linguists, so I now consider how one might make hypotheses about earlier systems, where we have no contemporary records. After all, some physicists seek laws that work both forwards and backwards, time-neutral, enabling us to consider the current state of the universe and to see how it might revert to the primeval Big Bang in a giant reversal of the arrows of physical or thermodynamic processes, and biologists hypothesize ancestral species, which they suppose must have existed at certain periods; Richard Dawkins (2004) has sought to retrace the path of evolution to the origin of life four billion years ago, wondering how evolution might turn out if we could re-run it another time.

Only a small number of the world's languages have any kind of recorded history over more than a few generations, and in no case do records go back more than a few thousand years. From some perspectives, this doesn't matter. There are plenty of grammars to hypothesize and plenty of changes to describe accurately and then to explain within these recorded histories. Explanations for structural changes may be grounded in grammatical theory and careful examination of historical changes, where the goal is explanation for how and why they happened, sometimes leads to innovations in grammatical theory. That has been the focus of the work I have described in this book and analyses of changes have been used to argue for claims not only about grammatical theory but also about language acquisition, that children learn only from simple structures and that acquisition is cue-based. That is not to say, of course, that these propositions could not have been based on other kinds of data, but the fact is that they were based on analyses of historical change. From analyses of historical changes, we have learned things about the nature of the language faculty and about how it develops in children, unhampered by the limited inventory of changes.

The limits on the records of human language history, however, are a problem if one is interested in a full history of human languages, seeking to recover what has been lost. In that case, one might seek to extend the available data about change by reconstructing changes that occurred prehistorically, i.e. before we have attestation in written records. This involves postulating a hypothetical language, a "proto-language," and the changes that mapped that proto-language into the languages that are attested more directly. There are other reasons to seek to reconstruct a proto-language: one can express genetic relationships among languages or learn more about the internal history of an individual language by considering its possible prehistory. In any case, there has been a vast amount of work on the reconstruction of proto-languages. It was a major focus of nineteenth-century linguistics and the enterprise continues to have popular appeal; the most extreme ambitions, reconstructing Nostratic (the supposed ancestor of the Indo-European, Semito-Hamitic, Uralic, Kartvelian, Altaic, and Dravidian families, and sometimes other phyla) and Proto-World have featured in lengthy articles in *The New York Times* and popular magazines in the last few years. This work embarrasses historical linguists who believe that we cannot reconstruct reliably over time-depths of more than a few thousand years. Certainly the greater the time-depth, the more speculative the reconstructions. Whatever the reasons to reconstruct and whatever the popular interest in the enterprise, reconstruction of aspects of Proto-Indo-European (PIE) was one of the great intellectual achievements of the nineteenth century and it is useful to ask what is being reconstructed.

First, let us distinguish two kinds of reconstruction. For Old English, Old Spanish, etc., we have only partial records and we hypothesize and "reconstruct" what M I G H T have also occurred in the language beyond what is recorded. This does not involve change directly; scholars practice this kind of reconstruction extensively, and teachers often expect students of Latin, Classical Greek, and Old English to compose new writings in these languages. We follow our intuitions and exploit what we know of Old English and the nature of languages and of language change quite generally. Our success varies tremendously depending on the richness of the records. Where the records are extensive, and where there are daughter languages, as with Latin, we can develop a fairly full picture of the language and, we think, reliable intuitions about what might occur. If the records are slim, our hypotheses are more tenuous. This is a bit like reconstructing the skeleton of a dinosaur, projecting from a small number of bones.

At other times, there are no bones and no fragmentary records, only descendants and daughter languages. In such cases, one reasons from the properties of the descendants and deduces what the properties of the parent must have been, the proto-language, in the same way that biologists deduce the properties of missing links. The proto-language that has received the most work is Proto-Indo-European and we have rich hypotheses about the nature of PIE. But what is PIE?

There are two kinds of reconstruction, as we just saw, and, in addition, two fundamentally different views of what is reconstructed in the second case, where we have no records: they are often called N O M I N A L I S T and R E A L I S T. The nominalist view sees reconstructions as artifacts that express the historical relationships between daughter languages precisely and abstractly and involve various idealizations. The realist view is that one can reconstruct some prior reality, learn about how people spoke prehistorically, before our records begin, and even learn something about the nature of change from the reconstruction. The possibilities for reliable reconstruction of this latter type, I argue, are quite limited, because getting beyond the limitations requires a theory of change that is unattainable. Let us examine the nominalist and realist views in more detail.

First, the nominalist view is that the function of reconstructions is to express relationships precisely. If Greek and Latin are historically R E L A T E D, that relationship is expressed by the properties of the parent language from which they descend and changes that produced the two daughter languages. The parent language is an abstraction with no particular claim to historical reality, a myth, but a useful myth with a specific function, to express historical relationships. Antoine Meillet (1937: 41, 47) expressed the view forcefully that a reconstruction is an abstract representation of similarity (the emphasis is Meillet's):

> la seule réalité à laquelle elle ait affaire, ce sont les correspondances entre les langues attestées. Les correspondances supposent une réalité commune; mais de cette réalité on ne peut pas se faire une idée que par des hypothèses, et ces hypothèses sont invérifiables: la correspondance seule est donc objet de science. On ne restitue pas par la comparaison une langue disparue: la comparaison des langues romanes ne donnerait du Latin parlé au IVe siècle ap. J.-C. ni une idée exacte, ni une idée complète . . . ce que fournit la méthode de la grammaire comparée n'est pas une restitution de l'indo-européen, tel qu'il a été parlé: *c'est un système défini de correspondances entre les langues historiquement attestées.*

> 'the only reality to which [a reconstruction] relates are the correspondences between the attested languages. The correspondences presuppose a common reality; but one can get an idea of that reality only by hypotheses, and these hypotheses are unverifiable; only the correspondence is the object of science. One does not reconstruct comparatively a language which has disappeared: comparing the Romance languages would not yield any exact or complete notion of Latin as it was spoken in the 4th century AD . . . what the method of comparative grammar yields is not a reconstruction of Indo-European as it was spoken; *it is a precise system of correspondences between the historically attested languages.*'

For Meillet, a reconstruction does not constitute a claim about a prior reality – "on ne restitue donc pas l'indo-européen" (1937: 41); it is simply an accurate and abstract statement of the historical relationship among languages. Under this view, one seeks to quantify the degree of historical relatedness among sets of languages and historical relatedness is expressed through tree diagrams or cladograms, introduced by Schleicher (1861–1862) (chapter 2, figure 2.1). As often pointed out, the Schleicher-style cladograms, familiar from all textbooks on historical linguistics, capture only what biologists call homologies, similarities that arise through historical commonalities, and not analogies, similarities that arise from common developments. So cladograms are supplemented by waves, indicating common developments. Even so, this kind of reconstruction involves several counterfactual idealizations.

One idealization is to take languages as the basic objects of reality, entities "out there," existing in their own right, waiting to be acquired by speakers – an

E-language approach, in our terms. A language for Meillet is a social construct, studied as a shared social phenomenon and located in society at large; this was the view of Durkheim, Saussure, and many of Meillet's contemporaries in France. However, there is no definable notion of a language as an external entity, such that one can show in some non-circular way that a certain sentence is "a sentence of English," as we have noted. There is no general algorithm that characterizes the sentences of English and there cannot be such an algorithm if particular sentences may or may not be sentences of English depending on whether one is in Cornwall or Tennessee. Languages, rather, are conglomerations of the output of various grammars, all represented in the mind/brains of individual speakers. Languages are not coherent or systematic entities themselves and, in that case, one cannot suppose that there was a single form of Latin from which the various Romance languages descended. Therefore, there can be no single form of Latin that one can reconstruct through a comparison of the daughter languages. Rather, Latin, as it was spoken in Gaul, developed into various forms of French, while the somewhat different Latin spoken in Iberia developed into forms of Spanish, Portuguese, Galician, etc.

Schleicher-style cladograms, employing idealizations of this type, were developed to capture relatedness among certain kinds of morphological elements and among lexicons, which were taken to be pretty much unstructured inventories of words. Nineteenth-century linguists were successful in establishing historical relationships between words in different languages. Words, after all, are transmitted more or less directly from one generation to the next. We refer to *shoes* because our models used that word. Words may change their form somewhat as they are transmitted. We have already noted the way in which the wave theory (*Wellentheorie*) was introduced in the nineteenth century to capture similarities resulting from relationships between geographical neighbor languages.

However, if one thinks beyond the lexicon and if one thinks of relatedness more broadly, not just in terms of similarities resulting from a common history, one would arrive at very different relations. Individual sentences are not transmitted in the way that words are. I don't say *Individual sentences are not transmitted in the way that words are* because one of my models used that sentence. If one thinks of grammars, acquired on exposure to some relevant linguistic experience, and emerging according to the prescriptions of the linguistic genotype, as children identify predefined cues, one could compare the grammars of German speakers with those of English speakers and ask whether those grammars are more or less similar to each other than to the grammars of Italian speakers. German grammars are quite different from English grammars: they are object–verb (*Ich glaube, dass Gerda Claudia liebt* 'I believe that Gerda loves Claudia'), verb-second (*Im Dorf gibt es nicht viele Hunde* 'In the village there are not many dogs'), and have very different word-order possibilities inside VP. In fact, it is quite possible, even likely, that the syntax of English grammars might be more similar to grammars with which there is less historical connection. After all, the child acquiring a language has no access to the historical sources of the linguistic forms in the input, and accordingly no bias toward having linguistic ontogeny recapitulate phylogeny, in Ernst Häckel's famous phrase: the stages of acquisition do not retrace the steps of history. From this perspective, and looking at cues in the current linguistic literature, English syntax may be more similar to Italian than to German, and French syntax may be more similar to German than to Spanish. Similarly, languages that have split relatively recently may differ in some very important cues: for example, Polish allows null subjects and Russian does not. There is no reason to believe that structural similarity should be a simple or even an approximate function of historical relatedness, . . . assuming that there is a coherent, non-circular notion of historical relatedness to be discovered; we shall return to this point later.

Meillet emphasized in our quotation earlier and repeatedly elsewhere that one cannot reconstruct spoken Latin by a comparison of the attested Romance languages – one simply cannot capture the parent language; rather one reconstructs an abstraction that characterizes relationships in the most efficient way, a kind of algebra. Whatever the viability of Meillet-style reconstruction and whatever the idealizations used, it is important to recognize the ontological status of the hypotheses under the nominalist view: they are abstractions designed to express historical relatedness and not claims about prior reality; they do not seek to recover what was lost and they do not face the problems that the realist view of reconstruction faces.

There was a time when this was the standard view of reconstruction and I could have cited many people adopting what I have presented as Meillet's nominalist view. Pulgram (1959: 423) claimed that

No reputable linguist pretends that Proto-Indo-European reconstructions represent a reality, and the unpronounceability of the [reconstructed] formulae is not a legitimate argument against reconstructing. To write an Aesopian fable or the Lord's Prayer in reconstructed Proto-Indo-European is innocent enough as a pastime, but the text has no doubt little if any resemblance to any speech ever heard on earth. In other words, reconstructed Proto-Indo-European is not a language at all, at least not according to any defensible definition of the term language.

Under the nominalist view, one reconstructs a system that states the precise relationships between languages. The system consists of a proto-language and operations mapping its forms into those of the daughter languages. The most closely related daughter languages share the greatest number of mapping operations.

Second, a very different view, the one criticized by Pulgram, holds that reconstructions do, in fact, express prior reality. This was the realist view of

Schleicher, who in 1868 wrote the Indo-European fable to which Pulgram referred.[2] It was called *The Sheep and the Horses*.

Avis akvāsas ka
Avis, jasmin varnā na ā ast, dadarka akvams, tam, vāgham garum vaghantam, tam, bhāram magham, tam manum āku bharantam. Avis akvabhjams ā vavakat; kard aghnutai mai vidanti manum akvams agantam.
Akvāsas ā vavakant: krudhi avai, kard aghnutai vividvant- svas: manus patis varnām avisāms karnauti svabhjam gharmam vastram avibhjams ka varnā na asti.
Tat kukruvants avis agram ā bhugat.

'[The] Sheep and [the] Horses
[A] sheep, on which wool was not, saw horses, one [a] wagon heavy pulling, [another] one, [a] load great, one, [a] man swiftly carrying. [The] sheep to the horses said: heart pains me seeing [a] man horses driving.
[The] horses to the sheep said: listen sheep, hearts pain us seeing: man, [the] master, wool of the sheep makes for himself [a] warm garment and to the sheep the wool not is. That having heard, [the] sheep to the plain fled.'

One is struck by the number of Sanskrit-inspired *a* vowels instead of the *a, e, o* triad. Hermann Hirt, one of the foremost post-neogrammarian Indo-Europeanists, gave a new version of the same fable in 1939, which looked very different. Then Winfred Lehmann and Ladislav Zgusta provided another reinterpretation in 1979, very different again from Schleicher's original, particularly in the use of laryngeals (discovered only in 1879 by Ferdinand de Saussure, just twenty-one years old at the time), particles, and in the Delbrück-style syntax.

Owis eḱwōskʷe
(Gʷarēi) owis, kʷesyo wḷhnā ne ēst, eḱwōns espeḱet, oinom ghe gʷr̥um woǵhom weǵhontm̥, oinomkʷe meǵam bhorom, oinomkʷe ǵhm̥enm̥ ōḱu bherontm̥.
Owis nu eḱwobh(y)os (eḱwomos) ewewkʷet: "Ḱēr aghnutoi moi eḱwōns aǵontm̥ nerm̥ widn̥tei." Eḱwōs tu ewewkʷont: "Ḱludhi, owei, ḱēr ghe aghnutoi n̥smei widn̥tbh(y)os (widn̥tmos): nēr, potis, owiōm r̥ wḷhnām sebhi gʷhermom westrom kʷr̥neuti. Neǵhi owiōm wḷhnā esti.
Tod ḱeḱluwōs owis aǵrom ebhuget.

One observes big differences in the reconstructions, and further variation again if one seeks to reconstruct the PIE of 2500 BCE or of 3200 BCE. This is not just a function of greater understanding after a century of research, but also of matters of taste and emphasis. Lehmann and Zgusta also note considerable variation amongst contemporary Indo-Europeanists in the kinds of reconstructions they offer. So even in PIE there is much disagreement about what gets reconstructed. We have no instances of reconstructed proto-languages being confirmed by the subsequent decipherment of a newly discovered language, as sometimes happens when a new fish fossil is discovered.

---

[2] Schleicher's 1868 article is not easily accessible and short. It is reprinted in its entirety in Lehmann & Zgusta (1979).

All this variation despite the use of the same tools. There are two traditional tools for reconstruction (everything is coming in two's in this section): internal reconstruction and, by far the more important, the comparative method. Internal reconstruction involves examining the properties of a single language and eliminating superficial oddities, in the way that Grassmann explained why certain Greek nouns show an alternation between aspirate and non-aspirate consonants in their stem (chapter 2). It is not really a historical method, as often noted, and it is used mostly as a prelude to the comparative method, to eliminate the effects of recent changes. Recall that Grassmann argued that one could understand the variation in the stem of words like Greek t^hriks 'hair,' which is t^hrik- in the nominative and $trik^h$- in other cases, by taking it to have been earlier t^hrik^h-; that was an elegant hypothesis and internal reconstruction would postulate an earlier t^hrik^h-. However, there is no reason to believe that earlier speakers used a t^hrik^h- stem.

The comparative method requires a notion of a CORRESPONDING form. We have intuitive notions about what these might be in the area of the lexicon, and these are words that are cognate, having the same historical source: French *père* corresponds to Portuguese *pai*, to Sardinian *patre*, to Catalan *pare*, and to Spanish *padre*, and one reconstructs a proto-form on the basis of such correspondences. Most people would reconstruct initial *pa-* but there would be differences: not everybody would reconstruct *-ter* if they did not know that the actual antecedent was Latin *pater*. There are limits and one cannot reconstruct Latin from the data of the Romance languages, as Meillet noted. For instance, French *cinq*, Italian *cinque*, Spanish *cinco*, and Portuguese *cinco*, all with an initial fricative or affricate, do not yield Latin *quinque*, with an initial stop.

Corresponding forms are the basic wherewithal of the comparative method but it is impossible to know what a corresponding form could be in syntax, hard to know how one could define a sentence of French that corresponds to some sentence of English, and therefore hard to see how the comparative method could have anything to work with. It certainly cannot be keyed to cognateness, since there is no sense in which two particular sentences are historically cognate, coming from the same historical source. If there are no correspondences, the comparative method cannot be applied in the domain of syntax.

Instead of using notions of correspondence and the comparative method, some linguists have used different, non-traditional methods, based on harmonic properties and theories of directionality.

Many reconstructions have been based on theories of typological change emanating from Greenberg's harmonic universals, discussed in section 2.6 (Greenberg 1966). Pure object–verb languages are said to have the harmonic word-order properties of verb–auxiliary, noun–preposition, adjective–noun, etc. Indeed, with the new interest in syntactic change in the 1970s, almost all the papers in anthologies like Li (1975, 1977) and Steever, Walker, & Mufwene (1976) dealt with changes affecting unattested proto-languages, for the most part established by following the Greenbergian harmonies. In 1976 Calvert Watkins provided a devastating critique of contemporary efforts to reconstruct in this way the syntax of Proto-Indo-European, the best supported of the world's major proto-languages. Watkins pointed out that almost all Indo-Europeanists agree on the presence and the precise shape of a relative pronoun (*yo*) and a comparative morpheme (*-tero*) in the parent language, because cognate forms are attested robustly in the daughter languages. However, Greenberg's typology prescribes that "pure subject–object–verb languages" lack such forms and therefore they do not occur in the Procrustean reconstructions that Watkins was criticizing. Watkins' point was not just to criticize particular pieces of work but to raise fundamental methodological issues.

The theories of change were so various and the desire for reconstruction was so strong that we witnessed a curious event: within a year around 1975, three books were published on the syntax of Proto-Indo-European, all based on different harmonies; one argued that PIE was underlyingly subject–verb–object, one that it was subject–object–verb, and one that it was verb–subject–object (Lehmann 1974, Friedrich 1975, Miller 1975). It was like the competing PIE versions of the fable of *The Sheep and the Horses*. The problem was that the three hypotheses could not be compared productively, because there were no agreed criteria or established methods. Matters of taste were involved and anybody's guess was as good as anybody else's, there being no agreed effective method of reconstruction. Watkins (1976), in fact, used the comparative method in examining relative clauses dealing with athletic events in Hittite, Vedic Sanskrit, and early Greek, but in a restricted context. He was dealing with constructions where the daughter languages had common properties. He concluded that "the syntactic agreements are so striking and so precise, that we have little choice but to assume that the way you said that sort of thing in Indo-European could not have been very different."

However, problems arise when the most archaic patterns are not alike in the daughter languages. What can a comparativist conclude from a demonstration that Hittite and Germanic had an underlying subject–object–verb order, Celtic verb–subject–object, and other early grammars subject–verb–object? The answer is nothing, unless one has a rich theory of change, which might say, for example, that a subject–object–verb language may change to subject–verb–object, but not vice versa. That is why rich, deterministic theories of change predicting long-term changes, such as those typological theories based on Greenbergian harmonies, go hand-in-hand with work on reconstruction. If one has no such theory, one's reconstructions will be limited to the kind of similarities discussed by Watkins.

That is, indeed, about as far as we can go, in my view: one can reconstruct syntactic patterns where the daughter languages show identity; and sometimes one can reconstruct identity. That, of course, may enable us to make a guess about the prehistory of an individual language: if a language Anglish, lacking property *p*, is related to a set of languages all manifesting property *p*, we may guess that prehistoric Anglish had that property and lost it. There is no secure basis for that reasoning, but the guess might turn out to be productive and might help us to understand other properties of Anglish, which might then be seen as fossils, remnants of a prehistoric system.

As an example: one might try to identify relics and archaisms, on the one hand, as distinct from innovative forms, on the other. Harris & Campbell (1995) give a simple example. Germanic languages have the following words for 'adder.'

(1)   English   German   Gothic   Old Norse
        adder   *Natter*   *naðr-*   *naðra*   'adder'

English is clearly deviant, because there was a reanalysis of *a nadder* as *an adder*, as with *napkin/apron*, etc. If we set aside this innovative form of English, we can reconstruct an initial **n-* in the proto-language (Harris & Campbell 1995: 367). This seems to be a perfectly appropriate strategy. What Harris & Campbell did is set aside certain data until they had identity among the daughter languages: if the word for 'adder' is *n-* initial in all the remaining daughter languages, it is reasonable to suppose that that was true of the corresponding word in prehistoric speech. Where one has identity is where the skeptics of the 1970s said that reconstruction was possible (Jeffers 1976, Lightfoot 1979, 1980, Watkins 1976); when the archaic forms are the same, the proto-language could not have been very different. Identity among several languages may lead one to make a hypothesis about the prehistory of one deviant language, English in this case.

The conceptual problems in reconstructing a proto-syntax are profound and most successful reconstruction deals with phonological forms and certain morphemes, as often noted (e.g. Hock 1986: 570). This is not surprising. Words are transmitted from one generation to another; a child calls certain objects *tables* because that is what her models call them. Therefore, it is not incoherent to suppose that French *père* and Spanish *padre* are in some sense the same word, "corresponding" forms, and cognate with Latin *pater*. If words are transmitted, then maybe some prehistoric forms can be reconstructed with some reliability. Even in this domain, Meillet's point about the impossibility of reconstructing any known form of Latin by a comparison of the Romance languages remains valid. Reconstructing a proto-syntax, on the other hand, lacks the basic wherewithal of the comparative method, the existence of corresponding forms.[3]

---

[3] Hock (1986: 568–573) offers a valiant defense of realism in reconstruction, but ultimately defends a notion that we can "recover linguistic prehistory, in so far as it APPROXIMATES earlier linguistic reality" (p. 568, my emphasis) and then weakens the notion of "realistic"

To take a different tack, we might ask what we might be able to reconstruct at a different level. Children acquire grammars when exposed to some kind of triggering experience. A grammar emerges as a function of that triggering experience and the demands of the linguistic genotype, Universal Grammar, and that grammar generates an indefinite number of structures and sentences.

In that case, we might, in principle, seek to reconstruct a set of simple sentences for our proto-language, the PLD, or the grammar more or less directly. I know of no claim in the literature that we can reconstruct the sentences of PIE. That would involve claiming that there is some general algorithm that maps a set of sentences into another set and the generality of that algorithm would enable us to reconstruct proto-sentences. Since there is demonstrably no algorithm that generates the sentences of English, it is hard to imagine that there could be an algorithm mapping the sentences of a language into the sentences of a descendant language, least of all the PLD of one language into the PLD of another (2). Outside certain formulaic expressions, people don't learn to say particular sentences because they heard that sentence uttered by somebody else; rather, people acquire systems that they use freely. Schleicher didn't reconstruct the sentences of his fable from corresponding sentences in the daughter languages; rather, he had concocted a system from which he thought he could generalize.

(2) $PLD_x \rightarrow PLD_y$

There are claims, however, that we can reconstruct proto-grammars (Schleicher's approach, in a sense), and we will come to those claims in a moment. But there is an intermediate position. The most articulated recent claim that reconstruction of proto-syntaxes is possible is in chapter 12 of Harris & Campbell (1995). They do not claim that it is possible to reconstruct proto-sentences or proto-grammars but that they can reconstruct the "sentence patterns" of a proto-language. However, their claim is overblown. When one looks at their analyses carefully, one sees that they provide only a highly intuitive notion of corresponding forms and that they reconstruct in two contexts: when the daughter languages have identical patterns, as the 1970s skeptics allowed, and when one can appeal to notions of directionality, like the 1970s

---

still further, conceding that one can "reconstruct systems which are maximally 'realistic', i.e. 'possible' in natural language" (p. 572) (in other words, which correspond to the demands of UG). Hock & Joseph (1996: 470–471) note that "we are more successful in reconstructing basic morphological elements . . . than we are able to reconstruct complete, complex words. . . . Reconstructing specific sentences runs into even greater difficulties than reconstructing complex words." They go on to observe that "All reconstructions are HYPOTHESES about the nature of the proto-language . . . True, we try to exclude questionable hypotheses by appealing to such principles as Occam's Razor and naturalness. But these are only very general guidelines. They really do not help us in dealing with many specific issues . . ." (Hock & Joseph 1996: 474).

typologists. Recently, the *Journal of Linguistics* conducted a debate on these matters: Lightfoot (2002b,c) and Campbell & Harris (2002).

Grammaticalization theory is the newest attempt to explore the alleged unidirectionality of change and might provide a basis for reconstructing protogrammars. Grammaticalization, a notion first introduced by Meillet, is taken to be a semantic tendency for an item with a full lexical meaning to be bleached over time and to come to be used as a grammatical morpheme. Such changes are said to be general and unidirectional; one does not find changes proceeding in the reverse direction, so it is said, when bound forms become independent lexical items. Grammaticalization of this type does undoubtedly occur and there are many examples (Hopper & Traugott 2003). One example is the recategorization of the English modal auxiliaries like *must* and *can*, which were verbs in Old English grammars but are Inflectional elements (or "auxiliaries") for present-day speakers (chapter 5).

Grammaticalization is a real phenomenon but it is quite a different matter to claim that it is general, unidirectional, or an explanatory force. Rather, when grammaticalization takes place, it is explained when one points to local factors that promoted the new grammar, new triggering experiences, changes in cues, or what Kiparsky (1996) called the "enabling causes." If one observes a lexical verb being reanalyzed as a functional category in one language, one needs a local cause and it is not appropriate to explain the change by invoking a general theory of change or some principle of UG that favors the new grammar. There was no re-categorization of "modal" verbs in Swedish or French, and one wants to understand why the change happened in English when it did; what was the specific, local cause? Simply saying that there is a universal tendency for this to happen provides no understanding of what happened to English grammars in early Modern English and is false (Lightfoot 2003). Grammaticalization, challenging as a PHENOMENON, is not an explanatory force. We have no well-founded basis for claiming that languages or grammars change in one direction but not in another, no basis for postulating algorithms mapping one kind of grammar into another kind (3). The fact that we observe locative case endings coming to be used with partitive force in some language does not mean that it cannot be otherwise. Recall again that we have historical records for only a tiny fraction of human language history and any inductive generalizations are perilous. Van Gelderen (1997), Newmeyer (1998: ch. 5), Janda (2001), Joseph (2001), and others offer careful studies showing changes that run counter to grammaticalization, DE-GRAMMATICALIZATION, where affixes or minor categories become full lexical items.[4] Blanket assertions that such changes do

---

[4] Janda (2001) offers many references. He also has good critical discussion of how fundamental the issue of unidirectionality is for grammaticalizationists and how cavalier some of them have been in dismissing changes that appear to run counter to their predispositions. Newmeyer (1998: ch. 5) examines studies that use reconstructions as EVIDENCE for "grammaticalization theory," despite the fact it was ASSUMED in the very reconstruction.

not occur, as in the writings of Haspelmath (1999a,b), do not remove them from history. We saw examples in chapter 6, where an old genitive case ending was reconstrued in English as an *'s* clitic on DPs and even as *his* (*Mrs. Sands his maid*), prepositions may become verbs (*to up the ante*), etc.

(3) $G_x \rightarrow G_y$

The general idea here is that if we had a strong theory of change, incorporating historical laws that certain things can change in certain ways but not in others, then perhaps reconstruction might be possible. However, if languages did progress in the way that grammaticalization theory suggests, then one might reconstruct more or less ungrammaticalized proto-systems, in which the functional elements of the daughter languages correspond to lexical categories in the proto-system. One would still be left with the problem of determining which functional categories derived from which lexical categories and of explaining why particular changes occurred at particular times and under particular circumstances.

Again, problems come where there is variation in the daughter languages, object–verb order in one language and verb–object in the other. Where there is variation in the daughters, Campbell (1990, 1997), like his predecessors in the 1970s, appeals forthrightly to notions of directionality. If one language has property *a* and the other language has property *b*, one reconstructs proto **a* if one knows that *a → b* is a possible change, but not *b → a*. For example, Harris & Campbell assume that partitives may emerge from genitive or locative cases but not vice versa (Harris & Campbell 1995: 362–363). On the basis of this notion of directionality, they reconstruct an ablative case in Proto-Finno-Ugric, which becomes a partitive case in Lapp and "Finnic," but the presuppositions are perilous.

Reconstruction of earlier grammars or languages, where our most ancient records show variation, can happen only where we have a substantive theory of change, to the effect that a language or grammar with some property can only develop from an earlier language or grammar with some other property. Linguists have sought such theories for 200 years with no success, and grammaticalization theory fares no better. My own view has been that the search is misconceived; there is no theory of change to be had independent of theories of grammar and acquisition.

Yet another approach is to reconstruct a proto-grammar on the basis of parametric variation, as suggested by Roberts (1998b). His idea was that "the parameters of UG provide a way of determining syntactic correspondences." If parameter values are expressed as 0 or 1, Roberts proposed to use "the traditional methodology of reconstruction" to deduce that *p* is 0 in the proto-language in (4).

(4)   proto-language: p=?

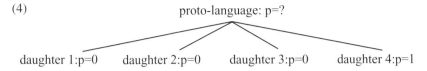

daughter 1:p=0   daughter 2:p=0   daughter 3:p=0   daughter 4:p=1

However, given that the traditional methods do not depend on majority rule, this conclusion does not follow. We can reconstruct $p=0$ in the proto-grammar only if we have reason to believe that the parameter in question may change from 0 to 1, but not vice versa, directionality again. The parameters of UG may provide another way of establishing correspondences and therefore a way to reconstruct proto-grammars by the comparative method. To say that Italian is a null-subject language and English is not represents a point of correspondence between the two grammars. So a positive/negative setting of a parameter is the correspondence between two grammars. However, this is very different from saying that *père* and *padre* are corresponding words, in fact cognate; furthermore, it doesn't help with reconstruction unless one also has a theory that predicts the direction of change, that a positive setting may change diachronically to the negative setting and not vice versa, for example. It is said that notions of markedness might be relevant in this regard, if unmarked settings can be shown to change over time to marked and not vice versa. But this has not been shown and is unlikely to be true. MARKEDNESS is used variably to indicate an initial, default setting of a parameter at the level of UG or to indicate the statistically most common property, when one surveys the grammars of the world. But in neither interpretation can one suppose that unmarked settings change unidirectionally to marked over the course of time.[5] Nor is it likely that parameter settings will be shown to change in the reverse direction, from marked to unmarked, although that is sometimes said to be a "natural" development (Roberts 1998a). In that case, in the absence of some such theory of change, parameter settings provide no special basis for reconstruction.

To see the problems, consider some specific cases. Rizzi (1982: 73, n25) postulated a subjacency condition limiting syntactic movement to crossing at most one bounding node, where the bounding nodes might be (i) DP, IP, and CP, (ii) DP and IP (English), or (iii) DP and CP (Italian, French). We discussed this in sections 4.1 and 7.1. The variation was marked in the order given: if children begin with hypothesis (i) (hence the unmarked value), one can show

---

[5] The practice of reconstructing unmarked forms and assuming that languages may change from unmarked parameter settings to marked is the reverse of the nineteenth-century practice of reconstructing highly complex morphological forms incorporating all the idiosyncrasies of the various daughter languages. The assumption then was that languages tended to simplify over time. These represent very different hunches about the direction of change, but unfortunately it is hard to find evidence to indicate which hunch is more plausible. In my view, that is because neither view is correct and there are no sustainable generalities about the directions of change.

how they may be driven to hypothesis (ii) and then to (iii) (the most marked setting) by available positive data, PLD, but not vice versa. Subjacency now seems to be less well understood than we once thought, but it serves to illustrate the point of logic. I see no basis for concluding from Rizzi's markedness claims that earlier languages, analyzed in his way, must have been the most restricted, allowing movement only within an unembedded clause and that there was a general progression to long-distance movement. It is not difficult to imagine that early speakers might have had the least restricted grammars, allowing long-distance movement and that subsequent grammatical reanalyses yielded grammars where movement became more restricted, perhaps changes involving complementizer projections. Nor do Rizzi's markedness claims entail the reverse development.

Kayne (1994) has argued that grammars always have an underlying verb–object order and that surface object–verb order results from a marked adjunction operation moving object DPs to a higher position to the left of the verb. I see no reason to conclude that early prehistoric speakers must have had verb–object order, only acquiring the adjunction operation later, on the grounds that unmarked operations are precursors to marked. Nor the reverse. At a minimum, this would be a separate claim. If the adjunction operation is morphologically driven (Roberts 1997), and if the proto-grammar had viable case endings, then the adjunction would be available. Indeed, Newmeyer (2000) argued that the earliest human languages must have had the (marked) object–verb order, with the adjunction operation; this is motivated by the claim that object–verb grammars have functional advantages: they reveal the thematic roles of syntactic positions more directly. Whatever the merits of Newmeyer's argument, he notes, surely correctly, that there is no inconsistency with Kayne's adjunction analysis.

Some grammars (French, Dutch, etc.) have an operation overtly raising verbs to a higher functional position, while other grammars do not have that operation but rather one lowering inflectional elements on to the verb. Furthermore, some grammars may have both options, as we noted in section 5.2. We know, of course, that English used to have the overt V-to-I raising operation and lost it, in favor of a morphological operation of Inflection Lowering. But suppose that we did not know that and that we had Shakespearian texts, manifesting both operations, and data from German and Dutch, all of which could be construed as resulting from a V-to-I operation. I don't see how one could conclude anything about Proto-Germanic from such variation, unless there were a theory of change stipulating that V-to-I grammars may change to Inflection-lowering grammars but not vice versa.[6] Again directionality.

---

[6] Roberts (1998a) posits that V-to-I grammars may change to Inflection-lowering grammars but not vice versa, on the grounds that I-lowering is less marked than V-to-I raising and that grammars generally change from marked to unmarked operations.

One final example: Roberts & Roussou (2003) argue that UG encompasses a bias against movement operations, such that, if there is no positive reason for postulating movement, grammars will tend to lose such operations over time. Thus elements tend to be base-generated in their surface positions, rather than moving there in the course of a derivation. They argue that English had infinitival inflections that required base-generating certain elements as verbs, heading a VP. As those inflections were lost, there was no reason for these items to be base-generated as verbs and they came to be base-generated in higher functional positions, not moving there. This UG bias is postulated as a way of explaining grammaticalization phenomena, but it does not follow in any way that proto-grammars lack the inflectional markers which required elements to be base-generated as verbs (and Roberts & Roussou do not suggest that it follows).

In short, I do not see that postulating UG cues and parameters changes the problems in reconstructing proto-grammars. I have argued that there is little basis for recovering much of the syntax of what has been lost, when we have no records and the daughter languages disagree. However, parametric variation opens another way of expressing the relatedness of languages, in fact I-languages. Recall Meillet's nominalist view that reconstructions are ways to express relatedness among languages and do not recover earlier, unrecorded languages.

In recent work, Pino Longobardi (2002, 2003) has developed an approach to defining relatedness between systems by quantifying the degree of correspondence among parametric settings, i.e. without invoking reconstructions or any kind of change. He has identified parameters in the syntax of noun phrases and analyzed the parametric settings for noun phrases in several European languages: Italian, Spanish, French, Portuguese, Latin, Classical Greek, Greek, Gothic, Old English, English, German (D), and Bulgarian (table 8.1). We need not concern ourselves here with the content of the parameters, just with the differences in the settings. 0 marks a parameter that is irrelevant in the language, resulting from partial interactions among parameters: either there is no trigger manifested for that parameter (0) or the parameter is necessarily set to a certain value ($0+$ or $0-$), as a consequence of other settings.

In that case, the distance between any two languages can be expressed by an ordered pair of positive integers <n,m>, where n is the number of identities and m the number of differences. Call such pairs "coefficients" (table 8.2).

A short form for coefficients (obscuring the relative weight of identities and differences) can sometimes be the integer resulting from subtracting m from n (table 8.3).

Now we have a means to quantify the degree of similarity between grammars. The relative distance among three or more languages can be computed by comparing the coefficients of each subpair. We observe from Longobardi's

Table 8.1 *Parameter settings (Longobardi 2002, 2003)*

	It	Sp	Fr	Ptg	Lat	ClGr	Grk	Got	OE	E	D	Blg
1. ± gram. Count ('null article')	+	+	+	+	−	−	+	−	−	+	+	−
2. ± gram. def in D	+	+	+	+	−	+	+	−	+	+	+	+
3. ± Enclitic def (D or H)	−	−	−	−	−	−	−	−	−	−	−	+
4.												
5. ± def. on As	−	−	−	−	−	+	+	+	−	−	−	+
6. ± high Dem	+	−	+	+	−	−	+	−	+	+	+	+
7. ± high Dem+Art +2	−	−	−	−	0	+	+	0	−	−	−	+
8. ± n (strong H1)	+	+	+	+	+?	+	+	+	+	−	+	+
9. ± transparent As +8	+	+	+	+	+	−?	−	+	−	−	−	−
10. ± postnominal As +9	−	−	−	−	−	−	0	−	0	0	0	0
11. ± strong ref in D	+	+	+	+?	?	?	+	?	?	−	−	+
12. ± number N (BNs)	+	+	−	+	+	+	+	+	+	+	+	+
13. ± ambiguous singulars	−	−	−	−	−	−	−	−	−	−	−	−
14. ± GenO	−	−	−	−	−	−	+	+	+	−	+	−
15. ± GenS	−e	−e	−	−	−	−	−	+	+	+	+	−
16. ± Free Gen (non−agr.)	+	+	+	+	+	+	−?	−	−	+	+	+
17.												
18. ± prep.Gen (inflect. Gen) +16	+	+	+	+	−	−	−	0	0	+	+	+
19. ± D Poss (weak)	−	+	+	−	0−	−	−	−	+	+	+	−
20. ± A Poss (strong)	+	+	+	+	+	+	−	+	+	−	+	+

Table 8.2 *Coefficients (Longobardi 2002, 2003)*

	It	Sp	Fr	Ptg	Lat	ClGr	Grk	Got	OE	E	D	Blg
It		16.2	16.2	18.0	11.4	10.6	10.7	8.7	8.7	11.6	12.5	11.6
Sp	16.2		16.2	16.2	12.3	10.6	8.8	8.7	8.7	11.6	12.5	9.8
Fr	16.2	16.2		16.2	10.5	8.8	8.9	6.9	8.7	11.6	12.5	9.8
Ptg	18.0	16.2	16.2		11.4	10.6	10.7	8.7	8.7	11.6	12.5	11.6
Lat	11.4	12.3	10.5	11.4		11.3	6.8	10.4	6.7	6.8	7.7	9.5
ClGr	10.6	10.6	8.8	10.6	11.3		11.5	9.5	6.8	7.9	8.8	14.2
Grk	10.7	8.8	8.9	10.7	6.8	11.5		8.6	10.5	8.9	9.8	12.5
Got	8.7	8.7	6.9	8.7	10.4	9.5	8.6		8.6	4.1	7.7	7.7
OE	8.7	8.7	8.7	8.7	6.7	6.8	10.5	8.6		11.4	12.3	7.8
E	11.6	11.6	11.6	11.6	6.8	7.9	8.9	4.10	11.4		14.3	7.10
D	12.5	12.5	12.5	12.5	7.7	8.8	9.8	7.7	12.3	14.3		8.9
Blg	11.6	9.8	9.8	11.6	9.5	14.2	12.5	7.7	7.8	7.10	8.9	

Table 8.3 *Simplified coefficients (Longobardi 2002, 2003)*

	It	Sp	Fr	Ptg	Lat	ClGr	Grk	Got	OE	E	D
It											
Sp	14										
Fr	14	14									
Ptg	18	14	14								
Lat	7	9	5	7							
ClGr	4	4	4	4	8						
Grk	3	0	−1	3	−2	6					
Got	1	1	−3	1	6	4	2				
OE	1	1	1	1	−1	−2	5	2			
E	5	5	5	5	−2	−2	−1	−6	7		
D	7	7	7	7	0	0	1	0	9	11	
Blg	5	1	1	5	4	12	7	0	−1	−3	−1

chart that there is a loose relationship between structural correspondence and agreed historical relationships, as we anticipated earlier in this section. On one hand, the Romance languages have a high degree of correspondence, less so with Latin, still less so with Classical Greek, and much less so with other, non-Romance languages. The closely related English and German show a fair degree of correspondence. On the other hand, Classical Greek is quite different from Modern Greek and closer to Bulgarian, Gothic is very different from the closely related Old English, and from German and Modern English, and Old English from Modern English.[7]

8.3   Conclusion and manifesto

This takes us to a point where we can conclude that the possibilities for recovering structures that have been lost are very limited, where we have no records for a hypothetical proto-language. There are possibilities for reconstructing where we have partial records or tentatively in those cases where the daughter languages show the same properties or we can reconstruct agreement in the daughter languages (as with the *adder* example). Otherwise, the limitations are severe and we can reconstruct neither sets of sentences nor properties of I-languages, the systems.

We have observed two kinds of reconstruction, realist and nominalist, and two motivations for reconstructing: to recover what has been lost or to

---

[7] Gianollo, Guardiano, & Longobardi (2004) provide a more recent and more elaborated comparison, dealing with 38 parameters. I have drawn from the earlier, published material, which is more compact and is based on the same logic.

express relationships among languages. The former is far more difficult than is often supposed. As for the latter, Meillet and others sought to express the HISTORICAL relationships among languages. However, we have found an alternative, whereby we can express the STRUCTURAL relationships among languages, following the lead of Longobardi; we do that by identifying shared cues or parameter settings. It remains an open question to what extent structural relationships reflect historical relationships. We may be limited to establishing historical relationships on the basis only of correspondences between sounds and the shape of words, and we may have no basis for establishing historical relations for the syntactic structures.

Under this view, we would not expect to reconstruct a proto-syntax nor to express historical relationships by reconstructions and the corresponding changes into the daughter languages. Instead, we establish the structural relationships among I-languages by identifying shared cues. It is an empirical issue whether relationships among I-languages so defined will match the historical relationships provided by historical linguists comparing words. This matter was discussed by Humboldt (1836/1971) and he and I would bet against that eventuality; Longobardi bets in favor.

Indeed, this is just one way in which our activities differ from those of traditional historical linguists. Under the perspective developed here, we study language change through differences in I-languages, linking them to changes in E-language in a way that the new E-language can be shown to trigger the new I-language, which, in turn, contributes to new E-language. That involves good theories of grammatical structures and grammatical variation, and of language acquisition. It also involves the study of language use, speech comprehension, social variation, and discourse analysis. We have taken specific approaches to these matters here, but those specific approaches will almost certainly be revised as work progresses. A student of language change must be a generalist, in control of many branches of linguistics, understanding the revisions to theories in all these domains of the field.

In this perspective, historical linguists are not aging gentlemen at the end of the departmental corridor, working on etymologies and reconstructing proto-systems for all-inclusive phyla like Nostratic. Rather, they are at the center of the linguistics department, engaged with all aspects of the field, benefiting from and contributing to discussions of syntactic theory, language acquisition, parsing, the use of grammars, social variation, computer modeling, and creoles. By studying language change from this perspective, they learn what it takes for a child to identify a different cue in the acquisition process, where we are lucky and have appropriate records. They learn how social variation and the varying use of grammars may influence the next generation of speakers and lead them to identify different cues. In addition, just as understanding aspects of language change in the nineteenth century contributed to the work of people trying to understand biological and political change, so too the new historical linguists participate in discussions of change in other domains, engaging with other disciplines.

In particular, they will help us understand how new languages emerge, both new E-language at the group level and new I-languages at the individual level, the two being intimately related. In this way, linguists have a more sophisticated treatment of history than has been obtained in biological or political history.

References

Allen, C. 1997 Investigating the origins of the "group genitive" in English. *Transactions of the Philological Society* 95.1: 111–131.

　2002 Case and Middle English genitive noun phrases. In Lightfoot, ed. 57–80.

Anderson, S. R. & D. W. Lightfoot 2002 *The language organ: linguistics as cognitive physiology*. Cambridge: Cambridge University Press.

Baker, M. A. 2001 *The atoms of language*. New York: Basic Books.

Bean, M. 1983 *The development of word order patterns in Old English*. London: Croom Helm.

Bejar, S. 2002 Movement, morphology, and learnability. In Lightfoot, ed. 307–325.

Belletti, A. 1994 Verb positions: evidence from Italian. In Lightfoot & Hornstein, eds. 19–40.

Berlin, I. 1996 *The sense of reality: studies in ideas and their history*. London: Chatto & Windus.

Berwick, R. C. 1985 *The acquisition of syntactic knowledge*. Cambridge, MA: MIT Press.

Bickerton, D. 1984a The language bioprogram hypothesis. *Behavioral and Brain Sciences* 7: 173–188.

　1984b Creole is still king: response to commentary. *Behavioral and Brain Sciences* 7: 212–218.

　2004 Reconsidering creole exceptionalism. *Language* 80.4: 828–833.

Bloomfield, L. 1933 *Language*. New York: Holt.

Bobaljik, J. D. 2001 The Rich Agreement Hypothesis in review. Ms, McGill University.

Briscoe, E. 2000 Grammatical acquisition: inductive bias and coevolution of language and the acquisition device. *Language* 76.2: 245–296.

Brugmann, K. 1918 *Verschiedenheiten der Satzgestaltung nach Massgabe der seelischen Grundfunktionen in den indogermanischen Sprachen*. Leipzig: Trübner.

　1925 *Die Syntax des einfachen Satzes im Indogermanischen*. Berlin: de Gruyter.

Brugmann, K. & B. Delbrück 1886–1900 *Grundriss der vergleichenden Grammatik der indogermanischen Sprachen*. Strassburg: Trübner.

Buck, L. & R. Axel 1991 A novel multigene family may encode odorant receptors: a molecular basis for odor recognition. *Cell* 65: 175–187.

Campbell, A. 1959 *Old English grammar*. Oxford: Oxford University Press.

Campbell, L. 1990 Syntactic reconstruction and Finno-Ugric. In H. Andersen & K. Koerner, eds. *Historical linguistics 1987: papers from the 8th International Conference on Historical Linguistics*. Amsterdam: Benjamins. 51–94.

1997 Typological and areal issues in reconstruction. In J. Fisiak, ed. *Linguistic reconstruction and typology* (Trends in Linguistics: Studies and Monographs 96). Berlin: Mouton de Gruyter. 49–72.

Campbell, L. & A. Harris 2002 Syntactic reconstruction and demythologizing "Myths and the prehistory of grammars." *Journal of Linguistics* 38: 599–618.

Canale, M. 1978 Word order change in Old English: base reanalysis in generative grammar. PhD dissertation, McGill University.

Chambers, J. K. 1992 Dialect acquisition. *Language* 68: 673–705.

Chaudenson, R. 1992 *Des îles, des hommes, des langues*. Paris: L'Harmattan.

Chomsky, N. 1957 *Syntactic structures*. The Hague: Mouton.

1959 Review of B. F. Skinner *Verbal Behavior. Language* 35: 26–57.

1965 *Aspects of the theory of syntax*. Cambridge, MA: MIT Press.

1973 Conditions on transformations. In S. R. Anderson & P. Kiparsky, eds. *A festschrift for Morris Halle*. New York: Holt, Rinehart, & Winston. 232–286.

1975 *The logical structure of linguistic theory*. New York: Plenum.

1980 On binding. *Linguistic Inquiry* 11: 1–46.

1981a *Lectures on government and binding*. Dordrecht: Foris.

1981b Principles and parameters in syntactic theory. In N. Hornstein & D. W. Lightfoot, eds. *Explanation in linguistics: the logical problem of language acquisition*. London: Longman. 32–75.

1986 *Knowledge of language: Its nature, origin and use*. New York: Praeger.

2002 *On nature and language*. Cambridge: Cambridge University Press.

Cinque, G. 1999 *Adverbs and functional heads: a cross-linguistic perspective*. Oxford: Oxford University Press.

Clahsen, H. & K.-D. Smolka 1986 Psycholinguistic evidence and the description of V2 in German. In H. Haider & M. Prinzhorn, eds. *Verb-second phenomena in Germanic languages*. Dordrecht: Foris. 137–167.

Clark, R. 1992 The selection of syntactic knowledge. *Language Acquisition* 2: 83–149.

Clark, R. & I. G. Roberts 1993 A computational model of language learnability and language change. *Linguistic Inquiry* 24: 299–345.

Cohen, G. A. 1978 *Karl Marx's theory of history: a defense*. Princeton: Princeton University Press.

Crain, S. & R. Thornton 1998 *Investigations in Universal Grammar: a guide to experiments on the acquisition of syntax and semantics*. Cambridge, MA: MIT Press.

Crystal, D. 2004 *The stories of English*. London: Allen Lane.

Curtiss, S. 1977 *Genie: a psycholinguistic study of a modern-day "wild child."* New York: Academic Press.

Davies, A. M. 1998 *Nineteenth-century linguistics* [*History of Linguistics*, ed. G. Lepschy, vol. 4]. London: Longman.

Dawkins, R. 2004 *The ancestor's tale: a pilgrimage to the dawn of life*. London: Weidenfeld & Nicolson.

DeGraff, M., ed. 1998 *Language creation and change: creolization, diachrony and development*. Cambridge, MA: MIT Press.

2001 Morphology in creole genesis: linguistics and ideology. In M. Kenstowicz, ed. *Ken Hale: a life in language*. Cambridge, MA: MIT Press. 53–121.

2004 Against creole exceptionalism (redux). *Language* 80.4: 834–839.

Dixon, R. 1997 *The rise and fall of languages*. Cambridge: Cambridge University Press.

Dresher, B. E. 1999 Charting the learning path: cues to parameter setting. *Linguistic Inquiry* 30: 27–67.

Dresher, B. E. & J. Kaye 1990 A computational learning model for metrical phonology. *Cognition* 34: 137–195.

Ekwall, E. 1943 *Studies on the genitive of groups in English*. Lund: Gleerup.

Fikkert, P. 1994 On the acquisition of prosodic structure. PhD dissertation, University of Leiden.

 1995 Models of acquisition: how to acquire stress. In J. Beckman, ed. *Proceedings of NELS 25*. GLSA, University of Massachusetts. 27–42.

Fodor, J. D. 1998 Unambiguous triggers. *Linguistic Inquiry* 29.1: 1–36.

Friedrich, P. 1975 *Proto-Indo-European syntax. Journal of Indo European Studies* monograph no.1, Butte, Montana.

Frisch, K. von 1967 *The dance language and orientation of the bees* (transl. L. E. Chadwick). Cambridge, MA: Harvard University Press.

Gelderen, E. van 1997 *Verbal agreement and the grammar behind its "breakdown": Minimalist feature checking*. Tübingen: Max Niemeyer.

Getty, M. 2002 *The metre of Beowulf: a constraint-based approach*. Berlin: Mouton de Gruyter.

Gianollo, C., C. Guardiano, & G. Longobardi 2004 Historical implications of a formal theory of syntactic variation. Paper presented at DIGS VIII, Yale University. Ms, University of Trieste.

Gibson, E. & K. Wexler 1994 Triggers. *Linguistic Inquiry* 25.3: 407–454.

Goethe, J. W. von 1790 *Versuch die Metamorphose der Pflanzen zu erklären*. Gotha: C. W. Ettinger.

Goldin-Meadow, S. 2003 *The resilience of language: what gesture creation in deaf children can tell us about how all children learn language*. New York: Psychology Press.

Goldin-Meadow, S. & C. Mylander 1990 Beyond the input given: the child's role in the acquisition of language. *Language* 66: 323–355.

Gopnik, M. & M. Crago 1991 Familial aggregation of a developmental language disorder. *Cognition* 39: 1–50.

Gorrell, J. H. 1895 Indirect discourse in Anglo-Saxon. *PMLA* 10.3: 342–485.

Gould, S. J. 1985 A clock of evolution. *Natural History*, April: 12–25.

Greenberg, J. H. 1966 Some universals of grammar with particular reference to the order of meaningful elements. In J. H. Greenberg, ed. *Universals of language*. Cambridge, MA: MIT Press. 73–113.

Grimes, B. F. & J. E. Grimes 2000 *Ethnologue*, vol. 1: *Languages of the world*; vol. 2: *Maps and indexes*. Dallas: SIL International.

Grimm, J. 1848 *Geschichte der deutschen Sprache*, vol.1. Leipzig: Weidmannsche Buchhandlung.

Haeberli, E. 2002 Inflectional morphology and the loss of V2 in English. In Lightfoot, ed. 88–106.

Haegeman, L. 1994 *Introduction to government and binding theory* (2nd edn). Oxford: Blackwell.

Hall, R. 1966 *Pidgin and creole languages*. Ithaca, NY: Cornell University Press.

Harris A. & L. Campbell 1995 *Historical syntax in cross-linguistic perspective*. Cambridge: Cambridge University Press.

Haspelmath, M. 1999a Are there principles of grammatical change? *Journal of Linguistics* 35.3: 579–595.

1999b Why is grammaticalization irreversible? *Linguistics* 37.6: 1043–1068.

Hawkins, J. 1979 Implicational universals as predictors of word order change. *Language* 55.3: 618–648.

Hickey, R. ed. 2003 *Motives for language change*. Cambridge: Cambridge University Press.

Hiltunen, R. 1983 *The decline of the prefixes and the beginnings of the English phrasal verb*. Turku: Turun yliopisto.

Hock, H. H. 1986 *Principles of historical linguistics*. Berlin: Mouton de Gruyter.

Hock, H. H. & B. D. Joseph 1996 *Language history, language change, and language relationship: an introduction to historical and comparative linguistics*. Berlin: Mouton de Gruyter.

Hockett, C. F. 1965 Sound change. *Language* 41: 185–204.

Hoenigswald, H. 1978 The *annus mirabilis* 1876 and posterity. *Transactions of the Philological Society*: 17–35.

Holmberg, A. & C. Platzack 1995. *The role of inflection in Scandinavian syntax*. Oxford: Oxford University Press.

Hopper, P. & E. Traugott 2003 *Grammaticalization* (2nd edn). Cambridge: Cambridge University Press.

Hornstein, N. 2001 *Move! A minimalist theory of construal*. Oxford: Blackwell.

Hróarsdóttir, Þ. 2000a *Word order change in Icelandic*. Amsterdam: Benjamins.

2000b Interacting movements in the history of Icelandic. In Pintzuk, Tsoulas, & Warner, eds. 296–321.

Hubel, D. 1978 Vision and the brain. *Bulletin of the American Academy of Arts and Sciences* 31.7: 28.

Hubel, D. & T. Wiesel 1962 Receptive fields, binocular interaction and functional architecture in the cat's visual cortex. *Journal of Physiology* 160: 106–154.

Humboldt, W. von 1836 *Über die Verschiedenheit des menschlichen Sprachbaues und ihren Einfluss auf die geistige Entwicklung des Menschengeschlechts*. Royal Academy of Sciences of Berlin [*Linguistic variability and intellectual development*, transl. G. C. Buck & F. A. Raven 1971. Philadelphia: University of Pennsylvania Press].

Hyams, N. 1986 *Language acquisition and the theory of parameters*. Dordrecht: Reidel.

1996 The underspecification of functional categories in early grammar. In H. Clahsen, ed. *Generative perspectives on language acquisition*. Amsterdam: Benjamins. 91–127.

Janda, R. D. 2001 Beyond "pathways" and "unidirectionality": on the discontinuity of language transmission and the counterability of grammaticalization. *Language Sciences* 23. 2–3: 265–340.

Janda, R. D. & B. D. Joseph, eds. 2003 *Handbook of historical linguistics*. Oxford: Blackwell.

Jeffers, R. 1976 Syntactic change and syntactic reconstruction. In W. Christie, ed. *Current progress in historical linguistics*. Amsterdam: North-Holland. 1–16.

Jerne, N. K. 1985 The generative grammar of the immune system. *Science* 229: 1057–1059.

Jespersen, O. 1909 *Progress in language* (2nd edn). London: Swan Sonnenschein.

Jonas, D. 2002 Residual V-to-I. In Lightfoot, ed. 251–270.

Joseph, B. D. 2001 Is there such a thing as grammaticalization? *Language Sciences* 23. 2–3: 163–186.

Kato, M. & E. Negrão, eds. 2000 *Brazilian Portuguese and the null subject parameter.* Frankfurt: Vervürt.

Kayne, R. S. 1994 *The antisymmetry of syntax.* Cambridge, MA: MIT Press.

Kegl, J., A. Senghas, & M. Coppola 1998 Creation through contact: sign language emergence and sign language change in Nicaragua. In DeGraff, ed. 179–237.

Kellner, L. 1892 *Historical outlines of English syntax.* London: Macmillan.

Kemenade, A. van 1987 *Syntactic case and morphological case in the history of English.* Dordrecht: Foris.

Kemenade, A. van & N. Vincent, eds. 1997 *Parameters of morphosyntactic change.* Cambridge: Cambridge University Press.

Kerswill, P. 1996 Children, adolescents, and language change. *Language Variation and Change* 7: 177–202.

Kiparsky, P. 1996 The shift to head-initial VP in Germanic. In H. Thráinsson, S. Epstein, & S. Peters eds. *Studies in comparative Germanic syntax,* vol. 2. Dordrecht: Kluwer. 140–179.

 1997 The rise of positional licensing in Germanic. In van Kemenade & Vincent, eds. 460–494.

Klein, W. 1974 *Word order, Dutch children and their mothers.* Publikaties van het Instituut voor Algemene Taalwetenschap 9. University of Amsterdam.

Koeneman, O. 2000 The flexible nature of verb movement. PhD dissertation, Univerity of Utrecht.

Kohonen, V. 1978 *On the development of English word order in religious prose around 1000 and 1200 A.D.: a quantitative study of word order in context.* Åbo: Åbo Akademi Foundation.

Koopman, H. 1984 *The syntax of verbs: from verb movement rules in the Kru languages to Universal Grammar.* Dordrecht: Foris.

 1986 The genesis of Haitian: implications of a comparison of some features of the syntax of Haitian, French, and West-African languages. In P. Muysken & N. Smith, eds. *Substrata versus universals in creole languages.* Amsterdam: Benjamins. 231–259.

Kouwenberg, S. 1992 From OV to VO: linguistic negotiation in the development of Berbice Dutch Creole. *Lingua* 88: 263–299.

Kroch, A. 1989 Reflexes of grammar in patterns of language change. *Language Variation and Change* 1: 199–244.

 1994 Morphosyntactic variation. In K. Beals et al., eds. *Papers from the 30th Regional Meeting of the Chicago Linguistics Society: Parasession on Variation and Linguistic Theory.* Chicago: Chicago Linguistics Society. 180–201.

Kroch, A. & A. Taylor 1997 The syntax of verb movement in Middle English: dialect variation and language contact. In van Kemenade and Vincent, eds. 297–325.

 2000 Verb–object order in early Middle English. In Pintzuk, Tsoulas, & Warner, eds. 132–163.

Kuhn, T. 1962 *The structure of scientific revolutions.* Chicago: Chicago University Press.

Labov, W. 1963 The social motivation of a sound change. *Word* 19: 273–309.

Lakoff, R. T. 1975 *Language and woman's place.* New York: Harper & Row.

Lasnik, H. 1999 *Minimalist analysis*. Oxford: Blackwell.

Lass, R. 1980 *On explaining linguistic change*. Cambridge: Cambridge University Press.
  1997 *Historical linguistics and language change*. Cambridge: Cambridge University Press.

Lees, R. 1957 Review of *Syntactic Structures*. *Language* 33.3: 375–408.

Lehmann, W. P. 1967 *A reader in nineteenth century historical Indo-European linguistics*. Bloomington: Indiana University Press.
  1974 *Proto-Indo-European syntax*. Austin: University of Texas Press.

Lehmann, W. P. & L. Zgusta 1979 Schleicher's tale after a century. In B. Brogyanyi, ed. *Studies in diachronic, synchronic, and typological linguistics: festschrift for Oswald Szemerenyi on the occasion of his 65th birthday*. Amsterdam: Benjamins. 455–466.

Lenneberg, E. H. 1967 *The biological foundations of language*. New York: John Wiley.

Lewontin, R. C. 1972 The apportionment of human diversity. *Evolutionary Biology* 6: 381–398.

Li, C. N., ed. 1975 *Word order and word order change*. Austin, TX: University of Texas Press.
  ed. 1977 *Mechanisms of syntactic change*. Austin, TX: University of Texas Press.

Lightfoot, D. W. 1974 The diachronic analysis of English modals. In J. M. Anderson & C. Jones, eds. *Historical linguistics*. Amsterdam: North Holland. 219–249.
  1979 *Principles of diachronic syntax*. Cambridge: Cambridge University Press.
  1980 Sur la reconstruction d'une proto-syntaxe. *Langages* 60: 109–123. [English version in P. Ramat, ed. *Linguistic reconstruction and Indo-European syntax*. Amsterdam: Benjamins. 128–142. Reprinted in I. Rauch & J. Carr, eds. *Language change*. Bloomington: Indiana University Press.]
  1989 The child's trigger experience: degree-0 learnability. *Behavioral and Brain Sciences* 12.2: 321–334.
  1991 *How to set parameters: arguments from language change*. Cambridge, MA: MIT Press.
  1993 Why UG needs a learning theory: triggering verb movement. In C. Jones, ed. *Historical linguistics: problems and perspectives*. London: Longman. 190–214. [Reprinted in A. Battye & I. G. Roberts, eds. *Clause structure and language change*. Oxford: Oxford University Press.]
  1994 Degree-0 learnability. In B. Lust, G. Hermon, & J. Kornfilt, eds. *Syntactic theory and first language acquisition: crosslinguistic perspectives*, vol. 2: *Binding dependency and learnability*. Hillsdale, NJ: Erlbaum. 453–472.
  1997 Catastrophic change and learning theory. *Lingua* 100: 171–192.
  1999 *The development of language: acquisition, change and evolution*. Oxford: Blackwell.
  ed. 2002a *Syntactic effects of morphological change*. Oxford: Oxford University Press.
  2002b Myths and the prehistory of grammars. *Journal of Linguistics* 38: 113–136.
  2002c More myths. *Journal of Linguistics* 38: 619–626.
  2002d Introduction to Chomsky 1957. Berlin: Mouton de Gruyter.
  2003 Grammaticalisation: cause or effect? In Hickey, ed. 99–123.
  2006 Minimizing government: deletion as cliticization. *The Linguistic Review* 23.2.

Lightfoot, D. W. & N. Hornstein, eds. 1994 *Verb movement*. Cambridge: Cambridge University Press.

Lilly, J. C. 1975 *Lilly on dolphins: humans of the sea*. Garden City, NY: Anchor Press.

Longobardi, G. 2002 Parametric comparison and historical relatedness. Paper presented at DIGS VII, Girona.

　　2003 On parameters and parameter theory. In E. Stark & U. Wandruszka, eds. *Syntaxtheorien: Modelle, Methoden, Motive*. Tübingen: Gunter Narr. 273–290.

Lorenz, K. 1961 *Evolution and modification of behavior*. Cambridge, MA: Harvard University Press.

Lumsden, J. 1998 Language acquisition and creolization. In DeGraff, ed. 129–157.

Marler, P. 1999 On innateness: are sparrow songs "learned" or "innate"? In M. D. Hauser & M. Konishi, eds. *The design of animal communication*. Cambridge, MA: MIT Press. 293–332.

Matthews, P. 2003 On change in "E-language." In Hickey, ed. 7–17.

Mayr, E. 2004 *What makes biology unique? Considerations on the autonomy of a scientific discipline*. Cambridge: Cambridge University Press.

Meillet, A. 1937 *Introduction à l'étude comparative des langues indo-européennes*. Paris: Hachette [reprinted 1964, University of Alabama Press].

Miller, D. G. 1975 Indo-European: VSO, SOV, SVO, or all three? *Lingua* 37: 31–52.

Muysken, P. 1988 Are creoles a special type of language? In F. Newmeyer, ed. *Linguistics: the Cambridge survey*, vol. 2. Cambridge: Cambridge University Press. 285–301.

Mustanoja, T. 1960 *A Middle English Syntax*. Helsinki: Société Néophilologique.

Nettle, D. & S. Romaine 2000 *Vanishing voices: the extinction of the world's languages*. Oxford: Oxford University Press.

Newmeyer, F. 1998 *Language form and language function*. Cambridge, MA: MIT Press.

　　2000 On the reconstruction of "Proto-World" word order. In C. Knight, M. Studdert-Kennedy, & J. Hurford, eds. *The evolutionary emergence of language*. Cambridge: Cambridge University Press. 372–388.

　　2003 Grammar is grammar and usage is usage. *Language* 79.4: 682–707.

Newport, E. L. 1998 Reduced input in the acquisition of signed languages: Contributions to the study of creolization. In DeGraff, ed. 161–178.

Newport, E. L., D. Bavelier, & H. J. Neville 2002 Critical thinking about critical periods: Perspectives on a critical period for language acquisition. In E. Dupoux, ed. *Language, brain and cognitive development*. Cambridge MA: MIT Press. 481–502.

Nichols, J. 1992 *Linguistic diversity in space and time*. Chicago: University of Chicago Press.

Niyogi, P. & R. C. Berwick 1997 A dynamical systems model of language change. *Complex Systems* 11: 161–204.

Nunes, J. 1995 The copy theory of movement and linearization of chains in the Minimalist Program. PhD dissertation, University of Maryland.

　　2004 *Linearization of chains and sideward movement*. Cambridge, MA: MIT Press.

Nunnally, T. 1985 The syntax of the genitive in Old, Middle, and Early Modern English. PhD dissertation, University of Georgia.

O'Neil, W. 1978 The evolution of the Germanic inflectional systems: a study in the causes of language change. *Orbis* 27.2: 248–285.

Otani, K. & J. Whitman 1991 V-raising and VP-ellipsis. *Linguistic Inquiry* 22: 345–358.

Paul, H. 1880 *Prinzipien der Sprachgeschichte*. Tübingen: Niemeyer.

Pearl, L. 2004 Addressing acquisition from language change: a modeling perspective. *Penn Working Papers in Linguistics* 11.1.

Pedersen, H. 1931 *The discovery of language: linguistic science in the nineteenth century*. Bloomington: Indiana University Press.

Piattelli-Palmarini, M. 1986 The rise of selective theories: a case study and some lessons from immunology. In W. Demopoulos & A. Marras, eds. *Language learning and concept acquisition: foundational issues*. Norwood, NJ: Ablex. 117–130.

Pintzuk, S. 1999 *Phrase structures in competition: variation and change in Old English word order*. New York: Garland.

    2002 Verb-complement order in Old English. In Lightfoot, ed. 276–299.

Pintzuk, S., G. Tsoulas, & A. Warner, eds. 2000 *Diachronic syntax: models and mechanisms*. Oxford: Oxford University Press.

Pires, A. 2002 Cue-based change: inflection and subjects in the history of Portuguese infinitives. In Lightfoot, ed. 143–159.

Plank, F. 1984 The modals story retold. *Studies in Language* 8: 305–364.

Platzack, C. 1988 The emergence of a word order difference in Scandinavian subordinate clauses. *Special Issue on Comparative Germanic Syntax: McGill Working Papers in Linguistics*, 215–238.

Popper, K. 1959 *The logic of scientific discovery*. London: Hutchinson.

Pulgram, E. 1959 Proto-Indo-European reality and reconstruction. *Language* 35.3: 421–426.

Quirk, R. & C. L. Wrenn 1955 *An Old English grammar*. London: Methuen.

Rask, R. 1818 *Undersøgelse om det gamle Nordiske eller Islandske Sprogs Oprindelse*. Copenhagen: Gyldendalske Boghandlings Forlag.

Renfrew, C. 2000 At the edge of knowability: towards a prehistory of languages. *Cambridge Archaeological Journal* 10.1: 7–34.

Rizzi, L. 1978 Violations of the wh-island constraint in Italian and the Subjacency Condition. In C. Dubuisson, D. W. Lightfoot, & C.-Y. Morin, eds. *Montreal Working Papers in Linguistics* 11: 155–190.

    1982 *Issues in Italian syntax*. Dordrecht: Foris.

Roberts, I. G. 1997 Directionality and word order change in the history of English. In van Kemenade & N. Vincent, eds. 397–426.

    1998a Verb movement and markedness. In DeGraff, ed. 287–327.

    1998b Review of A. Harris & L. Campbell, *Historical syntax in cross-linguistic perspective*. *Romance Philology* 51: 363–370.

Roberts, I. G. & A. Roussou 2002 The history of the future. In Lightfoot, ed. 23–56.

    2003 *Syntactic change: a minimalist approach to grammaticalization*. Cambridge: Cambridge University Press.

Robins, R. H. 1967 *A short history of linguistics*. London: Longman.

Rodrigues, C. 2002 Loss of verbal morphology and the status of referential null subjects in Brazilian Portuguese. In Lightfoot, ed. 160–178.

Rohrbacher, B. 1999 *Morphology-driven syntax: a theory of V to I raising and pro-drop*. Amsterdam: Benjamins.

Ross, J. R. 1967 Constraints on variables in syntax. PhD dissertation, MIT.

    1969 Auxiliaries as main verbs. In W. Todd, ed. *Studies in philosophical linguistics*, Series I. Evanston: Great Expectations. 77–102.

Sampson, G. 1980 *Schools of linguistics: competition and evolution*. London: Hutchinson.

Sandler, W., I. Meir, C. Padden, & M. Aronoff 2005 The emergence of grammar: systematic structure in a new language. *Proceedings of the National Academy of Sciences* 102: 2661–2665.

Sankoff, G. & S. Laberge 1973 On the acquisition of speakers by a native language. *Kivung* 6: 32–47.

Sapir, E. 1921 *Language*. New York: Harcourt.

1929 The status of linguistics as a science. *Language* 5: 207–214.

Saussure, F. de 1879 *Mémoire sur le système primitif des voyelles dans les langages européennes*. Leipzig: Teubner.

Schleicher, A. 1848 *Über die Bedeutung der Sprache für die Naturgeschichte des Menschen*. Weimar: Hermann Böhlau.

1861–1862 *Compendium der vergleichenden Grammatik der indogermanischen Sprachen*. Weimar: Hermann Böhlau.

1863 *Die darwinische Theorie und Sprachwissenschaft*. Weimar: Hermann Böhlau.

Schneider, E. W. 2003 The dynamics of new Englishes: from identity construction to dialect birth. *Language* 79.2: 233–281.

Senghas, A., S. Kita, & A. Özyürek 2004 Children creating core properties of language: evidence from an emerging sign language in Nicaragua. *Science* 305: 1779–1782.

Sievers, E. 1876 *Grundzüge der Lautphysiologie*. Leipzig: Breitkopf & Härtel.

Singler., J. 1988 The homogeneity of the substrate as a factor in pidgin/creole genesis. *Language* 64.1: 27–51.

Singleton, J. & E. L. Newport 2004 When learners surpass their models: the acquisition of American Sign Language from impoverished input. *Cognitive Psychology* 49: 370–407.

Smith, N. S. H., I. Robertson, & K. Williamson 1987 The Ijo element in Berbice Dutch. *Language in Society* 16: 49–90.

Sperry, R. 1968 Plasticity of neural maturation. *Developmental Biology Supplement* 2: 306–27.

Steever, S., C. Walker, & S. Mufwene, eds. 1976 *Diachronic syntax*. Chicago: Chicago Linguistic Society.

Stewart, I. 1998 *Life's other secret*. New York: Wiley.

Stockwell, R. P. & D. Minkova 1991 Subordination and word order change in the history of English. In D. Kastovsky, ed. *Historical English Syntax*. Berlin: Mouton de Gruyter. 367–408.

Stokoe, W. 1960 Sign language structure: an outline of the visual communications systems. *Studies in Linguistics, Occasional Papers* 8.

Sundquist, J. D. 2002 Object Shift and Holmsberg's Generalization in the history of Norwegian. In Lightfoot, ed. 326–347.

Supalla, S. 1990 Segmentation of Manually Coded English: problems in the mapping of English in the visual/gestural mode. PhD dissertation, University of Illinois.

Thackray, A. 1970 *Atoms and powers*. Cambridge, MA: Harvard University Press.

Thomason, S. G. & T. Kaufman 1988 *Language contact, creolization, and genetic linguistics*. Berkeley: University of California Press.

Thompson, D. W. 1917 *On growth and form*. Cambridge: Cambridge University Press.

Thornton, R. 1995 Referentiality and *Wh*-movement in child English: Juvenile D-*link*uency. *Language Acquisition* 4: 139–175.

Thornton, R. & K. Wexler 1999 *Principle B, VP ellipsis, and interpretation in child grammar*. Cambridge, MA: MIT Press.

Thorpe, W. H. 1957 The learning of song patterns by birds, with special reference to the song of the Chaffinch Fringilla Coelebs. *Ibis* 100: 535–570.

Thráinsson, H. 2003 Syntactic variation, historical development and Minimalism. In R. Hendrick, ed. *Minimalist syntax*. Oxford: Blackwell. 152–191.

Tinbergen, N. 1957 *The herring gull's world*. Oxford: Oxford University Press.

Turing, A. 1952 The chemical basis of morphogenesis. *Philosophical Transactions of the Royal Society of London* 37–72.

Vennemann, T. 1975 An explanation of drift. In Li, ed. 269–305.

Venter, C. 2002 Commencement address: Georgetown University Graduate School of Arts & Sciences.

Vikner, S. 1994 Finite verb movement in Scandinavian embedded clauses. In Lightfoot & Hornstein, eds. 117–147.

1997 V-to-I movement and inflection for person in all tenses. In L. Haegeman, ed. *The new comparative syntax*. London: Longman. 189–213.

Warner, A. R. 1993 *English auxiliaries: structure and history*. Cambridge: Cambridge University Press.

1995 Predicting the progressive passive: parametric change within a lexicalist framework. *Language* 71.3: 533–57.

1997 The structure of parametric change, and V movement in the history of English. In van Kemenade & Vincent, eds. 380–393.

Watkins, C. 1976 Toward Proto-Indo-European syntax: problems and pseudoproblems. In Steever, Walker, & Mufwene, eds. 305–326.

Weinberg, S. 1977 The forces of nature. *American Scientist* 65.2: 171–176.

Westergaard, M. 2005 What Norwegian child language can tell us about the history of English. In K. McCafferty, T. Bull, & K. Killie, eds. *Contexts – historical, social, linguistic: studies in celebration of Toril Swan*. Bern: Peter Lang.

Wexler, K. 1994 Optional infinitives, head movement, and the economy of derivations. In Lightfoot & Hornstein, eds. 305–350.

Whitney, D. 1875 *The life and growth of language: an outline of linguistic science*. New York: D. Appleton & Co.

Wurff, W. van der 1999 Objects and verbs in modern Icelandic and fifteenth-century English: a word order parallel and its causes. *Lingua* 109: 237–265.

Yang, C. 2002 *Knowledge and learning in natural language*. Oxford: Oxford University Press.

Zagona, K. 1988 Proper government of antecedentless VP in English and Spanish. *Natural Language and Linguistic Theory* 6: 95–128.

Index

Boldface items provide an introductory definition of the term.